WOMEN, MEDIA
AND CONSUMPTION
IN JAPAN

ConsumAsiaN Book Series
edited by
Brian Moeran and Lise Skov
and
published by
The Curzon Press and The University of Hawaii Press

WOMEN, MEDIA AND CONSUMPTION IN JAPAN

Lise Skov and Brian Moeran
Editors

UNIVERSITY OF HAWAI'I PRESS
HONOLULU

Published in North America by
University of Hawai'i Press
2840 Kolowalu Street
Honolulu, Hawai'i 96822

Published in the United Kingdom by
Curzon Press
St. John's Studio, Church Road
Richmond, Surrey TW9 2QA
England

Printed in Great Britain

Library of Congress Cataloging-in-Publication Data

Women, media, and consumption in Japan / edited by
Lise Skov and Brian Moeran.
p. cm. — (ConsumAsiaN series)
Includes bibliographical references and index.
ISBN 0–8248–1775–3 (alk. paper).
ISBN 0–8248–1776–1 (pbk. : alk. paper)
1. Mass media and women — Japan.   2. Mass media — Japan —
Marketing.   3. Consumption (Economics) — Japan.
I. Skov, Lise, 1965– .   II. Moeran, Brian.   III. Series.
P94.5.W652J38   1995
305.4'0952–dc20   95–19376
CIP

CONTENTS

CONTENTS

EDITORS' NOTE

ACKNOWLEDGMENTS

This book would not have been possible without the help of a number of people and organizations. Firstly, we would like to thank the Japan Foundation, John Swire and Sons, Cathay Pacific Airways Ltd. and the University of Hong Kong for providing the financial assistance which enabled us to hold a workshop on 'Women, Media and Consumption in Japan' at the end of November 1993. We are particularly grateful to Glen Docherty, Okazaki Kiyoshi, and Wang Gung Wu for their support at this time.

Secondly, we would like to thank those who at various stages sat in on the workshop and acted as discussants of papers – Hazel Clark, Mike Featherstone, Jonathan Hall, Kuah Khun Eng, Jeremy Tambling, and Matthew Turner – as well as the two anonymous readers who read through the papers with great care, commenting on them with a rare combination of critical insight and perceptiveness.

We are grateful, too, to Chan Lai Pek, Raymond Cheng, Lily Choi, Lai Mei Fong, Lee Chi Keung, and Wong Mei Ling for all their hard work in organizing and administering the less obvious but vital side of any academic gathering – including food, accommodation, transportation, slide projectors and other technical equipment, and ticket refunds.

All those who attended the workshop have contributed to this volume. We would like to thank them, not only for coming a long way during what was for some a Thanksgiving weekend, but for working so hard to finish their papers on time. Their cooperation has made our editorial task, never an easy one at the best of times, that much more pleasant.

Finally, we say *hej* to Marie Lenstrup, our super-efficient ConsumAsiaN Network Coordinator, office cohabitant and still – believe it or not – good friend.

Lise Skov and Brian Moeran

INTRODUCTION

Hiding in the Light: From Oshin to Yoshimoto Banana

Lise Skov and Brian Moeran

Exposure

We see them everywhere. So visible that we look right through them. Carefully made up faces, painted lips, plucked eyebrows – above all, perhaps, their hair, washed, conditioned, styled into perfect waves. We look right through their bodies, carefully rounded, straightened, padded, into the current shapes for breasts, waists, hips. We gaze past their expensive clothes – tailored business suits in pastel colours, designer scarves, high-heeled shoes – with just the right accoutrements: the Mikimoto necklace, Tiffany earrings, handbag from Ferragamo, Gucci or Lancel. And all we say is: 'Oh, is that the latest style?', or 'Is that what you're supposed to look like this season?' It is as if we cannot pick out women for themselves, and see them only as an incoherent flow of commercial trends.

These are the young working women of Japan's cities, the women who mix in with the commuter traffic in the early mornings; who administer the reception desks and offices in almost every Japanese corporation; who frequent the shopping streets, department stores, coffee shops, restaurants, art galleries, bars; who gather in Narita Airport to be conveyed to other cities, other streets, arcades, museums, in other countries as far apart as America and Australia, Switzerland and Singapore.

We hear women everywhere. So audible that we hardly listen to their carefully enunciated voices greeting us at the end of almost every telephone line, and on every visit to every commercial building in every city in Japan. Female are the voices of welcome at the foot of escalators or at the doors of lifts, behind the counters of stores, deep inside the cash dispensing machines in banks, at the entrance to soft-lit bars. Smiling, polite voices that match half-open pink-lipped mouths, assuring us that everything is under control. Recorded, broadcast and computer-simulated,

1

voices of information tell us at which bus stop to alight, what the weather will be like tomorrow, whether the person you wish to talk to is in or out, whether the planes at Narita will in fact take off on time for those exotic destinations abroad. Female are the voices of instruction, warning mothers and children to mind their hands and feet on the escalator, reminding passengers not to forget their belongings on the train, recommending consumers to purchase this detergent, that wine, those contact lenses, cleansing creams or leopard-spotted leotards. Anonymous images, anonymous voices, yet ever present.

The Japanese media, too, are full of women. The faces that gaze out from magazine covers lined on the counters of station kiosks, or which in fifteen second exposures try to attract television viewers' attention during commercial breaks, or which, more lengthily, stare across from rooftop hoardings at expressway drivers, are predominantly images of young women. During the daytime, television stations put on special programmes – cookery, Culture (with a capital C), aerobics, soap and serialized dramas – and gather audiences of women to applaud, laugh, talk at appropriate points and to receive, if they are lucky, special rewards in the form of advertised stockings, sauces, soaps, shampoos. In bookstores we find special sections devoted to romance novels and women's comics, to cookery, crochet, and dress-making manuals, to glossy books on interior decor, flower arrangement and anything else that will help convert a woman's daily household chores into a fine art – a task also taken on by various department store and national news-paper 'culture clubs' which see it as their main objective to cultivate the minds and bodies of Japanese women.

Women, too, are bathed in the media glare. There is a succession of pop idols, from Pink Lady to Wink, by way of Yamaguchi Momoe, Matsuda Seiko and Kyon Kyon (Kiyozumi Kyōko). There are models like Miyazawa Rie who was celebrated for turning soft-porn into art when posing nude in the desert of Arizona, only to attract the media spotlight once again during her short engagement to a young *sumō* wrestler. There once was, and now is again, the Crown Princess, this time cast as educated, intelligent, cosmopolitan. There was, too, a woman leader of the Socialist Party, Doi Takako, who then fell from grace with the shifting tide of political tastes. There are the fashion designers – Kawakubo Rei, Shimada Junko, Mori Hanae – who dress women models on the catwalks in fabrics of light and shade, while trendsetting academics like Ueno Chizuko or Nakane Chie write much discussed books on the theatre of underwear or the vertical nature of Japanese society with which anybody interested in Japan should be familiar. Then there are writers such as Kuroyanagi Setsuko, who writes a best-seller about her childhood, and Yoshimoto Banana and Sakura Momoko who name themselves after fruits and bring fame to girls' romantic fiction.

International media, too, have zoomed in on Japanese women, with English language magazines like the *National Geographic* printing ambiguous images of women soldiers in uniform learning the traditional bridal art of flower arrangement, and *The Face* featuring on its front cover a gaudily-clad and carefully made-up *geisha* apprentice blowing a billowing pink bubble out of her gum (Figure 1). More than anyone else, Japanese women seem to embody those contradictions which have been used so frequently to describe Japan: east and west, tradition and modernity, continuity and change – an elusive set of clichés, yet complex enough to be reinvented over and over again.

Women in Japan – so visible, so audible, and yet transparent. They are hiding in the light.

Hiding in the Light

Women have been, and still are, key figures in Japan's consumer culture – not only because they are their country's greatest spenders, but also because they form a group which has been most carefully observed, analysed and defined in marketing discourses. This volume will examine the images of women in Japanese consumer culture. It is not simply about women, nor about media, but about the relation between the two. The metaphor we have chosen to describe the media exposure of Japanese women is taken from a book by Dick Hebdige (1988), whose analysis of the way in which youth conflicts are simultaneously concealed and displayed in the British media, especially the process by which media presentations transform certain problems at the same time as enunciating them, seems to match the ambivalence of Japanese media's rendering of women. Japanese women are certainly hiding in the floodlight of media interest; but what do such images mean? Are they simply free-floating signifiers that circulate as media-invented phantoms without reference or relevance to the lives that Japanese women actually lead? Do the media really dress Japanese women in a straight-jacket despotically labelled 'the subject of consumption', where women themselves can only respond with inarticulate jerks of resistance to the consumer spectacles that surround them? Or is it rather that women, excluded – as they tend to be – from politics and industry, compensate for their subordination by living it up on the consumer scene? Could it

3

Figure 1 Hiding in the light (*The Face*, April 1993).
Courtesy of Norbert Schoerner

be, indeed, that women are riding on the seething wave of media proliferation – a wave which has borne them from the margins to the very
centre of Japanese society? Are they as dominated by the media as media
images are dominated by them? Where *are* Japanese women in these
exposures? The more the media's searchlights are directed at them, the
more invisible they seem to become.

This book consists of a collection of essays, each of which examines
representations of women in Japanese media – television, popular literature, and in particular women's magazines. These readings of women's

4

media are intended to give an overview of the Japanese media market which, in spite of its growing importance, has not yet been dealt with comprehensively in English. The focus is on media *for women*, and hence on the way in which women's media form a crucial part of what Inoue Teruko has called 'women's culture' (1985:80). Indeed, we would argue that media provide a cornerstone of feminine gender identity in contemporary Japan – not only as some kind of manipulation by the culture industries, nor only as a form of streamlined government propaganda, but as a pervasive presence which cannot be ignored (although it may be explicitly rejected) by women making sense of their lives. As would be expected of an analysis of women and media anywhere in the world, issues such as femininity, sexuality, love, age, family, food and fashion play a central role in the following chapters. All of the contributors to this book have, in one way or another, been poring over the shoulders of Japanese women – leafing through their magazines, reading their books, or watching their television programmes – to see how all these topics are dealt with in the intimate and personal, yet highly commercial, world constituted by women's media.

As in other countries where consumption is prominent, women are Japan's prime consumers but, as we will discuss in some detail, consumption is not simply an aspect of the social division of labour which happens to have been allotted to women. Rather, our argument is that being a consumer is a form of self-reflection offered to Japanese women by those media targeted directly at them. Such an identity ties women closely to consumer trends and simultaneously enables the market to address them in a very personal way. Yet, it is also an identity which – for a number of reasons that we will discuss during the course of this introductory essay – has been attractive to women. Here we are not saying that consumption is all there is to Japanese women. Far from it. Being a consumer is only one among many forms of self-reflection, but it is a form which is of sufficient significance to be analysed in its own right. In political terms, this consumer identity is highly ambivalent because it has made women very receptive to the controlling strategies of marketing, at the same time as they have been drawn into a central role in the Japanese economy and simultaneously increased their personal autonomy.

This leads us to argue from the beginning that there is no simple or uniform answer to the question of the media's 'manipulation' of women. It is clear that, in spite of the view of some academics that publishers and advertisers make a concerted and conscious effort to 'dupe' the readers of their women's magazines (e.g. McCracken 1993), no publisher concerned with its magazine's financial success can afford to ignore its readers entirely or to pander totally to their desires and expectations. Rather, there exists a two-way relationship between women and the market. And although power is not equally distributed in this relationship, women consumers are never, either as a group or as individuals, totally powerless in their responses to, or uses of, media images. The fact that different chapters in this book offer different perspectives on this relationship between media and women is not caused simply by authors' personal and theoretical inclinations, but also by different aspects of the media they study. In other words, it is the *interactive* nature of the relationship between media and audience which should be stressed.

There are certain topics which we would have liked this book to cover, but which for practical reasons we have been obliged to leave out. For example, we have been unable – regrettably – to include a chapter on Japanese pornography which, although consumed primarily by men, consists mainly of representations and interpretations of women's sexuality. Also, we would have liked to include more about feminism – both in terms of the ways in which Japanese women have expressed dissatisfaction with their socially defined womanhood, and of the ways in which Japanese feminists have criticized women's media. Not surprisingly, but – for our purposes – unfortunately, many Japanese scholars working in this local and political field are concerned more with current Japanese academic debates than with engaging with western scholars through English language publication. However, we believe that this book – along with other recent publications – marks an increased interest in such issues as media and consumption in the otherwise somewhat conservative field of Japanese Studies.

As it is, the essays published here cover media for women of all ages, starting with Paul Harvey's analysis of the television series *Oshin*, the most popular *asadora* morning show ever aired, and named after its main character who was presented at the time as 'all of Japan's grandmother'. The essay discusses the role played by national television in re-telling Japan's wartime and postwar history from a woman's point of view. From *Oshin*, we move to Brian Moeran's in-depth content analysis of the illustrated monthly *Katei Gahō*, targeted especially at housewives in their 40s. This magazine excels in a particularly luxurious and tradition-oriented style, and the self-conscious staging of Japaneseness, here analyzed in relation to recurrent themes in Japanese Studies, raises the question of the role played by women's media in preserving and presenting the canons of Japanese culture.

Next we shift to younger age segments of the market, first to the growing number of unmarried women in their late twenties and thirties. Nancy Rosenberger examines a selection of magazines aimed at this group which she identifies as 'elite cosmopolitans'. She shows how they simultaneously take part in a global consumer culture – through travel, fashion and so on – and in a local culture which lays claim on them to fullfill their roles as wives and mothers. She then makes use of a number of interviews to show how older unmarried women cope with being single *vis-à-vis* the media's constructions of femininity, marriage and lifecourse. Lise Skov then provides a detailed instance of the way in which a wide range of magazines, targeted at unmarried women, has taken up the issue of environmentalism in relation to media design, fashion and consumption, especially during the so-called 'ecology boom' in 1990. This she analyzes in the context of the global integration of environmental concerns with consumption in order to paint a distinct picture of Japanese women's consumer culture with its rapid turnover of trends. Through a reading of the way in which women's magazines have dealt with environmentalism, she discusses young Japanese women's ambivalent position as trendsetters for the whole of society while being largely excluded from political decision-making power.

After this, John Clammer presents a survey of ways in which the female body is represented in Japanese print media. He takes a sample of three types of magazine – women's, men's and weekly current affairs publications targeted at various age groups – which he finds contain broad similarities. The essay analyzes Japanese media representations of women in relation to recent western developments in the sociology of the body. From this, we move to an analysis of cute (*kawaii*) in Japanese consumer culture – an all-encompassing trend which has included almost anything from food to clothes, by way of personal items, idols and music. In her comprehensive analysis – the first of its kind – Sharon Kinsella traces cute back to the early 70s' emergence of a Japanese youth culture. She analyzes childlike cuteness in relation to cultural notions of childhood and adulthood, before criticizing the moral panic articulated by conservative critics who, though highly condescending toward the trend, have until now had the last word in analyzing it.

From this we shift to a still younger market segment of high school students in their teens. Merry White argues that teenagers as a distinct age group have evolved during the last decades in close interaction with the consumer market, and she analyzes the ways teens' magazines construct a 'curriculum' for the lives and concerns of this age group.

Finally, in an essay on Yoshimoto Banana's *Kitchen*, John Treat outlines the main features of this first novel by a young girls' fiction writer, before interpreting it in connection with its highly ambivalent appraisal by the Japanese literary establishment, as well as with perceived changes in the libidinal economy, and – by implication – Japanese families. Through this analysis he poses the question of whether profound cultural change is taking place in the context of consumption and postmodernism in Japan.

Our intention in presenting the chapters in this order is twofold. Firstly, we explicitly want to avoid creating a sense of chronology: the age categories employed by the media are *not* stages in Japanese women's lifecourse (even though they are frequently made out to be), but stills based on marketing data from the late 80s and early 90s. The elderly women who every morning dutifully followed the trials of *Oshin* on their television sets during the mid-80s have not moved through age-slots in the media in the same way as younger women now do. Indeed, when today's grandmothers were in their teens, the category of – and market for – Japanese teenagers did not even exist. Similarly, young *Cutie* readers, for their part, are unlikely to end up appreciating that brand of Japaneseness in which a magazine like *Katei Gahō* revels, and a safe bet is that some kind of change in taste will occur before they reach their forties. During the past twenty years, the consumer market has been transformed – and is still being transformed – so radically that it is impossible to predict the ways in which its present shape will continue to change beyond anything but the immediate future. Even though prognoses based on identification of generations have come to play a major part in Japanese market research, the age segmentation presented here is only valid in relation to the *current* grid used by market analysis. Hence, we are not attempting to forecast the future, but to analyse recent changes in Japanese society and to diagnose the present.

Secondly, the 'old age end' of the media market is characterized by what – with a friendly reference to Hobsbawm and Ranger (1983) – we might call the 'consumption of tradition'. This is relatively congruent with most textbooks about Japanese culture, and thus, by starting with *Oshin* and the middle-aged housewives of *Katei Gahō*, we are able to present a widely recognizable image of Japan. So we start out by fulfilling our ambivalent duty as Japanologists, before moving on to the disruptions, fads and cross-currents which have turned the young people's market into a dynamic whirl, often fueled by an explicit rejection of 'typically' Japanese values. Frequently, western goods and styles take on special significance, as in unmarried women's consumption lifestyle, according to which *western-ness* – symbolizing work and personal freedom – is pitched against the expectation that a 'Japanese woman' ought to sacrifice herself to husband and children in marriage. Thus, international influences in the Japanese consumer market contribute to creating specifically Japanese phenomena that simply do not accord with 'traditional' Japanese values. An example of this is young people's craze for cute writing, clothes and foods which Sharon Kinsella labels the first truly Japanese postwar style, and which has already become an international force, particularly in Asia.

In this introductory essay, we will start by arguing that the close link between women and the media is brought about by complex social and economic changes which have affected the whole of Japanese society. In order to clarify this link, we will present an overview of women's recent history in relation to work, family and consumption. Our aim is to show that *qua* their roles as consumers, women have moved from the margins of society to its centre in a long-term process which has been considerably speeded up during the last three decades. However, their central position in contemporary consumer society, carefully recorded in the mirror cabinet of the media, is highly ambivalent because it is still based on their subordinate position in the labour market. In contrast to most marketing analyses, as well as to some recent sociological studies, we wish to emphasize strongly that women nevertheless have gained their consumer identity through *work* – usually badly paid work outside or subordinate work within Japan's famous large corporations. Even though Japanese women continue to be financially dependent on men during most of their lives, having an income of their own has allowed them a corner of privacy. It has also included an admission ticket to their country's consumer market which has in the meantime taken upon itself the special task of analyzing their behaviour, enunciating their problems and providing them with appropriate solutions.

In the second half of this Introduction, we will focus on the way in which, during the last twenty years, Japanese media and consumer markets have grown more segmented and differentiated in close interaction with changes in women's lives and outlooks. Here we will present extensive data – collected during field research on Japanese media and consumption from 1990 onwards – in order to analyze the way in which women are conceptualized in marketing discourses and to discuss the implications of the complex symbiosis between women, media and consumption in Japan.

Implicit in this introductory essay is a periodization of the development of Japanese consumer culture which deserves a few comments before we proceed. In terms of consumption, the 'postwar' period can be said to have ended with the Tōkyō Olympics in 1964. This event not only marked Japan's recovery from postwar poverty and its readmittance as a member of the international cold war community; it also marked an advance in media technology and distribution – whether in the film director Ichikawa Kon's careful staging of the cameramen who were relaying the Olympics to the world, or in the rapid permeation of television throughout Japan.[1] The 60s was also a decade which saw student riots against the renewal of the US security treaty AMPO (leading to the US return of Okinawa to Japan in 1972), ending up with further demonstrations against Japan's environmental pollution, and the Ōsaka Expo in 1970 – diverse changes which, together with the oil crisis in 1973, led to the restructuring of the Japanese economy.

The shift from the 'postwar' period to the so-called '70s' and '80s' for which we argue here, is in fact in line with Karatani Kōjin's periodization of the history of Japanese literature, where he points out (1993: 292) that the term 'Shōwa' lost its significance as a historical division once the term 'postwar' ceased to be used in literature in the mid-60s. In other words, after the Tōkyō Olympics, it became more common for Japanese to talk about the '60s', the '70s' and the '80s' and thus to place their country in a synchronic context with the rest of the world, rather than continue to delineate time according to a specifically Japanese imperial calendar. However, as Aoki Tamotsu (1994) has pointed out, it is also highly problematic to state that the 'postwar' period is over when war issues are still as politically explosive as they are in Japan today. This goes both for domestic politics – marked, for example, by the bitter and continuing struggles over the degree to which school text books should conceal Japanese imperialism – and for international relations, especially in the Asian region, where elderly Korean 'comfort women' demand damages from the Japanese government for their sufferings while the Japanese army's massacres in China are being recorded by new generations of journalists and filmmakers. It is clear that Japan's political development from World War II has been out of synch with its economic recovery, resulting in a time lag which in itself has also influenced contemporary Japanese consumer culture.

According to our periodization, we see the crucial rupture giving rise to the kind of consumption with which this book deals as taking place in the early 70s, born out of gradual postwar changes and further fueled by the international oil crisis. In Japan, the main trend of the 70s was marked by a rediscovery of tradition as 'a truly national, pervasive, *mass* phenomenon' (Ivy 1988:21), which included going back to roots that led either into the dim and distant past (NHK's Silk Road documentary series), or straight into the present-day Japanese countryside – witness the National Railways' *Discover Japan* ad campaign, or the *mingei*, folk craft, 'boom' (Moeran 1984).

This playing on tradition by Japanese media was also accompanied by the revitalization among thinking elites of *nihonjinron* 'discussions of the Japanese' throughout the 70s (Yoshino 1992), when – paralleling Huyssen's discussion of postwar Germany – history and the past were abandoned to 'tradition-mongering neo-conservatives bent on reestablishing the norms of earlier industrial capitalism: discipline, authority, the work ethic and the traditional family' (Huyssen 1986:172).

The 80s, on the other hand, were marked by a celebration of the city and of a more self-conscious consumer culture. At the same time, liberalization of financial markets and Nakasone Yasuhiro's 'grand design' for an internationalized Japan-in-the-world in the 21st century (Pyle 1987) – together with a variety of ambitious technological projects that marked the Japanese government's drive towards an information society (*jōhō shakai*) – produced a consumer boom which has, in retrospect, been dubbed the 'bubble period' (*bubble jidai*). No doubt it was the strength of the Japanese economy, together with the international political situation, which brought the country to such a position, but Japanese women consumers, with their taste for western brand-name goods and international travel, were among the first to take advantage of these changes.

The 90s can be said to have begun with the bursting of the financial bubble in 1991. Well before the full implications of the economic crisis had manifested themselves, there was a shift in consumer trends away from the conspicuous and outgoing consumption of the 80s towards a more inwardly oriented 'pursuit of authenticity' (*honmono shikō*), as interpreted in such advertising keywords as 'handmade' (*tezukuri*), 'home party', and the ever recyclable notion of 'tradition' (*dentō*) (Moeran and Skov 1993:124–9). The economic crisis has, at the time of writing, brought with it cutbacks in employment – firstly affecting women, though eventually posing a threat to the overall employment structure of Japanese companies.

Politically, uncertainty has arisen from the failure of the Liberal Democratic Party to maintain control of government after more than four decades of uninterrupted power, and from a consequent series of shifting alliances between unlikely partners. At the same time, pressure from foreign governments has led to the further opening up of the domestic market, so that Japanese consumers can now purchase – among

11

other things – American apples, Thai rice and German beer at competitive prices. In this way, imported goods are moving into the medium quality, medium price range of the market. It is likely that the various strategies employed to overcome the economic and political crisis will bring about new changes in consumer culture, with an increased influx of labour away from the manufacturing and into the service industries. As we shall see, this would in fact be a further development of an on-going process in the postwar Japanese economy.

In this Introduction we will first provide a brief historical overview of Japanese women as workers, consumers, mothers and daughters during the past 125 years, before moving on to a critical discussion of the notion that Japanese women have been marginal to the central dynamic of their society. Then we will examine the way in which women were conceptualized as consumers during the 80s – a process which was closely linked to the increase in the number of women working outside the home. After that we will take a closer look at the slippery notions of power and sexuality which have accompanied Japanese women's recent exposure as consumers, before going on to examine the gradual segmentation of Japan's homogeneous 'mass market' during the same decade. We will then present an analysis of the relation between market segmentation and the development of women's magazines from the 1970s onwards. By way of conclusion, we will discuss some of the contradictory implications of the close relationship between women and the market.

Work, Family and Consumption

Let us start with what seems to be a contradiction. From their very beginning, women's studies have focussed on the task of making women visible – by writing the unrecorded history of women, by giving voice to women's experiences, and by revealing aspects of women's lives and labour that had previously been overlooked in a male-dominated society. At the same time, until a few years ago, women were for the most part defined in Japanese Studies as peripheral to the main dynamics of Japanese society. This seems to counter the high visibility of women in the 1980s and 90s, but our argument is that it nevertheless acts as a precondition for people's understanding of the recent changes that have occurred in Japanese society.

Here we will address this paradox and take issue, firstly, with the idea that women have been both marginal and conservative until their apparent 'emergence' in the vanguard of social change in the 1980s.

Secondly, we will criticize the notion underlying this discussion: that women have been little more than consumers during most, if not all, of Japan's history since the Meiji era (1868–1912). By examining the historical background of Japanese women's employment and the complex ways in which they have been marginalized since the mid-to late-19th century, we should be better equipped to grasp some of the ambiguities of the media's celebration of Japanese women as consumers from the start of the 1980s onwards.

The view that Japanese women are marginal has been strongly supported by what can be described justifiably as a male-biased model of social organization that has focussed on 'groupism', 'vertical relations', 'harmony' and various other cultural attributes which scholars and journalists have long listed in their promotion of the idea that Japan is different from other industrialized countries of Europe and the Americas. Thus, all of us nowadays, whether we are employees in international conglomerates, MBA students at university, or devoted Japanologists, can reel off a list of qualities that are said to distinguish Japanese companies from their counterparts elsewhere: lack of differentiation between managers and workers, a system of 'permanent' employment, and enterprise rather than trade unionism – to name but a few features that are the result of, and contribute to, a 'homogeneous' workforce. It is also quite well known that even now less than half of that workforce enjoys such benefits from its employers, even though in Japan they are widely recognised as desirable, and that this half includes less than five per cent of all women workers.[2]

The so-called 'group model' should be criticised for focussing so narrowly on relations of production in a manner that further marginalizes women. On the one hand, as workers Japanese women are usually excluded from permanent employment in large Japanese companies, and thus also from the core values constituting what Clark (1979:95–7) has described as Japan's 'society of industry'. On the other, as wives, mothers and consumers, they have been relegated – like women elsewhere (Myers 1986:136) – to a marginal position of 'non-productive labour' in the home or supermarket. They have thus been overlooked at the same time as their contributions to both work and family have been crucial to Japan's successful economic development and social stability.

Moreover, the fact that the group model presents an idealized vision, rather than actual analysis, of social relations has been wrongly used to conflate all those aspects of Japanese society which it ignores into a single complementary image: that of women as primarily an *under-used* labour resource in Japan's economic development. This is a misconstrual.

13

Rural women, for example, have always worked and, until the mid-60s when the majority of the Japanese population was living in the country, the proportion of Japanese women working was considerably higher than that in, for example, the United States. Indeed, figures suggest that, without women to work in them, rural industries like agriculture, forestry and fishing would no longer exist (Sōrifu 1993:84–87) (Figure 2). Even today, the proportion of Japanese women in the workforce is not much lower than that of American women, except – significantly – between the ages of 25 and 35 (HILL 1987:142). Japanese women's

Figure 2 Without women to work in them, rural industries would no longer exist

14

lowest participation in the workforce was in 1970, but even at that time they still made up one third thereof (Iwao 1993:157). It is higher now than that of either France or former West Germany (Sōrifu 1993:62–3).[3] So, despite the fact that being a housewife is a feasible career in Japan today, the idea that women should be characterized as not participating in the labour force has very limited historical or social validity.

Let us cite one early example of Japanese women at work, in order to show how important their labour has been to Japan's manufacturing economy. At the beginning of the country's industrial development in the Meiji period, in particular between 1890 and 1910, women made up over two thirds of the labour force employed in private companies – mainly in the textile industry where they were employed as silk reelers, cotton spinners and weavers (Tsurumi 1990:9). In response to in-creasing labour instability and the economic crisis of the 1880s, when factory girls were the first to call industrial strikes in support of better working conditions and higher wages, factory owners began to issue employment contracts for periods of from one (in the silk mills) to three or even seven years (Tsurumi 1990:176). These contracts were not signed by the women workers themselves, but by their fathers – typic-ally poor peasants badly in need of cash to pay their land taxes. Factory agents deliberately recruited women from remote areas where there was no knowledge of the terrible working conditions then found in the textile industry. They handed over advance payments that were then turned into overpriced loans which daughters – sometimes no more than ten years old – would be obliged to repay by working through their contractual period. Women workers themselves would often incur further debts as a result of a rigid system of fines devised by mill operators to keep them under strict control. The gates to the women's quarters were usually locked at night to stop any worker from running away, and long working hours, poor lighting, unprotected machines, bad nutrition, as well as sexual assaults, were commonplace in the mills. Many women con-tracted tuberculosis and other respiratory diseases and a large number eventually took their own lives (Tsurumi 1990).

The young women working in the textile industry played a crucial role in Japan's early industrial development for, once the spinning mills and weaving shops were established, cheap textiles became the country's major export, thereby enabling Japan to pay for its imports of western technology. This it then used to develop its industries further. At the same time, the option of 'selling' their daughters enabled many tenant farmers to stay on their land and so secure a certain stability in the country during a transitional period when their livelihood, based on an old feudal order, was gradually being undermined (Tsurumi 1990:192).[4] Though severely exploited and abused, women were thus crucial for their contribution to the development of Japanese industry in world markets, and to the maintenance of social order at home. That they themselves were aware of their double importance for the nation can be seen, for example, in their work songs (Tsurumi 1990:97).

Japanese economic development gradually brought into existence a service sector which offered new kinds of employment to women – from the first women office clerks and telephone receptionists in the 1890s, to a much broader range of jobs that became available in the Taishō period (1912–1926). These included 'mannequin girls', 'depart(ment store) girls', 'manicure girls', 'bus girls', 'elevator girls', 'train girls', 'one yen taxi girls', 'gasoline girls', 'mahjong girls', and 'golf girls' (Shimamori 1984:54). In contrast to those working in the textile industry who had remained hidden in the factories, women who took up these new jobs were very visible in the communication, transportation and consumption of modern urban life. Japanese used the English word 'girl' (gāru) to describe women working in these new service sector jobs and, as indicated by the word, they tended to be young and unmarried, and often wore uniforms in western style as a sign of their, and their country's, 'modernization' (Figures 3 and 4).

With the growth of the service sector came Japan's first consumer culture. Conceived perhaps in victory in the Russo-Japanese war, early consumer culture was marked by events such as the creation of a 'Genroku revival' staged by Mitsukoshi to celebrate its reopening as a department store. This harking back to a golden age of Japanese feudalism (1688–1703) was expressed in a flamboyant Genroku design on a number of items – from combs and bags to wooden clogs, by way of towels and a Japanese-style 'Genroku dance' performed by a 'Genroku Study Association'. Three years later, in 1907, a cosmetics company was making use of celebrity endorsement in its advertising, while other companies were creating tie-ups with other media such as theatres and magazines. Japan then held its first national Beauty Queen competition and – true to shōjo form – selected a 16-year-old cutie, Suehiro Hiroko, who was then promptly thrown out of school. The full emergence of consumer culture as such, as well as that of the bourgeoisie, is seen to have coincided with the outbreak of the First World War in 1914 (Shimamori 1984:18–28).

Women's visibility during the early part of the century is recorded in the Tōkyō Asahi Newspaper's *Changing Japan Seen Through the Camera* published several years later in 1933. This album sets out to

Figure 3 Train girl (from *Changing Japan Seen Through The Camera* 1933)

show images of Japan to 'the reading public of the Occident' in order to give them a chance to 'be better acquainted with the many and rapidly changing aspects of Japanese life, which registers a continually quickening pace' (unpaginated preface). Its photos strike a fine, though even at that time well-tested, balance between the monuments of modernization (motor cars caught in a traffic jam, factory production of silk stockings), on the one hand, and modest markers of Japaneseness (a woman in kimono carrying a paper umbrella in the evening snow, a thatch-roofed village), on the other. This meeting of contrasts is also

17

LISE SKOV AND BRIAN MOERAN

Figure 4 Elevator girls (from *Changing Japan Seen Through The Camera* 1933)

presented in a fascinating collage of feet walking along a street, where Japanese *geta* clogs and *zōri* sandals intermingle with western-style women's high-heeled pumps and men's long black military boots. Similar to this is the haunting image of kimono-clad geisha practicing in pairs the seemingly unfamiliar steps of the fox-trot (cf. Savigliano 1992) (Figures 5 and 6).

For all this visibility, physical labour, though commonplace for women at the time, is represented in just one picture: that of a group of women photographed on a construction site doing the work of a bulldozer.

18

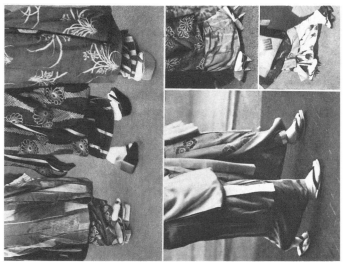

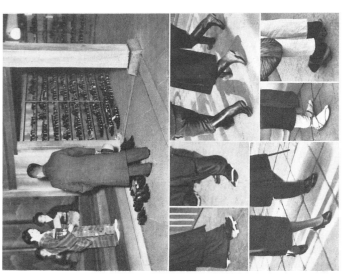

Figure 5 Footwear collage: east meets west (from *Changing Japan Seen Through The Camera* 1933)

Figure 6 Geisha practising their foxtrot (from *Changing Japan Seen Through The Camera* 1933)

Dressed in traditional work clothes, their bodies are short and broad, and their heads are covered, making their appearance completely different from that of the slim and fashionable 'girls' working in the service sector. The caption informs us: 'On account of their patience and low wages, women labourers are indispensible in driving piles, or levelling the ground with a primitive device' (Tōkyō Asahi Shinbun 1933:142) (Figure 7).

In contrast, images of these smiling women working in the new service sector take up a substantial part of the book and merge im-

Figure 7 Working women (from *Changing Japan Seen Through The Camera* 1933)

21

perceptibly with those of women as *consumers* – looking at market stall photographs of film stars (Figure 8), shopping in department stores, sitting in coffee shops, or camping in the mountains. It was precisely the expansion of the service sector which gave rise to those leisure-oriented 'modern girls' who first appeared in the 20s with their passion for the fashions of Greta Garbo and Marlene Dietriech. Popularly known as *moga* – a double pun on the hybrid form of 'modern girl' and on *mōdan*, 'hair cutting' (referring to their short hair styles) – these young women were urban flaneuses who would cruise along the Ginza shopping street (*ginbura*, in the slang of the time). They devoted themselves to films, jazz, dance and sports, all of which were seen to constitute 'modernism' (Shimamori 1984:52–55; Silverberg 1991).

However, with Japanese militarism in the 30s and early 40s, there was an important shift in the social perception of women when the government began to emphasize their *reproductive* roles. Even some feminists, who had previously promoted the independence of the modern girl, supported the state's view on motherhood for the simple reason that it was the first time that it had promoted a *positive* image of women (Miyake 1991:273; Yamazaki 1985:138–45). Whereas the Meiji government had regarded women within the family as simply inferior, subject to the moral authority of the father, the Shōwa government recognized women as the cornerstone of the family system. The obvious aim here was to assure the stability of the family and a sustained population growth in a period when men were needed as soldiers and administrators for Japan's colonial expansion. But an important side-effect was that, by promoting women as the mothers of the nation, the state also associated its own power with notions of fecundity and pro-ductivity. It was precisely because of the significance that it attached to motherhood that the Japanese government – unlike the British and US governments – did not systematically mobilize women's labour until the very end of the war. This is not, however, to ignore the fact that a large number of women, especially unmarried women, did find jobs in the military industry in spite of the lack of incentive for them to do so. After the war, three million women workers were laid off to make way for soldiers returning from the front (Miyake 1991).

The definition of women as *mothers* during the early part of the Shōwa period (1926–1989) marks the beginning of a conservative trend which lasted at least until the 1970s, and which saw women as up-holding the social order through their back-stage command of their families, and yet not being credited for the work that they continued to do. One effect of this policy towards women was to facilitate a transition

Figure 8 Buying pictures of film stars (from *Changing Japan Seen Through The Camera* 1933)

from a patrilineal household system based on the relationship between father and son (biological or adopted), to a woman-centred nuclear family in which the most important relationship was that between mother and children, rather than between spouses. In this way, men's dominance in the public sphere was neatly complemented by women's power at home. As Cho (1986:292) has pointed out in her discussion of the Confucian family in Korea, legitimizing what she calls 'mother power' in this way is probably 'the most successful way of accommodating women under the male-dominated social system'. It was *qua* their function as mothers and housewives that Japanese women gained national significance, supported by a widespread notion that they did not become 'real women' until they married and bore children, preferably sons. In contrast to some other Asian countries, very few Japanese have employed domestic workers to help women handle their double burden of family and work, even if they have had the financial wherewithal to do so (*Far Eastern Economic Review* 1992:37–8).

There is little doubt that this postwar definition of women as mothers has succeeded in making Japanese women the repositories of conservatism and nationalism. At the same time as marginalizing them from production, it has given rise to the idea that women contribute best to their country's economic development by serving their husbands at home so that *they* can go out and work hard for their companies. Although such ideas are being questioned, in most homes women have ideally got up first in the morning to make breakfast and prepare clean clothes for their husbands, while in the evening they have waited with food and hot bath prepared, however late their husbands came home. So women frequently find themselves praised as mothers of the nation, the key to Japanese success – only to be blamed in the next breath for not devoting themselves fully to this task and thereby for jeopardizing the welfare of the nation.[5] Given the prevalence of this idea, we find considerable attention paid to the 'absent father', the hard-working company employee. Indeed, the many stories about silly dads, clumsy and alien in their own homes, are partially verified by the fact that about one third of all husbands temporarily live apart from their wives and children, mainly because of their career structure (Iwao 1993:102).

Other factors support the notion that women are conservative elements in Japanese society. There are two areas in particular that we need to look at here: Japanese Culture with a capital C, and the education system. Firstly, women can be said to manage cultural heritage in the sense that they are the ones who practise the so-called 'bridal arts' – for the most part adopted from the former samurai class: tea ceremony, flower arrangement, and the wearing, making and maintaining of kimono. Significantly, most of these arts were formerly performed by men and sustained a masculine ethic of selflessness and harmony which was, and still is, very much part and parcel of the group model. Costume traditions are, of course, exempt from this, but in recent years, as the kimono has become an area of specialized knowledge, it, too, has been reinvented along the lines of the group model (Goldstein-Gidoni 1993). One significant result of this gender crossover, then, has been the fact that women have been turned into the guardians of, and specialists in, Japan's cultural heritage, though usually supervised by male 'masters' (O'Neill 1984). It has also marked a democratization in which elitist art forms with their masculine ethic have been transformed into nationally significant pastimes, in principle open to everybody. For young middle-class women, bridal arts have also provided a tuition in the 'good wife, wise mother' ideal which contributes to their value on the marriage market, at the same time as preparing them for a married life of idle boredom and the bliss of Japaneseness. Even though such training is not a criterion for getting married today, it is fair to say that the survival of many of Japan's traditional arts still depends on the interest women show in them.

Apart from their duties as wives, women have been obliged by the pressure on children in schools to spend a lot of time on their sons' and daughters' education. This has meant arranging extra lessons for them at cram schools and helping them through their homework which from an early age tends to take up a lot of time, although it is only for women whose husbands' income is high enough for them not to work that *total* devotion to their children's schooling is feasible. Their involvement in their children's education has given rise to the frightening concept of *kyōiku mama* (education mama), for whom a child's performance in school becomes her own *raison d'être*. As Lebra (1984:198) points out, children's success or failure in university entrance examinations has in some cases come to be seen as the success or failure of those children's mothers, especially, of course, in families which pass on academic ambitions to their children. Japan's education system thus keeps women firmly in their middleclass nuclear family place, and is a strong force for conservatism.

The semantically dense notion of motherhood has led to a gap between mothers, on the one hand, and young, unmarried women-in-the-making, on the other. In the postwar period, there was a strong social ideal that urban women should work outside the home only during those years leading up to marriage. During the 60s, most women were in fact required by their employees to quit their jobs in preparation for their weddings – a practice changed only as a result of a series of cases brought to court by women (Brinton 1993:230–1). It was at this time that the proportion of non-working housewives was highest in Japan, but the shortage of unskilled labour in the high growth economy created a demand that began to be filled by married women in their thirties and forties (Brinton 1993:10). Since then, the number of working married women has increased steadily, but still only 24 per cent continue to work without any breaks for marriage or childbirth (HILL 1987:143), while the majority of mothers begin to work again after their children have started going to school. In the mid-70s more young women began to continue their work after marriage and childbirth, and still more married women began to seek employment outside their homes. This process was facilitated by a renewed labour shortage brought about by the restructuring of the economy after the 1973 oil crisis, as well as by a falling birth rate (Smith 1987:16).

The point about Japanese housewives, therefore, is not that they do not work for a salary, but rather that they have poorly paid jobs with little or no chance of promotion or career advancement. Many work on a part-time or temporary basis and are not entitled to the kinds of benefits or compensation afforded full-time permanent employees, even though 'part' time (*pāto*) can signify as many working hours as does full time. Another large group consists of women who are self-employed, often as piece workers, typically assembling electronic parts in their homes when their children are at school (Brinton 1993:140). Women who were once highly visible and highly desirable *OL*s (office ladies) thus find themselves unable to go back to their former jobs. Moreover, like other mid-career recruits generally in Japan, they often cannot make use of their former work experience in a new job and are obliged to start from scratch when looking for re-employment as married women. Very often, they have little alternative but to take up unskilled work of a largely invisible kind, usually at home or close to the neighbourhoods in which they live, and with a pay scale which, on average, comes to just half of that enjoyed by men.[6]

There is a strong tendency to identify married women as *housewives* (*shufu*), thereby reinforcing the notion that home and family are, or ought to be, their main concern. This label, which has all too often been reproduced in Japanese Studies, shows a curious disregard for the fact that paid labour is an increasingly important part of married women's lives. For example, in his discussion of gender inequality, Smith (1987: 16) writes: 'work is not an alternative to homemaking; it is an extension

26

of the domestic role'. According to such a line of thought, it is easy to regard women's lives as being structured by a logic of leisure from which economic necessities are absent, at the same time as being up-holstered by an unquestioned nest-building instinct. It thus seems that whatever women do is determined by a desire for personal development, self fulfillment, and pleasant ways to spend their days (cf. Iwao 1993: 153–5) – concerns which, needless to say, hardly figure in discussions of *men*'s employment.

In this way, work has frequently been presented as yet another form of consumption to which women turn now that it is in vogue. It is also clear that the equation of men with production and women with con-sumption – or men with work and women with leisure – can only come about through considerable simplification of the current situation, for – as we will show in the following section – women's work and consump-tion condition each other. In our opinion, it is the decision-making power over their own salaries which is the main factor allowing women, and marketers, to create space for individualized consumption. At the same time, it is women's participation in public processes, whether related to work or leisure, which has made them visible in the streets, in the media and, not least, in marketing strategies.

Women as Consumers

In this section we will take a closer look at the economic and social changes which have turned women into key figures in contemporary consumer culture, paying special attention to the ways in which these changes have been conceptualized in marketing research. The so-called oil shock in 1973 marks the turning point after which more women began to work outside the home at the same time as beginning to play a more prominent role in consumption. Both government and industry responded to the crisis by implementing a number of structural changes in the Japanese economy which came into effect around 1975. Accord-ing to the Hakuhōdō Institute for Life and Living (HILL), these included, among other things, men's decreasing opportunities for promotion at work and a change in criteria from relatively more emphasis on seniority to one on merit; more women going to work outside their homes; the growth of the service sector and a shift towards convenience goods and services; the spread of high tech innovations; greater job mobility; a shorter working week; and increasing affluence (HILL 1987:234). A wide range of changes along these lines brought about a shift in power balances between work and leisure, production and consumption, as well as men and women, all coinciding with the shift from a high to stable-growth economy in 1975.

Until then, the proliferation of consumer goods had tended to be seen in terms of improvement of life in the Japanese household: for example, the 'three sacred treasures' of television, refrigerator and washing machine which were all the rage in the late 50s; followed by the '3 Cs' (car, cooler [air conditioning] and colour TV) in the 60s. The marketing of such goods was targeted at women as representatives of their families, rather than for their personal purchase, and the aim of the marketers was to place specific products in *all* Japanese homes. In addition, after a period of rapid urbanization, marketers realized that urban consumer markets no longer consisted primarily of young people who had come up from the country to live in large cities like Tōkyō. Instead, they found 'new families', a term coined by Marui Department Store's PR department (Yamaki 1992:306), who lived either within the Yamanote circle line, or in nearby suburbs within easy striking distance of the city's centre. Their children had been brought up as what the marketers liked to perceive as the first truly postwar generation in Japan in that they had no direct experience of hardship or poverty. It was to this generation that marketers turned their attention from 1975, as they made sure that products suited the new urban lifestyle. An illustration of this change is Seibu Department Store's decision not to rebuild immediately in its old established centre of Ikebukuro in the north west of the capital, but to set up a store in the trendy young people's area of Shibuya further south (Ueno 1991:8–9). The diversification that it and other stores sought to exploit led to the growth of specialized retail outlets which sold co-ordinated, rather than one-off, products. In other words, the new masses were not being asked to buy *things* so much as *ways of life* which were classified as home improvement, hobbies and leisure, fashion, Culture, tradition, and convenience (Ueno 1991:27). While increasing the emphasis on consumption, the development of the service sector also provided women with a wide range of opportunities for work and careers.

In this period, there was a major shift in emphasis in the way in which the media represented and addressed women, from 'women in the household' to 'women as individuals'. In married women's magazines, this change had already been on its way for some years,[7] but it was strongly enhanced by the emergence of young women's magazines, and was epitomized by the 1970 advertising headline by Parco, *From volume to beauty* (*mōretsu kara beautiful*), which heralded the shift from quantitative to qualitative consumption. At the same time, women's experiences and outlooks were also promoted at the international level as a result of western feminism. The fact that 1975 was designated an International Women's Year, and the decade that followed the Decade of Women, meant that Japanese media began focussing their attention on women – what they thought, how they lived, how they fared *vis-à-vis* men – and this general attention was eventually followed up in 1986 by the promulgation of the Law of Equal Employment Opportunities.

The interest in women promoted by feminism was taken up in a very literal way by Japanese industry. An illustration of this is a Tōkyō Gas advertising campaign in 1984 for a series of cookers, water heaters, and gas leak alarms. The ads showed visuals of women in the home in stereotypical situations – wearing an apron in the kitchen, or putting on lipstick in front of a mirror – yet pandered to by the headline, '*City gas is a feminist, isn't it?*' As Tanaka (1990:81) points out, this unexpected use of the word here implies that the gas company is feminist because it 'helps' women by supplying them with household goods to make their daily chores easier and safer. Tōkyō Gas's interpretation of feminism is perhaps only an extreme case of media appropriation of a range of concepts and problems that have sprung out of the women's movement – from notions of independence and individualism, to the urge that women should do what they themselves really want.

Some of the first to respond to the changing environment of the 70s were young people who would meet on Sundays near Yoyogi Park in Harajuku in Tōkyō and dance to rock music. The emergence of youth groups like this (quickly dubbed the *takenozoku* 'bamboo tribe') was accompanied by a growing consumer market for their generation, and the media – in particular, the new magazines – soon began delivering an integrated vision of fashion, lifestyles, music and idols. By the early 80s, Japanese commentators were suggesting that economic, social and political changes had given rise to a so-called 'new breed' (*shinjinrui*) in the offices of Japanese corporations.[8] What was new about these young men and women was that they were *not* willing to sacrifice themselves for their companies without getting anything in return, and that they regarded leisure as almost as important as work. They were associated with 'an ethos of individuality and self-actualization, a need for instant gratification, a concern with fashion, an absorption with leisure-time pursuits, and a tendency towards looser social ties, both at home and at work' (Anderson and Wadkins 1992:147). The 'new breed' was seen to mark a 'generation gap' dividing an older generation, which accepted the hitherto unquestioned work ethic, from a rising younger age group whose members were more concerned with their own lives. However, the gap cannot simply be summed up as a difference between work and leisure, for the 'new breed' of yuppies certainly worked hard. Rather, it lies in the emphasis on an individual perspective from which to understand work and career as well as the enjoyment of the here and now – whether related to work or leisure (Figure 9).

In young people's search for more immediate gratification, consumption came to be viewed in a *positive* light. Replacing a postwar version of the neo-Confucianist attitude which saw primary social value

Figure 9 Young women in Harajuku station,
Tōkyō, 1986

30

in endurance, the smothering of personal desires, and hard work for the development of the Japanese economy as a whole, younger Japanese opted for a more relaxed outlook which permitted, accepted, and highly evaluated *pleasure*. This shift has exposed, in particular, women whose work in Japanese corporations has been marginalized and who therefore have had little to lose by devoting themselves to the thrills of consumption. Despite obvious ambivalences, the identification of women as consumers has been widely celebrated as emancipation and empowerment at the same time. Commercial media have realized their own interest in promoting this shift in values – a shift which has proved to be the main growth area in the Japanese consumer market in the last twenty years.

This does not mean, of course, that men are absent from Japanese consumer culture. The popularity throughout the postwar period of bars, golf courses, mahjong clubs, and race courses bears witness to the fact that salarymen did not work all the time and that they used their leisure hours for something other than sleep (impressions from commuter trains notwithstanding). More recently, other preserves of male consumerism have been highlighted – from cars and motor bikes to the latest hi-fi equipment and electronic gadgetry, by way of all kinds of goods and services provided by Japan's busy sex industry. Some young men's magazines also promote body care in a manner similar to that found in women's magazines, with step-by-step instructions about how to clean, bathe and protect one's skin with an emotional intensity which is for the most part quite unimaginable in European and American magazines (cf. Winship 1987:154). The transformation of men as company workers or as out-of-place dads into leisure-oriented consumers has been a major area of potential growth for the advertising industry, and there are indications in the early 90s that such attention has begun to pay off (Figure 10). So far, however, women have dominated the consumer scene.

Let us now turn to marketing discourses. The Hakuhōdō Institute of Life and Living (HILL) is a research institute attached to one of Japan's biggest advertising agencies, Hakuhōdō. Its members have conducted research and published widely on the subject of Japanese women and its findings have consequences for Japanese women in three ways. Firstly, they are used directly by the advertising agency in designing advertising campaigns and in advising its clients about the structure and development of the consumer market. Secondly, HILL's research is often quoted in the news media as evidence of current trends and changes and so influences public perceptions. Thirdly, related to this, HILL's work is widely recognized and referred to as social research, so that HILL

Figure 10 Young men in Yoyogi Park, Tōkyō, 1986

researchers often work together with sociologists and anthropologists employed in academia. In other words, it is impossible to maintain a clear distinction between market research, news, debate, and social sciences. There is good reason, therefore, to take a closer look at the way in which changes related to women and consumption are conceptualized in this marketing-cum-sociological discourse.[9]

HILL (1987:9–15) lists four main reasons underlying the sudden attentiveness paid to women in the 1980s, and allowing the consumer market to target them. The first of these is their 'pioneering role': even as housewives whose sole job was to look after the family, women have always been finely attuned to matters affecting what is now referred to as 'lifestyle'. The Hakuhōdō Institute of Life and Living argues that they have almost invariably been ahead of men when it comes to surveys of trends such as the shift from supposed materialism to what it calls 'spiritual abundance' (*kokoro no yutakasa*), or desired changes in lifestyles generally. They have also been more conscious of the time available to them and so 'learned' much earlier than men how best to make use of those precious hours when they did not have to work on behalf of their husband and children.

Secondly, the change in the Japanese market from production-led mass consumption to a consumer-oriented segmentation permitted women – once the underlings in terms of Japan's economic growth – to emerge in a stronger position. According to HILL, this position was sustained by the fact that their husbands' incomes were no longer increasing in the way that they once had, so that women began contributing their own incomes towards overall household expenditure. In the decade between 1975 and 1985, we find that households in which both men and women worked had an income fifteen per cent higher, and an overall expenditure ten per cent higher, than those where men only worked.

Thirdly, HILL argues that women constitute the core of what it sees as the 'new needs' of Japan's consumer economy. Compared with other changes in society, women's 'power up' was extremely rapid – so much so that the system as a whole was unable to keep up. The biggest change here was the fact that women went to work outside the home, thereby causing a knock-on effect first on the household economy, then on the corporate economy, and finally on the Japanese economy as a whole. For example, the fact that they had less time available for their families, but two incomes to make up for it, meant that such households spent more money on eating out, entertainment, education, the arts, travel, fashion, cars and so on. In the absence of proper government-provided facilities or social security generally, says HILL, 'baby hotels' emerged for mothers who worked. In the absence of husbands to help at home, instant foods, household electric goods and service industries proliferated.

Finally, from the late 70s, a 'woman's view' began to be appreciated and desired in the Japanese business world generally. Companies – especially those operating in the spheres of distribution, food and interior decor – needed women to advise them. Some appointed women to important positions; others employed whole teams of women to dream up new hit products. In this way, there emerged a general acceptance of men's *and* women's viewpoints.

Additional figures listed by HILL (1987:28) show that there was a long-term increase in women's life expectancy from 64 years in 1930 to 81 in 1982. Over the same period, the years devoted to giving birth to and rearing fewer children decreased from 35 to 26 years. This seems to have resulted in an immense increase in women's 'private time', at the same time as their educational level had gone up, making them likely to seek cultured pastimes.

The line of thought adopted by the research institute outlined here is problematic in a number of ways. Firstly, even though women have fewer children than before, bringing up a child in Japan today is more time-consuming, costly and lonely than ever before. Secondly, washing machines and electric rice cookers may allow women to save time previously spent on washing clothes by hand and boiling rice in an iron cauldron, but in return the purchase of household goods may be conditional on women's paid work. Finally, and most importantly, HILL's perspective on increases in women's 'private time' after they have dealt with housework and childcare, seems to reinforce the idea that women are always and only consumers – to the extent that even women's work is seen as a preferred way to spend leisure time.[10]

The Hakuhōdō material shows that, at the same time as Japanese women have changed drastically, stereotypical gender roles have in fact been strengthened. For example, the 'woman's view' cultivated by the industry has attracted attention to matters that have conventionally been defined as women's domain. Yet, the finding that women are 'ahead' of men, in the sense that the attitudes and values held by women today are also likely to be found among men in a few years from now, is interesting in that it seems to contradict the widely held idea that Japanese women are conservative. However, this should be seen as being closely linked to the fact that women in Japan tend to be more interested in cultural matters than are men, whether in literature, art or fashion. Finally, even though women's financial means have increased because they now have an income of their own, the marketing discourses have reinforced rather than questioned the idea that housework and childcare are a woman's responsibility.

For many married women, the ideal is that their husband's salary should cover household expenses, so that they can decide how to manage their own income. Yet it is not always easy to draw a line between household consumption, on the one hand, and women's private consumption, on the other. Iwao, for example, describes the case of one woman who could not make up her mind about whether to pay for (and so decide on) a special family holiday, or for her daughter's education in a private college, out of savings from her own work (1993:54). We have already seen, too, how instant foods and electric household appliances are targeted directly at women consumers in order, as the marketing jargon has it, to 'help' women through their daily chores.

Furthermore, in spite of the fact that their improved buying power seems to have increased women's authority in the family, as Iwao argues (1993:86), other studies show that while husbands have the decision-making power over a wide range of family matters – from the name and education of children to choice of newspapers, television programmes and life insurance schemes – women only fully decide on two issues: the menu of the family dinner and how much pocket money they spend (HILL 1993b:56–7). No wonder then that they should treasure their private time and money spent on personal consumption!

Our argument here is exactly this: that, along with the reinforcement of women's responsibility for family and housework, women's increased spending power has brought with it a new type of consumer market for married women which caters to their own experiences, looks and tastes in a manner similar to that found in the explosive market for young single women. Whether watching a television series in the morning after all other members of the family have left the house, or reading through their magazines, married women often find personal consumption a lonely, though valuable, experience. It is true that the objects of mothers' and grandmothers' consumption may contain strong values of endurance and nostalgia – whether in the form of Oshin's retelling her life, and by implication Japan's history, or in a magazine like *Katei Gahō*'s impressionistic and ahistorical reinvoking of 'childhood memories'. But this alone does not make these different from younger women's media. For example, advertising for esthé salons presents an image of body discipline based on endurance and planning, while in shōjo literature nostalgia takes the form of the staging of the present as a memory of the future (Treat 1993). What these different forms of consumption indulged in by Japanese women of different ages have in common is the construction of an idealized dream world. In some cases these dreams seem to yield an immediate pleasure. In others they are bitter-sweet, based on the awareness of women's limited possibilities in a male-dominated society. Sometimes the dreams construct a kind of totality and overview in a woman's life which enable her to accept her outlook; at other times, they are the impetus that drives a woman to change her own situation. What all these visual and textual discourses share in common is their construction of women as individual consumers of a particularly emotional kind.

What, more specifically, are these types of individualized consumption? Travel and tourism form one important area. Even though more Japanese men than women go abroad every year, men tend to go on business trips while women travel as tourists. Except in the case of a newly-wed couple's honeymoon, it is common for a woman, whether married or not, to travel with another woman friend rather than with a male companion. Secondly, women's personal consumption is often combined with a desire to learn: tennis, swimming, 'jazz dance', aerobics are all consumed lesson by lesson. In department store art exhibitions and their 'women's salons', and in culture centres as well as adult universities, women pay in exchange for knowledge and experiences of Culture (HILL 1987:17–18). Of course, department stores which, together with coffee shops and restaurants, provide multiple possibilities for women to spend time, are all places of consumption in which respectable middleclass women have been seen throughout the postwar period. But in the 80s women also moved into areas of consumption which until then had been the domain of men. Young women began to ride motor bikes, for example, and go to bars to drink alcohol late at night, play golf and bet on horses – once all typically men's expensive and time-consuming leisure activities. *Oyaji girl* (uncle girl) is the name the media have given to the young women who poach on middleaged men's preserves in this way.

With their increasing consumer power, women have found themselves the focus of attention of other Japanese companies which have begun to treat them as what the Hakuhōdō Institute of Life and Living, in its quick-fix advertising jargon, calls 'VIPs' (1987:19–25). The keywords ascribed to this acronym are: *variety, venture, independent, instant, pleasure* and *peace* – by which is meant that women are seen to want to try out all kinds of different things in life, especially things that they find challenging and which give them economic and psychological independence. By 1982, half of all married women in Japan were working and half of those that were not wanted to work. Unmarried women, for their part, realized that living alone, independently of their parents, could be an enjoyable experience which made them question whether in fact they really wanted to get married at all (HILL 1987:218–231). Married or not, women generally were intent on getting the best out of life – primarily through fashion, leisure and Culture, in that order. According to the Hakuhōdō Institute of Life and Living, they regarded themselves as 'happy' and were prepared to do anything to stay that way.

In terms of figures alone, the women's consumer market is vast and varied. There are 60 million women in Japan, of whom 49 million are of working age. Of these, fifteen million unmarried, together with nine million married, women are employed full-time while a further 23 million married women are working part-time in one capacity or another. Only two million of working age are not engaged in any paid labour at all. Such are the statistics that market analysts like to use for shock effect, before proceeding to break down this market into five-year age cohorts, or to present it as consisting of students, unmarried OL, married OL, part-time housewives, full-time employees, and so on. These are then regrouped into lifestyles and given such trendy titles as: *Cinderella Mrs* (for the wife who has to be back home before her husband in the evenings), *Hobbusiness Woman* (for those who make their hobbies into businesses), *Playducation Mama* (the education mama who spends a lot of money on her child), *Part Mrs* (for the married woman working part-time), *Yenjoy Gal* (for the young woman at work who spends freely during her leisure hours), *Ms Anne Marie* (the punning nickname for unmarried women who have realized that they can live happily without a man), and finally the so-called *Mīhā* adult-child. These labels, and many more which were trendy in the late 80s, are part of the packages offered by advertising agencies to their clients as lifestyle maps of Japanese society.

In this section we have listed the socio-economic changes which have affected women, and have examined the way in which women are constructed as consumers in marketing and advertising discourses. What is particularly problematic from our point of view is the way in which marketing research sees women as always and only consumers, so much so that even their work – which eventually is what enables them to consume – is labelled as just one particular way of spending their 'private time'. We have also noted that at the same time as women's roles have changed dramatically since the early 70s, gender stereotypes have been reinforced by the consumer industry, in such a way that housework and childcare exclusively seem to be a woman's responsibilities. At the same time, however, women of all ages are invited to participate in consumer processes as personal experiences. We will now take a look at some of those areas in which women's lives have seen most change.

Power and Sexuality

As we have already seen, the Hakuhōdō Institute of Life and Living found that in the 80s women's 'power up' was faster than that of any other social group in Japan. Here we wish to take a closer look at this by examining how women fare in some areas where power is usually seen to lie: politics, work, and finally, marriage and divorce. In addition, we will discuss the ambivalent yet significant relationship between women's consumption and sexuality to see how it can throw light on Japanese women's perceived increase in power.

First, politics. In the 1970s, Susan Pharr (1981) looked at the role of political women in Japan and suggested that they were locked into a 'catching up' process, when compared with women in other advanced industrialized nations such as the United States, France, or England. Clearly, Japanese women have become much more involved in the world of politics in the sense that, on every count – from national to local government elections, by way of those for prefectural governors, city mayors, and village heads – a higher proportion of women than of men has been voting over the past 20 years. In her study, Pharr anticipated this trend and pointed out that this did not mean that women themselves would necessarily succeed to political posts. In fact, although a handful of Japanese women have been appointed to high office in international organizations such as UNESCO, UNICEF and the United Nations, at home they have had less success.

In March 1988, at the end of the Shōwa period, women occupied no more than seven out of 506 seats in the Lower, and 22 out of 251 seats in the Upper, houses of the national Diet. By July 1992, this number had increased to fourteen and 38 seats respectively (half of them members of the Japan Socialist Party), giving an overall proportion for women's representation of only 6.8 per cent. Elsewhere, Japanese women's participation in their country's governing process is much less marked. Less than one percent (64 of 8,745 employees) has managed to reach the ninth grade or higher in the civil service; six per cent of all judges, 2.8 per cent of prosecutors, and 6.1 per cent of lawyers in Japan are women. Figures for local government show that women are having even less success in influencing the political sphere (Sōrifu 1993:37–43). Such figures indicate that in terms of political power Japanese women are not about to 'catch up' with the type of gender (in)equality found in western countries, even less with Japanese men. It should be clear, therefore, that the perception that Japanese women's power is increasing is not directly related to the formal political institutions.

What, then, of work? Have women managed to obtain equality in their offices, shopfloors, and other places of work? We have already seen that the work that women do has for the most part been overlooked by those who wish to stress that women's place is in the home. A big

38

breakthrough for equal opportunities in the workplace came with the passing of the Equal Employment Opportunity Law (*Danjo koyō kikai kintō hō*) in April 1986. This bill removed a series of clauses which had hitherto protected women from working under the same conditions as men (for example, menstruation leave, restrictions on overtime and hazardous work). Although some of these clauses commonly were not heeded, the fact that they ceased to exist has encouraged many employers to offer women so-called dual track employment – either on exactly the same terms as those offered all men (with permanent employment, regular overtime work, probability of transfer, and so on), or along the lines previously offered to OL. However, the new law has failed to force employers to improve working conditions which have been arranged exclusively for male workers completely free from household responsibilities (Miyake 1991:294–5).[11]

This move towards greater equality between men and women in the Japanese labour market has come about by establishing a *male* norm for all employees regardless of sex. This holds true both for the contents of the Equal Employment Opportunity Law itself – which has abolished special treatment for women employees, but which also does not permit a man to argue against sexual discrimination in employment practices – and for the way in which the law has been implemented in companies, where women are offered the choice of working with men or in a separate women's group. In the case of the former, many women find themselves prevented from applying for a 'career track' job alongside male colleagues, because they would be obliged to accept long-term transfers during the early stages of their careers and so lessen their possibilities of ever living with a partner who is tied to his own work under similar conditions of employment (Iwao 1993:179–85).

In this context it is worth noting that *More*, *Croissant* and other new lifestyle magazines for women, which began to be published in the late 70s and early 80s and which made much of phrases like 'women's independence' and 'career woman', were actually addressed to freelance women who wished to lead 'elegant' lives, rather than to nurses, teachers and other women employed in corporate organizations. Like a few western magazines such as *Options*, which seem to focus on changes in women's new role in society but which are in fact predicated on consumption (Winship 1983:45–50), the new generation of Japanese women's magazines has ended up focussing on how to *consume*, rather than on work itself (Inoue 1992:117). Inoue goes on to point out that in fact magazines published later, such as *Orange Page*, *Lettuce Club* and *Esse*, shifted their attention away from 'career women' towards 'housewives' and, although they still focussed on their material consumption, it has been the social activizing of housewives (*shufuzō no shakaiteki kasseika*) which has been the main area of change among Japanese women since the 1970s (1992:118–9).

Let us now take a look at women's 'power up' in relation to marriage and divorce. It seems that even though women's life after marriage has changed considerably, young women are less eager than ever to get married. Both government statistical data and market analyses have recorded that the average marriage age – which in the postwar period has been relatively high in Japan compared to certain western nations – was increasing a little every year, especially in the metropolitan region. In 1975, 20 per cent of Japanese women aged between 25 and 29 years were unmarried. By 1990, this figure had gone up to just over 40 per cent, with the greatest increase registered in the late 80s, while the number of unmarried women aged between 30 and 34 during the same period had gone up to 13.9 per cent. These same data show that the proportion of unmarried *men* between the ages of 25 and 29 in 1975 was 48.3 per cent, rising to 64.4 per cent in 1990. The number of unmarried men in the 30 to 34 age group more than doubled over the same period to 32.6 per cent (Sōrifu 1993:5). While the number of those marrying after the age of 30 has doubled for women and tripled for men (HILL 1993b:12), we now find that more than 31 per cent of all Japanese men of marriagable age, and about ten per cent of those aged between 40 and 54, are unmarried (Sōrifu 1993:5). This is a comparatively high figure *vis-à-vis* the six per cent ratio for women (which is on a par with the United States and former West Germany).

In general, therefore, finding a partner has become a bigger problem for men than for women who have begun to make demands about the men they wish to marry. Hence we have the 'three high's' (*sankō*), as a popular description of the kind of husband sought by women: highly educated, with a high income, and physical height. While women have changed a lot over the past twenty years, men generally have not questioned their own role in a marital relationship, and basically seem to want a woman who will look after their home, manage their savings and bring up their children. This, of course, is a vast generalization that covers many different hopes and conflicts that individuals experience in their intimate relations, but such overall differences between men and women have been a key issue in the Japanese media.

Much is made, too, of divorce statistics, and most of the data we have examined interpret the increasing number of divorces as proof that women are becoming more 'liberated' from their families. For example, we are told that the number of divorces each year increased from 77,195 in 1965 to 179,191 in 1992 (when there were roughly 620,000 first and 134,000 second marriages) (Sōrifu 1993:3, 6). In 1990 the number of single mothers in Japan was 550,000, while single fathers made up 100,000. This increase in divorces is to be found in particular among couples in their late thirties and forties, when the children are well into their school education. Women who choose a life without a husband are often well-educated and have good career options, but even so, most women divorcees experience a considerable reduction in income when they begin to live on their own. The divorce rate of the 35–50 age group only amounts to five per cent (HILL 1993b:12). It would seem that such overall figures are so small that they only directly concern an in-significant proportion of the population. What they indicate is that a majority of Japanese women and men live on their own for a number of years before they marry, and that more and more can be independent if they wish to. All this is, of course, a result of women's work.

The possibility that women will not even need a man has brought about endless concern and fascination on the part of media. In Japanese, this ambivalence is expressed very well in a play on the word for women's 'sexual liberation' (*sei no kaihō*), where the Chinese character for 'freeing' is substituted by one that changes the meaning to the 'sexual opening' or 'revelation' of women (Tamiya 1992:102). Japanese women's increasing independence goes hand in hand with their increasing sexualization, and this ambivalent process is closely linked to their consumption as well. This applies not just to the types of consumption that are related to sexual experiences – from pornography to 'two shot' telephone sex, by way of love hotels where rooms are rented out for two hour sessions – but to women's consumer lifestyles in general, including the ways in which women are represented in women's magazines (Figures 11 and 12). It is hardly surprising that the ex-pansion of women's consumption in the 80s has been paralleled by a growth in the porn industry. In Tōkyō, where most of Japan's porn production is located, eleven adult videos are made every day. The central character in these tends to be a young woman, usually in her late teens. Reports suggest that a large proportion of the women who engage in the short careers offered by Japanese porn videos are students, OLs, and even housewives who are looking for a quick way to make money for 'shopping and travel and for living it up in Tōkyō's expensive nightspots' (Fornander 1992).

In general, young women have been widely represented as having an immense sexual appetite – whether as those scantily clad, often abused,

41

Figure 11 Similarities between advertising targeted at women and pornography 1: advertisement for watch and telephone club card

Figure 12 Similarities between advertising targeted at women and pornography 2: advertisement for jeans and telephone club card

bodies so ubiquitously promoted by all kinds of media, or as OLs turned into 'office fetishes' in a male-dominated work place. As Tamiya (1992: 103–6) has shown, Japanese media – particularly television and *manga* comics, but also advertising and, to a lesser extent, newspapers and magazines – are marked by a preponderance of visual images which portray women as sex objects. Car ads provide a convenient example of sexist advertising, in the way they are adorned with, and themselves adorn, women's bodies with cars – presumably to give credit to the idea that the metal body of a car is a shining phallus which can be used aggressively to hunt women (as in the Toyota *Chaser* or the Fiat *Uno* ad campaigns from 1990) (Bailey 1986:20)[12] (Figures 13 and 14). The prevalence of women in Japanese advertising is perhaps all the more striking because of the relative absence of both depictions of the female body in the Japanese aesthetic tradition, and of a cult of woman as a symbol of purity which are both pillars in western arts. Without any historical muddling, therefore, the female form has become a consumer icon.

In addition, Japanese media have a marked tendency to place women in typical housewife rather than working roles in fiction and drama. Furthermore, news broadcasts usually feature a man and a woman reporter together, where the latter has often been chosen because of her looks and youth, rather than for her knowledge and skills as a journalist. This is evidenced in the way in which she has been obliged to announce the lesser events of the day's news – the arrival of the school outing season in spring, for example, or the effect of the warm weather on budding cherry trees. Such appearances tend not be popular among women themselves (Tamiya 1992), but they have not been that widely debated in Japan (with such significant exceptions as Funabashi [1991] and Inoue et al. [1989]). In other words, the step women have taken out into the public space as workers and consumers has both loosened them from their backstage position at home, and recast them as floating signifiers of female form. In this process we find an ongoing displacement of women's desire for consumer goods with men's, indeed society's, desire for the female body.

The changes that Japanese women have experienced in the 80s also stimulated speculation about whether a popular feminist movement was in the making. Is it not reasonable – went the argument – to expect that the relative power that Japanese women have gained as consumers will make their overall subordination painfully clear, and thus give rise to a broad demand for real influence? As we have seen, this line of thought has hardly proved correct. Nor is it that feminism is completely absent in Japan which has one of the oldest and strongest women's movements

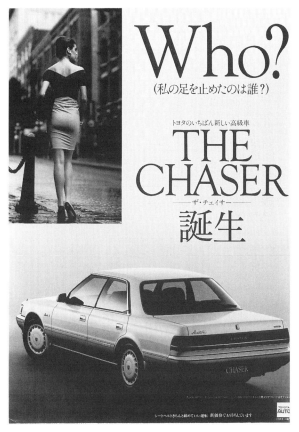

Figure 13 Advertisement for Toyota's The Chaser
(*Kigyō to Kōkoku*, May 1990)

in Asia and the region's highest level of feminist awareness (Sievers 1983; Jayawardena 1986:226–54). During the past 25 years, Japanese feminism has developed in close interaction with western feminism – from 1970–77 which (according to Ehara's periodization [1990]) marked the 'women's lib' movement, through 1978–82 when 'women's studies' were established, to 1983–90, the age of 'feminist debates'. However, as Jayawardena (1986:253) points out, feminist demands in Japan have only been granted in areas immediately compatible with capitalist growth – in particular those of education and employment.

Figure 14 Advertisement for Fiat Uno
(*Motor Magazine*, July 1990)

With this in mind, we can begin to understand the way in which feminism has come to be a part of the ambivalent cluster of consumption, independence and sexualization which acts as a backdrop to reinforce women's responsibility for family and housework. In this complex interplay of ideas and associations, feminist terminology has been co-opted as the means to utterly commercial ends, redressed as a way for advertisers to 'help' women. Given the relative isolation of feminists in Japan, this has been an easy game for media (at the same time as such a popularization can hardly be said to be limited to Japan).

Although we are critical of this 'domestication' of feminism, we still find that the 'loose use' (Tanaka 1990:82) of a range of feminist concepts does refer to real changes in Japanese women's lives – ambivalent changes which, sometimes invisible, sometimes over-exposed, can hardly be conceptualized in any straightforward manner.

Cultural Homogeneity, Media and Consumption

One line of thought that we have presented and criticized so far is that during the consumer boom the marginal position that Japanese women have had, and still have, in relation to the labour market has given them the power and freedom to shape their own lives to a greater degree than Japanese men whose time, lifestyle and future plans are determined by their work places. In a way, this very marginalization has generated cultural differentiation and creativity among consumers. However, as we have shown in the previous sections, such a line of thought is extremely ambivalent and has often been overshadowed by simplistic identifications of men with the group model, and thus with peer pressure and hierarchy in Japanese institutions, on the one hand, and women with consumption, living in happy disregard of social obligations, on the other. In this section, we need to examine the notion of homogeneity in Japan, its relation to consumption, and its implications for different forms of media: namely, television, newspapers and magazines.[13] We will then proceed to look at changes in the consumer market with reference to class, race and regionality, as well as gender and age.

Much has been made of the notion of homogeneity in postwar Japan. As, for example, H.D. Harootunian in his discussion of *Postmodernism and Japan* (1989) has trenchantly pointed out, quite a lot of this attention has been paid to creating and sustaining the idea that in Japan style, art, and aesthetic experience have come together to form a single, indivisible Japanese culture in which historicity is totally denied and regional, class and gender differences are ignored. In other words, the concept of homogeneity (often referred to as *tan'itsu minzoku*) has been used variously by politicians, intellectuals, media, and businessmen, as a means of coming to terms in their own specialized ways with a diverse population of 120 million inhabitants – primarily Japanese, but also including Ainu, Koreans, Chinese, and now Iranians and Filipinas – employed in occupations as varied as farming and computer programming, driving and accountancy, lumber and film directing, microchip processing, teaching, pottery, modelling, neighbourhood retailing, and road digging; and all living in regions as geographically different as

Hokkaidō, Nagano and Okinawa, with some as vast as the Tōkaidō megalopolis, and others as small as rural 'face to face' communities.

In spite of these obvious diversities, the notion of homogeneity, constituting what Hannerz (1992:16) has referred to as a 'replication of uniformity', still lies at the heart of much contemporary writing about the Japanese. However, this idea has less to do with a remote island people who, sheltered from external influences, have grown alike, than with an ongoing process of a strong social and cultural integration through the creation of a standard language, universal education, full employment, and nationwide media, reinforced by national political and business myths advocating social cohesion. Various scholars have commented on the notion of Japanese homogeneity – invoked in such phrases as *wagakuni* (our country, Japan), *kokumin* (the nation's citizens) and *kokutai* (an immutable, ageless ancestral tradition separating 'them' from 'us') – as a *political* concept used by state agencies to foster 'a sense of nation' in the late Meiji period, when social conformity was viewed as the binding principle of national loyalty; and again, between 1905 and 1915, to overcome what ideologues then saw as 'a crisis in the social order' brought on by 'city fever' and the threat to the stability of rural society marked by urban migration (Gluck 1985). They have also focussed on the way in which nationalist ideas have been further in-stalled in the minds of the Japanese through linguistic, psychological, aesthetic, cultural, social, and racial discourses (e.g. Dale 1986; Yoshino 1992).

And yet, underlying the political use of homogeneity and that bundle of other myths constituting 'Japaneseness' has lurked the inescapable presence of Japan's *economy* which, as we have argued, consists not simply of processes of production but also of those of consumption. Curiously, the inter-relatedness of the body politic and the economy, on the one hand, and of production and consumption, on the other, is overlooked, for example, by Harootunian who, in his attack on the political implications of the myth of homogeneity, presents a strangely one-dimensional argument about consumption and the postmodern. Ignoring Jameson's advice (1991:47; cf. Woodiwiss 1991:113) not to adopt a moral position on the issue of postmodernism, Harootunian follows Baudrillard in viewing consumption as generated by a system of objects standing in place of the social as an illusion:

> What is consumed is always new and everything is within the means of everybody, whatever one's capacity to pay for it. Every dream is marketable and directed towards everyone in society, not

48

merely the few, thereby effacing the difference between one consuming subject and another, since they are made to appear to belong to a common world populated by objects which they must consume.

(Harootunian 1989: 90)

There are crucial slips here which show that Harootunian has, firstly, failed to overcome the real challenge facing those theorizing about the postmodern: the acceptance of all possible values, courses of action and social situations as equally valid strategies. More importantly in this context, he also denies completely the dynamics of the consumer market which, in various ways, is closely related to postmodern culture.[14] As we have already pointed out, while every dream may indeed be marketable, no dream can any longer be directed towards *everyone* in the Japanese market economy of the 80s and 90s. To suggest otherwise is to assume, wrongly, not only that the market is both mass and homogeneous when it is clearly differentiated, but that the Japanese are themselves homogeneous – an argument of which, as we saw above, Harootunian clearly disapproves (and which, anyway, is immediately undermined by the issue of gender). Thus, in spite of his justifiable attacks on the likes of Nakane Chie, Doi Takeo and Kumon Shunpei for putting forward a sustained strategic argument about the homogeneous nature of the Japanese people, Harootunian himself ends up by presenting a similarly homogenizing view of the Japanese in his discussion of consumption.

This criticism of *Postmodernism and Japan* permits us to highlight a point that has received too little attention from scholars of Japan: the use in *marketing* of the idea that the Japanese form a homogeneous consumer society, in order to support and sustain economic growth (and, in passing, by focussing on the unique cultural attributes of that consumer society, to make it seem more difficult for foreign businesses to get a foothold in the Japanese market). The reason for marketers and advertisers espousing the homogeneous nature of their society lies, of course, in the fact that in a consumer market which is generally accepted as 'homogeneous', companies can produce and sell commodities which will be purchased ideally by more or less *everyone* in that market, and not just by a small part thereof. The equation of 'market' with 'society', both characterized by homogeneity, has thus encouraged the Japanese to participate in mass consumption as well as in the processes of mass production – a myth for which Harootunian himself falls when he argues that the marketing of desire effaces the difference between one consuming subject and the next. To add insult to injury, by stating that

49

consuming subjects *must* as a result consume, he falls into an old trap of assuming that consumers are somehow 'duped' into consumption.

Still, the idea of homogeneity needs to be examined more closely. After all, demographically, the Japanese consumer market is bigger than any national market in Europe; in terms of such variables as race, class and education, for example, it is also much more homogeneous than the US market, which is often used as a form of covert comparison by the Japanese. However, Japanese companies were also among the first to develop batch production, permitting small runs of particular items. This enabled different industries both to target highly specialized markets and to make possible a fast turnover of trends – thereby providing for a *temporal* segmentation of the market. We must thus see homogeneity as somehow not contrasted to diversity so much as forming a baseline of shared assumptions upon which market segmentation can proceed to proliferate.

Moreover, reconsidering homogeneity in terms of consumption does not entail exclusive concentration on economic institutions, since we also inevitably find ourselves having to take account of interaction between the state and market place. For example, an advertising agency would be unable to address the totality of the Japanese population in one single advertising campaign if it were not for the standardized and well-functioning education system which ensures literacy and common knowledge throughout almost the entirety of the Japanese population. It also militates against 'deviant' writing styles, however cute they may be, and ensures that everyone uses a 'common language' which is then further shaped by the media. Thus we find that a wide range of colloquial neologisms – from *skatto sawayaka* (totally refreshing)[15] to *sekuhara* (sexual harrassment), by way of such phrases as *body con* ('body conscious' clinging fashions), 'Nixon shock' (referring to that US President's floating of the dollar and rapprochement with China in 1971), *shinjinrui* (or 'new breed' of Japanese youth) and, more recently, *bubble jidai* (the 'bubble' period of the 1980s) – have first been coined in the media and then made part of everyday speech.

Another example of this kind of overlap between the state and the market place is NHK, the national broadcasting network, which is not dependent on advertising revenue as a source of income, but which nevertheless tends to assess the success of its programmes in terms of viewer ratings, in exactly the same way as do commercial channels in their attempts to attract advertising. It is clear that NHK sees itself as a competitor to, and is perceived as one by, such commercial stations as NTV, ABC and Fuji so that, though funded by the state licensing system, it also strives for market share by embracing as large an audience as possible for its programmes.

Newspapers also contribute in various ways to this penchant for national standardization, while allowing for some regional variation. Institutionally, they can link up with other media, so that each of the five major national dailies has its own television (and sometimes radio) network. Thus we find that the Yomiuri, Asahi and Mainichi have newspapers, magazines, television and radio stations by these names, while the *Sankei Shinbun* newspaper is part of the Fuji TV (CX) group and the *Nihon Keizai Shinbun* of the Tōkyō 12 Channel (or MegaTon) network. Each group shares news which it prints and broadcasts throughout the country, and many of these media have exclusive relations with certain advertising agencies. Some of the larger regional papers – the *Hokkaidō, Tōkyō, Chūnichi*, and *Nishi Nihon* newspapers – also form a 'bloc' along the same lines, sharing news and features. Similarly, when it comes to structuring the contents of newspapers, radio and television programmes, we find that there tends to be a format common to each group which tries to balance international, national and regional news, on the one hand, with sections on business, social, women, sports, Culture, and so on, on the other. The media diet is thus remarkable for its overall uniformity both among the same, and across different, media (see Moeran 1996; also Wolferen 1989:93–100).

Magazines, in contrast, have played a crucial part in the segmentation of the market because, unlike newspapers and television in particular, they are not a *mass* medium as such, but address their readers individually, focussing on their private lives or special hobbies. In this way, magazines have staged a remarkable comeback and shown the greatest comparative area of growth among the four main media during the past two decades, primarily because they can claim to provide advertisers with a more direct line to specifically targeted audiences. Although we will be discussing women's magazines which have been published since 1970 in the following section, we will here take a brief look at what we mean by 'individual readers', since this has a bearing on the notion of homogeneity.

At a micro level, homogeneity can be associated with 'creating sameness' among individuals, and processes whereby individuals and groups check and adjust themselves *vis-à-vis* others take place, of course, in all societies. What is remarkable about the way in which the Japanese tend to look to their neighbours, colleagues and friends is that such mutual adjustments have often not been used to set off individual differences so much as to enable an individual to immerse herself in her particular segment of society and there to impersonate her stereotype. This was true even in the 1980s, though, according to the Hakuhōdō Institute of Life and Living (HILL 1987:15–6), the number of people – particularly women – who said that they were 'embarrassed' if they did not do as everyone else in their everyday lives decreased from 33 per cent to eighteen per cent between 1982 and 1986, while the number of those who felt that it was all right to be 'individualistic' and different from others increased from ten to 31 per cent. Instead of 'hiding their suffering', women started turning towards 'strengthening their strong points' and so, ultimately, paying more attention to what *they* valued as important, rather than accepting what others valued, as hitherto. This recorded change thus points in a direction away from conformity.

At the same time, it is important to be aware of the fact that advertisers have been among the first to adopt the rhetoric of individualism which they address to women in particular (Moeran 1989:39–55). As part of a cluster of keywords describing women as independent and international, 'individualism' has also been used to signify different types of consumption. But, looking at women's magazines, we find detailed instructions to readers of *More*, *With* and so on, not just about which lipstick, eye make-up and foundation to put on for what occasion, or which accessories (from earrings to handbags and shoes) to wear with what clothes, but the best way to show off their legs, or how many buttons on a blouse should be left undone to look just right (Figure 15). The appetite for such detailed instructions has made advertising an easy task when millions of Japanese women have been eager to listen to the media's advice about how to dress, where to go, and what to buy.

Let us now take a look at the way in which the consumer market is structured by differences along the lines of class, race, region, age and gender. Firstly, differences in income and class affiliations are generally not addressed directly by the media, even though, of course, everyone knows that they exist and that different magazines tend to have readerships that are differentiated by their income. Figures that show that the vast majority of the Japanese people consider themselves to be middleclass are indirect evidence that they define themselves in terms of consumption, rather than of their relations to production. At the same time, advertising often tends to compensate for economic differences by taking an aspirational stance in the expectation that Japanese of different income levels will be united in their dreams of unattainable luxury. What we should not forget, however, is that there are also magazines, especially those for young people, which realize that their readers are not big spenders and so self-consciously promote street fashions, cheap garments and other goods.

Figure 15 Right-and-wrong instructions on how readers
with fat thighs should dress (*non-no*, December 1994)

So far as the issue of race is concerned, the consumer market consists
predominantly of Japanese, with tiny micromarkets for certain groups of
minorities and immigrants. Race is thus not a variable which stratifies
the market in Japan, but it has been included here because of the
frequency with which, in one form or another, foreign models and
images appear in the media. The use of white – rather than black
(Russell 1995) – models in Japanese advertising can also be interpreted
as part of this kind of aspirational strategy (cf. Inoue 1985:85). By
placing both actors and the settings in which they are located apart from

everyday Japanese situations, such advertising explicitly avoids representing anything specific to a class or region which might put off potential consumers. In this way, the representation of race in the media carefully avoids addressing ethnic divides within Japan, although – when used for Japanese products – western models can further create a sense of transnationalism that makes *all* Japanese seem to be part of global consumer capitalism. It is worth appreciating the irony that Japanese advertisers should use western celebrities like Arnold Schwarzenegger or Linda Evangelista as a means of uniting their own nation in front of their television screens.

Western dominance is, of course, at play in the way women's magazines hold up white models as ideals of beauty to which Japanese women should aspire. But that is only one part of the story. The western female body is also associated with nakedness and sex; it appears frequently in advertisements and photo reportages for underwear, and in recent years has also been widely used in esthé salon advertising. Magazine features with instructions on how to kiss or with illustrations of different positions for sexual intercourse almost invariably feature western faces and bodies, although their meaning is clearly not to encourage young Japanese women to find foreign lovers. Rather, the use of western models seems to allow for a subtle but ambivalent message to women readers who are encouraged to maintain a Japanese sense of decency at the same time as indulging in western sensual pleasures.

Japaneseness and western-ness are thus constituted as different *styles*, both of them belonging to the Japanese consumer market. As such, they can be mapped onto different market segments, with a dense foreignness found especially among women in their twenties, for whom western images are associated with a working woman's perceived independent and glamorous lifestyle. From the 80s onwards, the frequency of western, predominantly white, models in women's magazines has also been a consequence of Japanese economic command over and interest in international fashion. For example, in 1992 all front covers of the monthly magazine, *Classy*, featured the so-called supermodels – from Linda Evangelista (again) to Christy Turlington – photographed in in-house styles and Japanese poses. This marked a domestication of international fashion, rather than a kow-tow to foreign authority on style.

Thirdly, the emphasis on Japanese homogeneity has also led to disregard of local and regional differences, but at the same time there can be little doubt that Japan is an extremely centralized country, and that its consumer culture to a large extent radiates out from Tōkyō. The remoteness of the provinces is frequently experienced as a kind of 'belatedness' – as when the new styles only reach towns like Fukue in the Gotō islands or Asahikawa in Hokkaidō six months to a year after they have been all the rage in the metropolitan areas of Tōkyō and Ōsaka. This time lag may be most acutely felt by those teenagers who complain that they have to wait for up to three weeks before they can find newly advertised styles of clothing in their local shops. This, of course, is a result of the fact that the media, whether television, radio, newspapers, or magazines, reach the whole of Japan at the same time, often giving advance notice of new trends, whereas the distribution of goods tends to be a little slower.

In women's magazines, different regional tastes are often made to play off one another *au* Saussure within a structure of oppositions which ultimately coalesce like a magnetic field around Tōkyō. Thus, in the Kansai region, Ōsaka is viewed as *the* city of commerce, Kōbe as that of internationalization, and Kyōto as that of 'Japanese' tradition and culture. Each of these cities has its counterpart in the Kantō region, too, so that Ōsaka is to Tōkyō, as Kōbe is to Yokohama and Kyōto to Kamakura. But, once the two regions are compared, Ōsaka's commercial practices and people's lifestyle are suddenly interpreted as 'Japanese' and 'traditional' *via-à-vis* those of the capital which are more 'international' and 'modern', or – given the heterogeneous understandings available – *vice versa*. So, even though Tōkyō is the centre, it is possible for the media to promote a counter-identity based on difference from that centre.

Whereas differences of class, race and region are developed in only selective ways, gender and age have come to be the real playgrounds for market differentiation and segmentation. The categorical divide between men and women found in Japan has rarely been taken into account in discussions of the Japanese as a homogeneous nation. Rather, it seems to be assumed that the fact that men and women lead different but complementary lives (Edwards 1989:116) is not in itself a challenge to the notion that the Japanese are all the same, although it makes the notion that *everyone* buys the same things a little awkward, to say the least. One reason for this misleading idea is that gender segregation is not in itself a consequence of modernization, urbanization, industrialization or any other major social transformation. It can be found from time immemorial in even the smallest rural community in Japan, a fact which apparently has led some commentators to subsume gender segregation under the general idea that Japanese culture is somehow 'pre-modern'. In other words, gender has not generally been seen to challenge the 'replication of uniformity' view that Japanese society is essentially structured according to principles that belong in a small-scale community. However, as we have shown, gender categories and relationships are in the process of profound transformation, and even if the outcome can be seen as in many ways conservative, it is simply impossible to conceptualize Japanese women's contemporary leisure-oriented consumer lifestyles from the point of view of Confucian ethics or gender division of labour in traditional society.

Finally we come to age, which has been another important area for market segregation. Like gender segregation, age gradation has also long existed in small-scale communities in Japan, especially in the south west of the country, and has been reinforced continually through such socio-cultural constraints as a nationwide emphasis on 'vertical' relations of authority, a seniority system of promotion, and the 'proper' usage of honorific language. Such gradation applies both to men and to women who find that the difference between being a mother and being a daughter remains a critical threshold in their lives. These long-lasting gradations have been the backdrop against which media people and advertisers have generated and refined further age groupings and definitions of generations in terms of the consumer market, so that nowadays consumer age slots to some degree function as life-stages through which Japanese men and women find themselves passing (Figure 16).

Many of the transitions from one life stage to the next take place in April and are marked by particular consumer activities. A 'child' (*kodomo*), for example, becomes a 'student' (*gakusei*) on April 1 following her sixth birthday, at the same time as she also continues to be a child throughout her teens (White 1993). There is a tendency for all primary school students everywhere to want, and to get, a desk with built-in light and plastic pad on which to write. Within the category of 'student', the child proceeds from the state of 'primary' through 'middle' to 'high' school pupil, before entering the 'big student'-ship of university. Upon graduating, however, the student immediately becomes a 'member of society' (*shakaijin*), a role then occupied for the remainder of her life, of course, but particularly applied to young women and men between graduation and marriage. Young people may even be referred to as, for example, a '3rd year member of society' (*shakaijin san nen*) rather than by their age (usually 25 years old). Women then become 'wives' (*shufu-/okusan*) – usually in the spring and autumn – before embarking upon a new career as 'mothers' (*haha/okāsan*) which will give way, ultimately, to the status of 'grandmother' (*obā/obāsan*).

As we have argued elsewhere (Moeran and Skov *forthcoming*), much of the consumption in Japan centred round lifecourse takes the form of

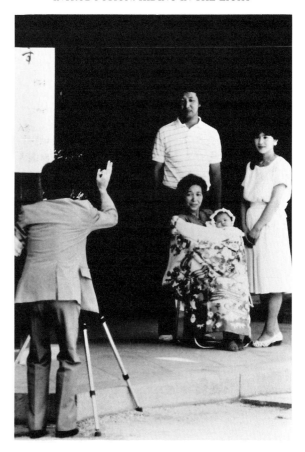

Figure 16 A newborn child is taken by its parents and
grandmother to the Meiji Shrine

a spiraling rhythm composed of cyclical and one-off events. These
include, on the one hand, regular calendrical events, such as Valentine's
or old people's day (*keiro no hi*), and, on the other, one-off affairs
marking – like the coming of age day (*seijin no hi*) – the rites of passage
from birth to death (and after-death, in the case of ancestors). Yet others,
such as the so-called 7-5-3 (*shichi-go-san*) festival for children of these
ages, are a mixture of the two. These events usually have important
psychological implications for the individual concerned in marking
certain stages in his or her life. They also have political implications for

the cultural integration of Japanese society. But, just as importantly, they provide marketers and consumers alike with a perfect frame for the production and consumption of goods. In the 80s, in particular, such events were promoted as festivals of consumption during which young people frequently exchanged expensive presents and went out on romantic dates together (Moeran and Skov 1993).

When examining the consumer market in relation to age, it is striking that most of the age differentiation that has taken place since the early 70s has been located at the young end of the market. Today there are more magazines targeted at twelve-year-olds than at 50-year-old women. This difference is not justified by the overall age distribution of the population. In contrast, the media has increasingly articulated concern for an 'aging' society in which one in four people is expected to be over 60 by the second decade of the next century. The proliferation of consumer culture has brought with it an articulate emphasis on youth, especially in relation to unmarried women's increased independence and sexuality. Frequently, the image of youth is also connected with the almost pre-sexual shōjo – just too old to be a child, but still far from adult decisions of marriage and career. This is, perhaps, a form of 'ageism' according to which desirable femininity is defined in terms of youth, appearance and (feigned) ignorance. At the same time, however, the market for more expensive prestige goods is sustained mainly by older women.

From this discussion of five sociological parameters, it is clear that the breakdown of the market has taken place most visibly along the two already-existing axes of gender and age, and that, in terms of consumption, the Japanese cannot simply be characterized as homogeneous. Add to this the highly advanced temporal segmentation brought about by booms and fads, and we get a picture of a dynamic whirl with shifting subcentres, not unlike the kind presented television viewers by an NHK weather forecaster during the typhoon season. The 70s and 80s were marked by the final fragmentation of cultural unity found in the 'mass market' consumerism of the postwar period. This process of differentiation seems merely to have been amplified in the 90s, following the end of the so-called 'bubble' period and a down-turn in the Japanese economy.

The fact that market segments are far more narrowly defined and managed in Japan than they are in Europe or the United States can be illustrated by the way in which Japanese cosmetics companies, like Shiseidō and Kanebō, produce different ranges of products for teens, young women in their twenties and thirties, and middle-aged women respectively. These are advertised in different styles that address problems specific to each age group, with the product range for middle-aged and elderly women making use of visuals of middle-aged models (often former models and actresses; for example, Shiseidō's *Revital* skincare product range). This is quite unlike European or American cosmetics companies such as Chanel or Revlon, which almost invariably use young models in globally standardized advertising campaigns, regardless of the audience that they may be addressing (either in Japan or elsewhere).[16]

Market analysis works largely by mapping emerging consumer lifestyles onto the sociological variables of gender, age, class and region. As we shall see in the following section, magazines – together with many of the brands and goods advertised in them – usually identify their readerships in terms of social groups already in existence. *Katei Gahō*, for example, is a magazine for middle-aged, well-off housewives. Not all of those, of course, who fall into the latter category will read *Katei Gahō*, but those with a conservative outlook, a special interest in high-class cooking and an insatiable appetite for glossy Japaneseness may well be attracted to the magazine. At the same time, distinct groups form round successful magazines. When they were first published, *an-an* and *non-no*, for instance, were not seen to have a clearly defined readership (Inoue 1985:83). Soon, however, their young readers crystalized into what marketers – by contracting the first two syllables of these magazines' titles – then called the *an-non* brigade. In other words, there is an ongoing interaction between social and market forces which continually affects the social maps underlying Japan's consumer culture (cf. Bourdieu 1984, Featherstone 1991a).

Women's Magazines

The range of glossy magazines directed at women of all ages in contemporary Japanese society is startling. There are almost one thousand 'commercial' (Winship 1987:5) or 'advertising' (McCracken 1993) magazines published in Japan, and out of them more than 140 address women exclusively.[17] Some of these are narrowly defined in terms of their subject matter – travel, motorbikes, cooking or TV – and are discussed and arranged in a manner to appeal to women's interests in particular. Most of them, however, follow a formula well-tested in women's advertising magazines of combining fashion with information about the urban scene: boutiques, department stores, restaurants and discos, together with current trends in art, film and literature, and articles about issues relating to women's lives. There is in all of them a strong emphasis on visuals, while the pervasive presence of advertising accounts for well over half the number of pages in some women's magazines and affects their editorial style and layout[18] (see Table 1). It is exactly as a vehicle for market segmentation through the close relation between advertising and editorial matter that what Inoue (1989) calls Japan's 'new women's magazines' have been successful. The first of these, *an-an*, was launched in March 1970. Aimed at a readership of 20 to 24-year-old women, it had the express editorial intention of linking ready-made cute fashions with the youth market (Ueno 1987:136). By creating all kinds of 'features' introducing new commodities to its readers, *an-an* soon attracted 30 per cent advertising (Yamaki 1992: 306–307), and by 1986 more than 85 per cent of its contents were devoted to advertising and editorial tie-ins (Inoue et al. 1989:51), while its readership had climbed to 650,000. Similarly, another publisher, Shūeisha, launched its new magazine, *non-no*, along more or less the same lines in February 1971. Aimed at a slightly younger readership of twelve to nineteen year old girls, *non-no* was soon selling 1.3 million copies and attracting 45 per cent straight advertising, though with fewer editorial tie-ins. The point to be made here is that narrowly targeted readerships have been invented by magazine publishers, not because there already exists some indefinable series of age divisions in Japanese society, but because publishers need *advertising* in order to keep their magazines financially stable.[19] In other words, the narrow segmentation of magazine readerships in Japan is as much for the benefit of those who wish to *sell* their products, as for those who wish to *buy* them.

Japanese magazines are published by a comparatively large number of publishers, each of whom vies with its competitors to put out very similar – what Winship (1987:41) calls 'me too' – publications aimed at a particular segment of the market[20] (Table 2). Some of them are given titles which directly address a certain reader type, such as *Fujin Gahō* (Housewives' Graphic). In this way, they resemble certain western magazine titles such as *Ms.*, *Working Woman* or *Playboy*. However, most Japanese magazines, especially the so-called an-non group, do not delineate a readership through their title (Inoue 1992:113). If anything, they prefer to demarcate their readers or the special style of their contents by means of subtitles. These often include English words in the *katakana* syllabary or in Roman writing. We thus find titles like *Cutie – for independent girl; éf – Fantastic monthly for young women;* and *Teen no fashion life mcSister* (teens' fashion life, *mcSister*); as well as *Onna no status magazine, 25 ans* (women's status magazine, *25 ans*); *Quality*

Table 1 Women's Magazines in Japan

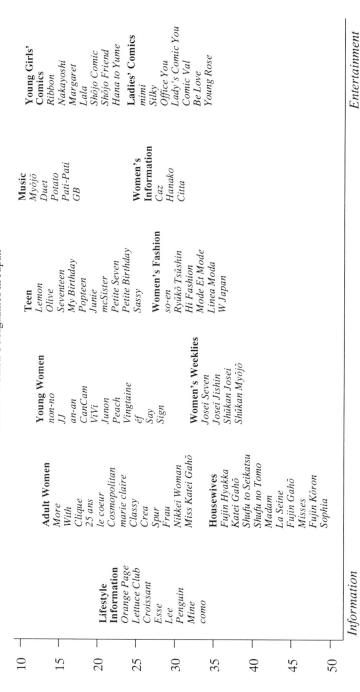

Lifestyle Information
Orange Page
Lettuce Club
Croissant
Esse
Lee
Penguin
Mine
como

Adult Women
More
With
Clique
25 ans
le coeur
Cosmopolitan
marie claire
Classy
Crea
Spur
Frau
Nikkei Woman
Miss Katei Gahō

Housewives
Fujin Hyakka
Katei Gahō
Shufu to Seikatsu
Shufu no Tomo
Madam
La Seine
Fujin Gahō
Misses
Fujin Kōron
Sophia

Young Women
non-no
JJ
an-an
CanCam
ViVi
Junon
Peach
Vingtaine
éf
Say
Sign

Women's Weeklies
Josei Seven
Josei Jishin
Shūkan Josei
Shūkan Myōjō

Teen
Lemon
Olive
Seventeen
My Birthday
Popteen
Junie
mcSister
Petite Seven
Petite Birthday
Sassy

Women's Fashion
so-en
Ryūkō Tsūshin
Hi Fashion
Mode Et Mode
Linea Moda
W Japan

Music
Myōjō
Duet
Potato
Pati-Pati
GB

Women's Information
Caz
Hanako
Citta

Young Girls' Comics
Ribbon
Nakayoshi
Margaret
Lala
Shōjo Comic
Shōjo Friend
Hana to Yume

Ladies' Comics
mimi
Silky
Office You
Lady's Comic You
Comic Val
Be Love
Young Rose

10
15
20
25
30
35
40
45
50

Information

Entertainment

(Source: A Japanese advertising agency, 1991. Translated and adapted by the authors)

Table 2 Women's Magazines Since 1970

Title	First Published	Publisher	Number of Copies
an-an	1970	Magazine House	650,000
non-no	1971	Shūeisha	1,500,000
Junon	1973	Shufu to Seikatsusha	480,000
JJ	1975	Kōbunsha	680,000
More	1977	Shūeisha	850,000
Croissant	1977	Magazine House	700,000
Cosmopolitan	1980	Shūeisha	300,000
25 ans	1980	Fujin Gahōsha	320,000
With	1981	Kōdansha	800,000
CanCam	1981	Shōgakkan	700,000
Olive	1982	Magazine House	550,000
Elle Japon	1982	Magazine House	350,000
Marie Claire	1982	Chūō Kōronsha	300,000
Lee	1983	Shūeisha	550,000
ViVi	1983	Kōdansha	580,000
éf	1984	Shufu no Tomosha	280,000
Classy	1984	Kōbunsha	300,000
Sophia	1984	Kōdansha	220,000
Orange Page	1985	Orange Page	1,200,000
Esse	1986	Fuji Television	610,602
La Seine	1986	Gakken	300,000
Mine	1987	Kōdansha	400,000
Lettuce Club	1987	Seibu Time	800,000
Nikkei Woman	1988	Nikkei Home Shuppan	240,000
Ray	1988	Shufu no Tomosha	350,000
Hanako	1988	Magazine House	350,000
Spur	1990	Shūeisha	100,000
Crea	1990	Bungei Shunju	300,000
Frau	1991	Kōdansha	250,000
Oggi	1992	Shōgakkan	?

(Adapted from Inoue *et al.* [1989: 20–1] and Dentsū [1991: 347–54])

life magazine, More; *Sophia – hi-quality magazine*; and *Global career no lifestyle fashion-shi, Oggi* (global career lifestyle fashion magazine, *Oggi*), with the added postscript, *oshare no tensai* (chic genius). More recently, lifestyle-oriented magazines have chosen even less descriptive subtitles, such as *Crea, Bunshun full of curiosity*; *Super Premium Magazine Serai*; and *Sign, suteki na ai to jibun ni deau* (*Sign,* meeting yourself and beautiful love). These subtitles function mainly to set the magazines apart from one another in the market place (Figures 17 and 18).

Many of the magazine publishers derive their main business from the publication of newspapers (for example, the Yomiuri, Asahi and Mainichi) or books (Shūeisha, Kōdansha and Chūō Kōronsha), but there are others (like Magazine House and Shufu no Tomosha) which have been first and foremost specialist magazine publishers. These publishing houses generally tend to print a series of titles targeted at different

Figure 17 Magazine front covers: *an-an*, *éf*, *Ryūkō Crea* and *Tsūshin*

Figure 18 Magazine front covers: *Cutie*, *25 ans*, *More* and *Lee*

market segments so that none of them competes with other magazines that it publishes. Thus, Shūeisha puts out *Lee* for women readers aged about 30 years and thus older than those taking *More*. Similarly, Kōdansha aims its *Mine* at an age group just above that of *With* and below that of *Sophia*. Sometimes publishers adopt a similar editorial line and visual style and may even use the same in-house models in order to create crossover readers – like Shūeisha's *non-no* for women aged 20 and *Men's non-no* for their brothers or boy friends, or Kōbunsha's *JJ* and *Gainer* for teenaged girls and boys respectively.

Throughout the 80s, the new women's magazines have been driven by advertising, so much so that older magazines have had little choice but to adapt to the changing market. For example, data provided by Inoue and her study group (1989:52) show that the an-non magazines have had a profound influence on, for example, *Shufu no Tomo* (first launched in 1917, and with a circulation in the mid-80s of 350,000 copies). In September 1981, *Shufu no Tomo* devoted almost 60 per cent of its space to editorial matter, one third to advertising and less than ten per cent to editorial tie-ins. Five years later, however, editorials amounted to less than, and tie-ins to considerably more than, one third of the magazine's contents, while advertising remained more or less constant. Although this strategy seems to have worked in the short-term, by the early 90s *Shufu no Tomo*'s circulation had dropped to just over 82,000 copies per issue (Dentsū 1991:348).

In many of the new women's magazines, the editorial line has been weak. A lot of articles have been commissioned or sub-contracted to 'creative houses' which put together packaged features, so that tie-ins now dominate the presentation of all 'editorial' matter, particularly new fashion trends. There are, of course, exceptions (such as *Croissant* and *Cosmopolitan*), but in general tie-ins now account for one third (*JJ, More, an-an, Shufu to Seikatsu, Fujin Club*) – occasionally as much as one half (*éf*) – of the editorial contents of most women's magazines (Inoue et al. 1989:51). Even so, studies have found that readers for their part tend to see magazine advertisements and articles as their most important sources of product knowledge and information.

At the same time, magazines gather information on their readers through numerous surveys about diverse aspects of women's lives. These include basic reader profiles (age, occupation, marital status, education), detailed breakdown of family economies (incomes, savings, property, home ownership, budget management, disposable cash, and so on), lifestyles (hobbies, leisure, qualifications, sports, overseas travel, matters of concern, future plans), and attitudes towards different kinds of advertising. Apart from supplying advertisers with precise knowledge about particular target groups, these surveys are also written up and presented in the magazines themselves, often with numerous figures and tables, as information about how readers lead their lives. They thus serve to enhance a sense of closeness between readers and publishers – a closeness which has enabled magazine publishers to create and sustain readerships which are extremely narrow in terms of age and interest grouping.

A more recent form of narrow-range targeting is to be found in the regional weekly, *Hanako*, launched by Magazine House in 1988, and aimed at 25 to 27 year old OL, with an average annual income of from ¥3 to ¥5 million, living in the greater metropolitan area around Tōkyō. This magazine is highly specialized, with detailed information about various trendy aspects of the urban scene both at home and abroad, and detailed descriptions, together with little maps, of new boutiques, restaurants and coffee shops. The fact that readers have been sighted carrying their copies of *Hanako* in New York, Hawaii, Hong Kong and other places that they visit (on average they make two trips abroad each year) has even led to advertising inquiries from companies located in these tourist centres (Kinameri and Ezaki 1989:269).

Finally, it should be noted that the fine-meshed grid through which publishers and magazine readers communicate with each other is relatively stable in the sense that magazines tend not to 'grow' too much with their readers. Although initially aimed at a late-teen readership, twenty years after it was first published *an-an* is still being read primarily by young women in their early twenties. The same is true for most other magazines. As they grow older, women will abandon one title (say *non-no*) for another that is pitched at a slightly higher age group (*More*), before graduating to yet another that features a married and more mature women's lifestyle (*Lee*). This means that magazines are to a large extent classified after the age group at which they are targeted, and subordinated to the specific style of a certain segment of that age cohort.

One problem that arises from magazine publishers' division of its women readers into such narrowly defined age ranges is one of definitions. This is particularly true of those aged between ten and twenty years. Whereas in England or the United States, most of us are quite happy to talk interchangably about 'teens' or 'youth', Japanese have a plethora of terms to describe their young people, among them 'child' (*kodomo*). Thus we find *jūdai* (*lit*, 'the tens') to refer to those aged between ten and nineteen, the English word 'teenager' or 'teen' for the thirteen to nineteen year old, *shōjo* or 'maiden' for girls aged anywhere between 8 and 20+, *shōnen* for boys in more or less the same age bracket, and *seishun* to refer to a period of 'youth' in general. Along with the concept of teen, Japanese marketing has borrowed other English concepts such as 'young' and 'adult' when carving out a specific market for unmarried women in their twenties to thirties. In terms of consumption, young people are something else both before and after being 'teenagers', so that 'teens' are themselves a sub-section of 'youth', and teenage culture a sub-sub-culture of the sub-culture of youth in general.[21]

This means that, by the time she reaches 35, a woman will, ideally at least, have 'graduated' (*sotsugyō*) through at least half a dozen magazines from the comics of her childhood and teeny-bopper days, through girlish and playful styles of teenage magazines, to the increasing seriousness of her early twenties, followed by the smooth and proper styles presented in magazines for working women. After marriage she will continue to move through a series of magazines – although the pace of the stylistic turnover is considerably slower at this older end of the market.

Cross-readings

Magazines can, of course, be read by more than one person and in all sorts of different ways (cf. McCracken 1993:7–8). This is no secret to those who produce women's magazines, and some magazines, such as *Miss Katei Gahō* and *Men's non-no*, have even been launched to capture a significant crossover readership of other magazines. In any household, it is likely that there will be some crossover reading of different magazines bought by individual members. For example, young single women who share a flat together may also share one another's magazines. A woman of any age will almost certainly leaf through and may well buy, magazines targeted at age groups different from her own, just to be able to peek into her own future or past, or out of curiosity for others' evolving lifestyles. So in families, daughters may read mothers', and mothers often borrow their adult daughters', magazines and on the basis of what they read there, talk about fashion and go shopping together.[22] Similarly, husbands are likely to leaf through copies of their wives' home publications, while teenage girls have been known to read their brothers' magazines. In coffee shops a variety of glossy magazines is available for leisurely reading by any customer. We also know of at least one elderly professor at a prestigious women's university who likes to read young women's magazines whenever he finds an issue on campus. In other words, women's magazines permeate contemporary Japanese culture.

One main attraction in reading Japanese magazines is that, unlike all-inclusive television, target readers are defined with such sociological and psychological realism that it seems as if we are being afforded a glimpse into a personal and hidden world of a selected group of people. A Japanese woman's magazine thus gives us a broad impression of what it may mean to be a Japanese woman of a specific age, educational background and income bracket; of what her emotional problems, her worries, her ambitions and her private dreams are likely to be, and with what she probably identifies: the way she cares for her body, for example, or how she has sex; whether her menstruation is painful; what she thinks of her boyfriend, and how she goes about finding a man; where she would like to go for her next holiday, and what she can buy there; where she might go over the weekend; what she has in her handbag, and how much it weighs; what kind of ring she would like her boyfriend to give her; how she looks at herself in the mirror, how she applies her make-up; what her underwear looks like; where she keeps things in her wardrobe; what kind of books she might read, the food she likes, the exercise she takes, the diet she can keep; and so on and so forth. She is described in such detail that she almost pales through overexposure.

Here we have depicted the Japanese women's media market as consisting of a fine-meshed grid which first categorizes a woman into a particular age, class, social status or lifestyle, and then presents her with a magazine produced specifically for her type. But does this really match the ways in which magazines and media are actually *produced* or, indeed, *read*? Hardly, for the grid of market analysis is constantly being twisted and manipulated by advertisers and editors who are always trying to adopt an advantageous position in the market place.

Let us take, as one example of such manipulation, the long-lasting campaign by Tōkyō Senkō International which introduced the French travel bag producer, Louis Vuitton, to the Japanese market in 1978. At the time, many of the young foreign models who worked in Japan used Vuitton products, and it was expected that they would appeal to a similar age group in Japan as well. But in order to avoid having the Louis Vuitton brand labelled as a fad, Tōkyō Senkō decided to create an image of exclusivity, romanticism and tradition for the product. 'The money was coming from young women, but we purposely avoided them. Normally you would address your consumers directly, but we maintained a different position,' the agency's president, Negishi Yoshiya, explained (Knibbs 1992: 20). In this way Louis Vuitton campaigns did not employ the kind of style that marketing has ascribed to young women, whose changing tastes themselves force companies to tow the fashion line in their advertising. Instead they focussed on brand name and corporate identity, presenting a purposely vague 'soft sell' approach which in turn managed to attract the attention of, among others, young women. This tactic met with great success. Louis Vuitton now has 23 shops offering its product line in Japan, in contrast to the two company stores it operates in France – where Japanese themselves account for 65 per cent of their sales. Indeed, Japanese customers now account for 75 per cent of Louis Vuitton's sales world wide, and yet its bags are still bought mainly by young Japanese women for use when they travel abroad. Louis Vuitton is thus an extremely popular brand in Japan, in spite of its image of exclusivity. Or is it, perhaps, precisely because of that exclusivity that it is so popular?

In this elusive, two-way process in which consumers and advertisers continually position themselves *vis-à-vis* each other, magazine editors often act as mediators. Sometimes, it seems more important for editors to sell their marketing niche of age, gender and style to potential advertisers, than to sell the magazine to those women belonging to the group which the editors have carved out for themselves. To some extent, this turns the media images of a 40-year-old well-off housewife, a 30-year-old single working woman, or a 20-year-old university student, into imaginary mirrors born out of a restless search to expand Japan's advertising market. Ironically, when advertisers become the target readers of women's magazines, they are also the first to be 'duped' by the types of women presented therein. By thinking that such types are real, or at least functional, advertisers proceed to place actual women readers in a secondary position as cross-readers, who can then leaf through their magazine pages with a thrill at seeing such a grotesque masquerade of Japanese femininity. In this way, the self-reflexivity offered by the magazines 'helps' women to stage themselves as female-to-female impersonators in a consumer society.

Once these first cross-readers, the so-called target audience, have consumed their magazines, women's media may then attract the attention of less foreseen readers. Later in this volume, John Treat describes the way in which Yoshimoto Banana's *Kitchen*, which can be seen as a 'translation' of the narrative style of girls' comic books into the form of the novel, has been received and given awards by the literary establishment – though not without a certain sense of ambivalence. In a similar vein, Sharon Kinsella describes another cultural critic Yamane Kazuma's extensive study of young people's cute handwriting in visitor books in tourist temples and love hotels. Japanese women's media have been recorded, analyzed and evaluated, sometimes in extremely disdainful ways and employing a vocabulary of pathology, by predominantly male cultural critics, who seem determined to ignore the role played by women both in Japanese consumer culture and in postmodernism (cf. Miyoshi and Harootunian 1989a). This pervasive attitude leads us to argue that women are indeed the 'hidden others' in debates which, more often than not, have been engaged in by men with an all-too-well-known depreciation of those kinds of commercial culture in which women participate so actively (Huyssen 1986:46–59). Hence we find an almost apocalyptic anxiety that the supposedly 'pure' and 'masculine' culture of Japan has been vulgarized, feminized, and infanticized to the point where it has become 'baby talk' beyond the comprehension of well-educated critics. Such moralistic cross-readings have played a crucial role in defining women's media, and as such they can hardly be ignored in an analysis of women, media and consumption in Japan.

This book is also based on cross-readings by a group of European and north American sociologists, anthropologists and literary scholars, both men and women, who for different reasons have found themselves studying various aspects of women's media in Japan. Our aim has been to avoid a moralistic approach, although we are acutely aware at the same time that – given the distances among us of geography and culture, as well as of age and gender – it may seem easy to label Japanese women as, in Orvar Löfgren's words (1990: 11), the 'other consumers', as passive victims of market manipulation. According to conceptualizations criticized by Löfgren, the 'other consumers' are the ones who seriously believe in the sugar-coated dreams and glossy images, who always hope that the purchase of things can bring them instant happiness, and who mirror themselves in the most recent consumer goods without ever discovering the hollowness and fragmentation of their identities. They are the 'other consumers' (for *we* are certainly not like them!) to the extent that their otherness makes them one-dimensional gorgons. But most of all, perhaps, they are an inverse sign of critics' own faith in the imaginary world of consumption.

Our sense of unease is here amplified by the fact that the spectacle of Orientalism looms over our shoulders when, as western academics, we present an account of Japanese women's media framed by yet another voyeuristic gaze from afar. The equally reductive paradigms of 'culture industry', on the one hand, and of Orientalism, on the other, seem to match and support each other only too well. As Tobin (1992c:37) rightly points out, in the context of Japanese Studies, 'to read Japanese consumption as meaningless, ridiculous, or parodic is to engage in a smug orientalist discourse'. This danger is something which, in writing this book, we have had to confront in both our methodology and style.

Still, our justification lies in the fact we are far from the only cross-readers of Japanese women's media, given all the *other* consumers, market analysts, and moralists who are doing precisely this. In a complex society such as Japan's, the production, distribution and consumption of media are themselves complex processes whose meanings are not fixed.

In the following chapters, along with our own interpretations, we try to pay special attention to some among the wide range of cross-readings present in the field, whether those of media audiences, or of editors, advertisers or critics. In some chapters, cross-readings themselves are even an object of inquiry; and eventually, what we present here is yet another cross-reading of contemporary media for Japanese women. We aim, of course, to present a series of adequate interpretations, but at the same time we do not pretend to provide a definitive explanation of the relation between women and media in Japan. In such a vibrant and dynamic field, all we can hope for is that our readers will want themselves to read, cross-read, and respond to our cross-readings.

NOTES

1 Regular television broadcasting in Japan (by NHK and the commercial channel, NTV) started in 1953. In the following year, 10,000 – and in the year following that, 100,000 – TV sets were sold. Distribution reached half a million in 1957, one million in 1958, and five million sets in 1960. By 1964, nine out of ten households in Japan owned a television set. The opening ceremony of the Tōkyō Olympic Games, together with certain events like the 100 metres sprint, were televised in colour for the first time in Japan (Yamaki 1992:232, 249–50, 493–5).

  It is interesting to note also that the term *information society* was actually coined by a Japanese anthropologist, Umesao Tadao, back in 1963 to describe the kind of society he was then living in.

  Many of the ideas presented here emerged during the course of discussion at the workshop on 'Women, Media and Consumption in Japan'. We would like to thank all the participants for their input, and also Eyal Ben-Ari, Marie Lenstrup and Merry White for taking the trouble to read and comment on various drafts of this Introduction.

2 In 1992, 53.2 per cent of women worked in enterprises with a workforce of under one hundred employees; 16.3 per cent in those under five hundred; and a further 20.9 per cent in large corporations that employed more than one thousand workers (Sōrifu 1993:66). In this respect, we should note two things: firstly, that it is only large corporations and the government sector which offer lifetime employment; secondly, that – as Brinton (1993:14) points out – it is very difficult to estimate precisely what proportion of the Japanese labour force enjoys permanent employment because it is not based on legal contract.

3 The highest ratio of employed women in Japan is for the 20–24 (75.6 per cent) and 45–49 (72.0 per cent) age groups; the lowest (52.7 per cent) for those aged between 30 and 34 (Sōrifu 1993:63).

4 The trade in young women was not limited to the textile industry. Many were recruited as so-called 'maids' to work as legal or illegal prostitutes (Dalby 1983:222–3; Tsurumi 1990:181–7). Here the initial loans offered by

recruiting agents were higher than those offered in the textile industry, so that women were often sold into prostitution when their parents or husbands fell seriously ill or died. These large loans often left the women concerned in lifelong debt, obliging them to renew their initial contracts against their will and making them *de facto* slaves of bordello owners.

5 A good example of this is provided by Glenda Roberts who quotes a speech by the president of an apparel company to his employees, most of them women, in which he talks of the angst-provoking breakdown of Japanese society when women 'no longer maintain the household' and begin to 'dislike raising children'. This he sees as leading to the 'fall' of men, so that the fact that there are few 'manly men' nowadays is to be attributed to women – an irony apparently not lost on those women workers present who found themselves having to listen to their employer telling them that their proper place was in their homes looking after their husbands and children (cited in Smith 1987:8–9).

6 81.2 per cent of all Japanese women aged over 35 years are employed part-time, mainly in the service and retail sectors. Only 4.5 per cent of these receive a monthly, only 5.8 per cent a daily, wage. The remaining 88.1 per cent work on an hourly basis. On average, these 5.92 million women work 5.8 hours a day over 20.9 days a month, and earn pay of ¥809 an hour (Sōrifu 1993:78–80).

7 Until about 1960, the magazine industry had been sustained by such titles as *Shufu no Tomo* (Housewife's Companion), *Fujin Club* (Wives Club), *Shufu to Seikatsu* (Housewife and Life) and *Fujin Seikatsu* (Wife's Life) – all of which were supported by household product advertising (medicines and foods) and which, in their editorial matter, promulgated the kind of Confucian 'good wife and wise mother' image typically expected of Japanese women at that time. With the publication of magazines such as *Misses*, *Young Lady* and *Madam*, however, there was more emphasis on women as individual consumers, and the main advertisers became fashion and accessory houses, travel agencies, real estate, car manufacturers, and the entertainment industry (Yamaki 1992:227–228).

8 The concept of *shinjinrui* is frequently and variously used by those discussing young people in Japan, and no single definition exists. Our usage here differs from that found in the chapter by Merry White later in this book.

9 We would like to thank Hidehiko Sekizawa, of the Hakuhōdō Institute of Life and Living, for his continued research hospitality – in particular, for making available to us two years' supply of all women's magazines published in Japan.

10 For example, in its concluding section 'The long lonely road' to an English language publication on Japanese single women, HILL (1993a:216–7) suggests that women work only to develop their interests, knowledge and experience – all of which are seen to lie primarily in the realm of consumption (hobbies, travel, education). This section is generally remarkable for its moral prescriptions: that women *should* commit themselves to responsibilities of one sort or another – whether of marriage or of an ill-defined 'long-term goal'; that they *should* sharpen their analytical abilities by going through higher education; and that they 'must develop the qualities necessary to help Japan meet . . . new challenges' (224).

11 In his discussion of gender inequality, published soon after the Equal Employment Opportunity Law was passed, Smith (1987:11) points out that at the time critics argued that, in its revised form, the law was far more favourable to the interests of employers than to those of employees. It does not, for example, specify punishment for an employer's discriminatory practices.

12 Car ads are a good example here because, once feminist ideas in western countries gained the kind of hegemony that made people generally recognize that an advertisement picturing a woman in silk dress as a (Renault) car was in bad taste (Dyer 1988:120–2), or which encouraged women themselves to rewrite headlines (for a Fiat ad) as eye-catching graffiti (Posener 1982), western advertisers found themselves obliged to search for different ways of presenting the things they wanted to sell.

13 Radio is also considered to be one of the four main advertising media in Japan, but since its total share of the market comes to less than five per cent, we have ignored it here.

14 It is clear from this and other comments that Harootunian and his fellow editor, Miyoshi Masao, are basically anti-commercialist and anti-consumerist. See, for example, phrases like 'all the gibberish gushing from advertising copywriters and store designers' (Miyoshi and Harootunian 1989b:xii).

15 An advertising slogan which, with the later *sawayaka tasty*, came to epitomize for Japanese the 'strategic tripod of taste, thirst and refreshment' represented by Coca Cola (O'Barr 1989:5, 12).

16 An exception may prove to be Lancôme's forty-year-old model, Isabella Rossellini, but at the time of writing the company was putting out photographs taken of her when she was much younger.

17 The Japanese Magazine Advertising Association in 1990 listed 903 advertising magazines, classified into the following headings: Agriculture (2), Annuals (28), Architecture (29), Business and the Economy (58), Children (97), Comics (84), Education (17), Employment (6), General (84), Government (8), Health and Medical (9), Hobbies (118), Literature, History and Art (39), Science (20), Sports (71), Television, Film and Entertainment (50), Women (144), and 'Young' (39) (Nihon Zasshi Kōkoku Kyōkai 1990).

18 In a thorough comparative study of Japanese, American and Mexican women's magazines in 1986, Inoue and her study group (1989, Chapter 2) calculate that, in the 'new' women's magazines in Japan (i.e. those first published after 1970), the average ratio of straight advertisements was 39.4 per cent and the ratio of visuals to print 78.3 per cent.

19 For an example of this trend elsewhere, see Winship (1987:38) who points out that the launching of *Options* in April 1982 involved 'two disparate but intimately linked selling operations: one to women, the other to advertisers'. The shift in financial emphasis from sales to advertising in the Japanese magazine market seems to have come much earlier, in 1969 when the newly launched *Nikkei Business* succeeded in attracting 45 per cent of its revenues from advertising (Yamaki 1992:277).

20 This is very different from the American or British magazine industry, where a common strategy is for a publisher to bring out a 'copy cat' version

of one of its *own* successful magazines, in order to *prevent* a competitor rushing in with a 'me too' publication (Winship 1987: 41).

21 The advertising agency Hakuhōdō divides Japanese magazines into five 'lifestages' or 'clusters': 'adult' (aged 35 and over), 'young adult' (24–35 years), 'young' (18–23 years), 'teens' (12–17 years), and 'junior' (under 11 years). It further classifies all magazines into three types: 'life' (women/men), 'entertainment' and 'general'.

22 Data compiled by the advertising agency Asahi Tsūshinsha show that the readership of *non-no* (which, it will be remembered, is aimed at girls in their teens) *rose* significantly among women aged between 35 and 49 years (circulation from 80,000 to 100,000 copies). The same was true, though to a lesser extent, of *éf, JJ, Olive, CanCam, ViVi* and *Say*. Similarly, magazines such as the weeklies *Shūkan Josei* and *Josei Jishin*, aimed at the older end of the market with peak readerships of women aged between 35 and 49 years, had second highest readership levels among the 12 to 19 age group.

1

INTERPRETING OSHIN – WAR, HISTORY AND WOMEN IN MODERN JAPAN

Paul A. S. Harvey

In terms of television drama in Japan, *Oshin* (1983–4),[1] produced by the Japanese national broadcasting corporation Nippon Hōsō Kyōkai (NHK – the Japanese BBC), was the success story of the 1980s. It achieved the highest levels of popularity since NHK began television broadcasting in 1953, and was the first Japanese television serial drama to achieve a global coverage, being seen in more than 40 different countries by 1993. The importance of *Oshin* is indicated in a full page article at the beginning of 1994, '*Onnatachi no ōenka: NHK asa no rendora 50 saku*' (Cheering on women: 50 years of *asadora*), where it is given the largest photo space (*Yomiuri Shinbun*, January 1, 1994, New Year's day supplement, p.1).

In this chapter I will examine the reasons for the success of *Oshin* in Japan, and the complex factors that stood behind its production. I will propose that there was a complicated and contradictory ideological input from NHK, which meant that the conservative appeal made by the drama – its overt content – included at the same time the presentation of a more ambiguous and less socially conservative message. This relation between overt content and covert meanings may be seen to be a variation on the function of wrapping as noted by Joy Hendry (1993:8–26). It is the argument of this chapter that the conservative packaging of the drama allowed the more innovatory social message to gain currency.

The innovatory nature of the message is to be linked to the fact that *Oshin* was written and produced by women, who made use of a women's genre, asadora (NHK morning serialised television novels), to make a powerful statement which reflected on the status of women in Japan, on women's history, and on attitudes to past Japanese military aggression, which was the subject of public debate in 1982–3.

The most remarkable aspect to the drama from a western point of view is that it provides data to stand alongside Okpyo Moon's (1992) contention that economic development in Japan can be allied to notions of a rise in women's status. Oshin, the protagonist of the drama, went from rice farming to hairdressing to retail and eventually to owning supermarkets. However, at the same time as being held up as an independent 'modern' woman creating prosperity for her family, Oshin was also an embodiment of traditional Japanese female 'virtues', primarily self-restraint and self-sacrifice. She was, in a sense, well wrapped in a very traditional kimono. Okpyo Moon is surely right when she complains that: 'in the study of gender relations, there has been [a] . . . powerful hindrance to the understanding of the reality of Japanese women: that is, the stereotypical image-making about Japanese women by western media as frail, submissive and mysterious beings' (1992: 206). *Oshin* provided a powerful demystification of this particular ideological package, for Oshin was neither frail, mysterious nor submissive, and the key to her success as a cultural icon was her ability to *endure*, a strength derived from her moral superiority to those who would inflict hardship upon her. Oshin's embodiment of 'endurance' forms a continuity with the kind of spiritual suffering that the high school baseball teams undergo in the presentation of the baseball tournaments on television throughout Japan every summer, and Brian Moeran describes *shinbō* (endurance) as one of the keywords contributing to group ideology in Japan (1989:62–3, 71).

I will divide the chapter into four sections. In the first section there is a brief sketch of *Oshin*'s storyline. In section two, I will discuss the asadora genre. In section three, I outline the issues which were addressed by NHK in *Oshin*, which included the 'school history book controversy' over description of past Japanese aggression (sparked by complaints from China and Korea) and social concerns in the early 1980s relating to delinquent Japanese youth. The fourth section concludes the chapter by examining the complex ways in which naming takes place in *Oshin*, and the way that *Oshin* owed its success both to its ambivalent ideological stance and the way that it was able to tap powerful nationalist sentiments. Oshin was, in a sense, Japan.

Plot Outline – *Oshin*

Oshin is a historical drama, set at the end of the Meiji period and finishing in present time (at the time of screening 1983–4). Through a series of flashbacks working up to the present, it tells the life-story of the lead character Oshin, beginning with the opening of the seventeenth Tanokura (Oshin's surname after marriage) supermarket, a link in the supermarket chain that Oshin and her children build from nothing after 1945. Oshin is absent from the ceremony. In the company of her grandson Kei, she has gone to revisit the village where she has spent her first seven years, and has suffered poverty and hardship, in order to reflect upon the 'meaning' of her prosperity. It is at this point that the flashbacks begin, with the first flashback sequence detailing the first time that Oshin was forced to leave home.

She was born in 1901 as the third daughter of a poor tenant farmer (*kosakunin*) in a village in the upper reaches of Yamagata prefecture's Mogami river. Owing to the injustice of the tenant farming system (whereby a large percentage of the rice is surrendered to the landlord), the family is forced to live close to subsistence. After a particularly bad harvest Oshin is sent away for a year by her parents, effectively *sold*[2] to a timber dealer to look after the baby and do chores in exchange for a bale of rice. The scene in which she leaves home has become one of the best remembered scenes in the drama. She is treated very harshly at the timber merchant's. Just before she is due to return home, she is falsely accused of stealing. This is too much for her and she runs away, collapsing into exhausted sleep in the snow in the Yamagata mountains. She is rescued by a deserter from the army, Shunsaku, who teaches her that war is wrong. (The time that Oshin spends with him is discussed later in this chapter, and is a key to the drama as a whole). Following this section Shunsaku is shot in the back by military police as he carries Oshin home in the early spring. His death affirms his anti-military stance.

Some months pass, and Oshin decides that she has to sell herself into service in order to provide food for her ailing grandmother, Naka, and because her mother, Fuji, has chosen to work as a geisha at a nearby hot spring to provide vital family income. Fuji is a pivotal reference point in the drama. Oshin's ability to endure is derived from her bond with her mother. Oshin moves to Sakata and is taken on by a rice dealer, Kagaya. The female owner of the business, Kuni, takes pity on her, and teaches her how to read and write, the basics of which she had picked up from Shunsaku. At Kagaya she also learns about class difference through her contact with Kayo, the daughter of the house.

In 1916 Oshin leaves Kagaya to be at the deathbed of her elder sister Haru, who has contracted tuberculosis while working in appalling conditions in a nearby silk mill (Hunter 1993:69–97). Haru encourages her to move to Tōkyō, which she does. She begins training as a Japanese-style hairdresser in Asakusa, a job which perhaps highlights the educative function that stands behind Oshin, since she is setting the hair of Japanese women *in the traditional way*, this being readable as a metaphor for the moral work done by the drama, which is teaching women to be '*women*'. But true to the complexity of the drama, it is an activity which serves only as one staging post on a long allegorical journey. There is more discussion of this later.

Before leaving Kagaya in Sakata, both Oshin and Kayo fall in love with Takakura Kōta, a wellborn young man who turns socialist in order to champion the rights of tenant farmers (i.e. Oshin's family). Kōta proposes to Oshin, but Kayo intervenes. Kōta and Kayo leave together for Tōkyō and Oshin follows.

In 1920, after a few years in Tōkyō, Oshin meets and marries Tanokura Ryūzō, third son of a comparatively wealthy farming family from Saga in Kyūshū, who owns a business selling textiles. The marriage is opposed by both Ryūzō's and Oshin's family on the grounds of class difference. In the years that follow Oshin and Ryūzō build Tanokura Shōkai, a textile factory (there is an irony here with regard to the death of Haru, Oshin's sister). However, soon after Oshin gives birth to her son, Yū, the 1924 Tōkyō earthquake reduces their home and the factory to rubble, leaving them bankrupt. They flee Tōkyō and join Ryūzō's family in Saga, Kyūshū.

Oshin is cruelly mistreated by her mother-in-law, and this is the period of greatest misery for Oshin, compounded by the fact that Ryūzō sides against her. She suffers without complaint for a year, up until the birth of her second child. The baby dies within a few hours, weakened by the bad diet and harsh treatment. As soon as she recovers, she leaves her husband and his family, and returns home to the north with her son, Yū. Her abandonment of the family is the second turning point of the drama, and is similar to her meeting with Shunsaku. This was also the highpoint of the drama's popularity, with a peak rating of more than 60 per cent. Up to the moment at which Oshin decides to leave, she has been a 'model wife' suffering in silence in the interests of family harmony, suppressing the self in the interests of the group, but by leaving she rejects this role and goes on to raise her children by herself and build a business on her own terms.

After a brief sojourn in Sakata, Oshin departs for Ise on the advice of Kōta, whom she has met again. In Ise she works as a fishmonger, peddling the day's catch in the streets. This goes well, and her husband rejoins her. The business expands and they open their own store. Kōta reappears, taking refuge from the *tokkō keisatsu*, the Japanese secret police. Kōta is a communist, working to subvert Japanese imperialism. He is arrested when he goes to visit Kayo's grave (Kayo had died in

Tōkyō working as a geisha to pay off family debts). We are informed that he will be tortured and probably put to death.

This forms the prelude to the 1930s, with increasing militarization as a background to Oshin's hard-won prosperity. Ryūzō changes from being a sympathetic young man (who buried his Kyūshū masculine (*danji*) pride and rejoined his wife after she had left him) to being an inflexible and authoritarian figure, sporting a Hitlerian moustache, and supporting Japanese expansion. War is pursued against China and the US, and within a short time the drama is filled with air raids, rationing and war. Yū leaves, and Hitoshi, the second son, though still under age, runs off to be trained as a pilot. The war comes to an end. The family is notified of Yū's death, and Ryūzō, who had amassed supplies for the army, takes responsibility for his part in the war, and commits suicide. Hitoshi returns home. Yū's friend Kimura visits the family and tells Oshin that Yū's death was a miserable one brought on by starvation and fatigue.

The last section of the drama concentrates on the rebuilding of the prosperity of the family in the postwar years, and in particular the founding of Tanokura supermarkets. This development spans 35 years, and was aired in the last three months of the drama from January to March 1984. The drama closes with Oshin and Kōta (who had survived after all) walking side by side on a hilltop overlooking the sea in Showa 58 (1983).

Asadora genre and history

NHK morning serialised television novels (NHK *Asa no Renzoku Terebi Shōsetsu* – asadora, literally 'morning drama') were first broadcast in April 1961. To date there have been over 50 different dramas, *Karin* (October 4, 1993 – April 2, 1994) being the fiftieth. These television dramas are the most popular drama on Japanese television, and have been so ever since their inception. This is a factor of the time of screening, which is 8:15 a.m. (with a repeat showing at 12:45 p.m.); the nature of the audience, which has been largely married women; and the content and format of the dramas themselves, which has shown continuity since 1966 when the genre began to achieve a recognisable shape. In recent years, these three factors – time, audience and content – have all begun to change. This chapter will focus on one of the most important participants in that change: the immensely popular *Oshin* (April 4, 1983 – March 31, 1984), the most successful of all the asadora (and thus of all Japanese television dramas since television began in Japan).

But before we look in detail at *Oshin*, it would be as well to consider how the genre became established in the 1970s, because *Oshin* was produced with very specific goals in mind; and its success was due in part to NHK's desire to revitalise asadora which had been in comparative decline since the popularity of the late sixties, when the ratings were regularly over 50 per cent (see Figure 1.1).

Makita Tetsuo (1976) and Muramatsu Yasuko (1979) have provided the most authoritative discussions of asadora up to the screening of *Oshin* in 1983.[3] The first asadora, *Musume to Watashi* (My Daughter and I), was screened from April 1961 for one year. It was designed to appeal to housewives who would be able to watch or listen to the story and dialogue as they did their housework. From the start, asadora included a narrator who filled in the gaps in the story and provided a non-visual continuity. In the first five years of asadora, NHK tried to fit well-known literary works into a televisual mode. The protagonist was often male, and the emphasis was on the man's perception of his world and his family. The literary works used as source material were the '*watakushi shōsetsu*' genre: autobiographical novels written largely by men. This early period of asadora was well summed up in an early publicity photograph for *Tamayura* (1965 – written by Kawabata Yasunari) showing Ryū Chishū with his wife and daughters gathered around him as he holds a *haniwa* (a clay figure from a burial mound) admiringly in his lap: the focus of the drama is male tradition and aesthetics which is to be *cherished* by the women, and of course the drama was produced, directed and written by men (*Stera* 1993.10.1). Kawabata himself put in a brief appearance in *Tamayura*, his first work produced on television, and it was the first time for Ryū, famous for his portrayals of Japanese father-figures, to appear on TV. *Akatsuki*, screened from April 1963 was similar: a story about a university professor who becomes a painter. Both of these were successful (there has rarely been an unsuccessful asadora), but it was felt that since the audience was largely female, a drama which spoke more directly to women's experience would be more popular. This was given impetus by the realisation that the potential audience was so great: the Tōkyō Olympics of 1964 had caused sales of televisions to rocket, and by 1966 televisions were widely diffused. This must have been one of the factors inducing the production team to put together a drama which would have more appeal to women, and *Ohanahan* (1966) was the result: it had no originating 'literary' source, but was based on a piece in the women's magazine *Fujin Gahō* and was written specifically for asadora (Makita 1976:86).

Both Makita and Muramatsu point out that *Ohanahan* had a mould-

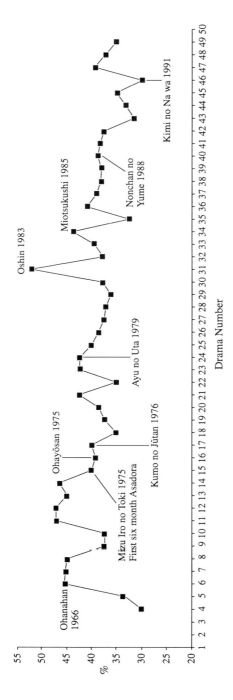

Figure 1.1 Graph of the popularity of Asadora 1961–1993

Source: Kantō ratings for Asadora 1961–1993 (data from *Stera Magazine* and *Video Research K.K.*)

ing effect on the genre. *Ohanahan* was not actually written by a woman,[4] but it took as its theme the life story of Asao Hana, centering on her and seeing the world through her eyes. In 1964, *Uzushio* had pioneered this format, delineating the protagonist as a woman with clearly defined characteristics, lighthearted and bold (*akaruku takumashiku*): a woman who remained undismayed by misfortune or economic hardship. *Ohanahan* developed and refined this, producing a heroine who was both bold and light-hearted, and at the same time free from prejudice and vigorous in defending the interests of her children and husband. Muramatsu characterises Ohanahan as cheerful, lighthearted and innocent (*yōki de akaruku tenshinranman*) (1979:4). After *Ohanahan* it became common for asadora to tell the life story of its heroine (*ichidaiki mono*) concentrating on the way the heroine interrelated with her family, and how she made the family a success. Not all of the early asadora (up to about 1980) focussed exclusively on a single woman: others focussed on the family as an entity (*kazoku mono*), without giving particular prominence to the heroine in the way that *Ohanahan* had done (Makita 1976:86). *Ohanahan*'s impact on the genre was due to its immense popularity: as can be seen from Figure 1.1, the average rating was 45.8 per cent and the peak rating (not shown on the graph) was 56.4 per cent. If we consider the way that the ratings for *Ohanahan* progressed through the year, we notice that they form an ideal upward tendency, showing that a high level of interest in the drama continued to increase up until the last three months of screening when there was a slight levelling off (Makita 1976:90). This was a pattern followed for a number of years, and for this period from *Ohanahan* (1966) to *Mizu Iro no Toki* (1975) the average daily ratings were most often over 45 per cent. From this period, and to a slightly lesser extent ever since, we can consider this television drama a phenomenon of social importance, speaking as it does from the corner of so many Japanese living rooms practically every single morning for the last thirty years.

Let me summarise Makita's six elements, which he suggests go to make up the characteristic shape of asadora following *Ohanahan*. The first is the creation of original material produced exclusively for the genre; the second, the tendency to focus on unknown 'ordinary' women; the third, to choose an unknown actress to play the part (and in the early years of asadora this was sufficient to guarantee national status as an actress); fourth, the change from a first person to a third person narration (and, we might add, an increasing tendency for women narrators – see Figure 1.2); fifth, as mentioned above, a new type of female personality on Japanese television who is straightforward, free from prejudice, able

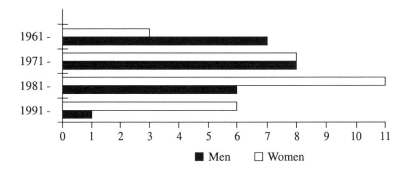

Figure 1.2 Number of female and male narrators for
Asadora 1961–1993

Source: Data adapted from information given
in *Stera* October 1993

to make things happen and knows how to survive (*sotchokusa, henken no nasa, jikkōryoku, ikite iku chie*); and sixth, the inclusion of various plot elements which are designed to maintain audience interest. Makita lists these as: enigmas (*nazo*), journeying (*hōrō*) which often means leaving the provinces to live in Tōkyō (*jōkyō*), war (*sensō*), death (*shi*) and, as Muramatsu points out, we might add romantic love (*ren'ai*), marriage (*kekkon*), and women and work (*onna to shigoto*), and a setting of the drama in the present or the past (within living memory) (Makita 1976:86; Muramatsu 1979:8). Indeed, when we consider Makita's list of plot elements, we may note immediately the novelistic background to the genre, for these are the same elements that serial novelists such as George Eliot or Charles Dickens made use of in *Middlemarch* or *Little Dorrit*.[5]

In Terebi Dorama no Josei Gaku, Muramatsu Yasuko is in broad agreement with Makita (they are colleagues at the NHK Hōsō Bunka Kenkyūjo in Atago, Tōkyō – a unit which researches trends in public opinion and television viewing), but she makes one or two important qualifications which are relevant to *Oshin*. Perhaps most importantly, Muramatsu highlights the potential for social innovation with regard to women that lies at the heart of asadora. She points out that female creativity was highlighted in both *Uzushio* (1964) and *Ashitakoso* (1968) where the protagonist was a female novelist. She also underlines the importance of the historical setting of the dramas: since the dramas are set in the past within living memory, it has meant that the majority of the heroines up to 1979 (as was the case with the majority of the viewers) have lived through the second world war. This allowed the dramas to develop an educative anti-war position, but also threw into relief the change in women's post-war social status after being given the vote, and benefiting from changes relating to inheritance and their legal status in the family. As asadora gained in confidence, the promotion of women's status became an essential aspect to the genre. Muramatsu sees a turning point with regard to a more definite promotion of women's status taking place in 1975 with *Kumo no Jūtan*, which was a story about the first woman pilot in Japan. 1975 was the United Nations International Year of Women, and the very theme of the drama formed a metaphor for the aspirations of Muramatsu and her generation, women taking the controls and beginning to fly. In line with this, Muramatsu comments on the departure of women for Tōkyō (a postwar phenomenon) in the dramas as symbolising a search for a life of independence and fulfillment, free of the obligations of the traditional family (*ie*) which maintained a robust existence, despite the increasing numbers of nuclear families and the increase in the number of married women working (1979:26).

One of the most valuable qualifications that Muramatsu makes about asadora is that it can also serve as a powerful tool for social conservatism. She comments on how the heroine, in search of independence, leaves the traditional family to recreate a family on her own terms, but that in the dramas in the 1970s this usually involved a strong relationship with her eldest son, who then went on to head the family and be the leading member of the upcoming generation. The energetic and socially innovative woman (we may remember Ohanahan deciding to become a doctor after the death of her husband) thus surrendered social innovation to her son. Baldly translated, social innovation for women was to proceed only so far as it would not interfere with their job of raising the future male leaders of society. The relationship between the bright, active and successful heroines and their daughters was thus severely underprivileged. Muramatsu makes interesting comments on the relationship between the heroines and their husbands, pointing out that the death of the husband is a common occurrence because it allows the drama to give more focus to the women, obviating the subsidiary female role in marriage at the same time as maintaining the degree of 'social realism' appropriate to the genre. The husband must die so that the woman can head the family, but following this it is common for the heroine to have one son (*hitori musuko o motsu hiroin ga ōi*) (1979:32).

In the 1980s, however, the relationship between the heroine and daughter and/or heroine and mother was placed at the centre of the drama (as in *Oshin* in 1983, or *Nonchan no Yume* in 1988), so that in this respect we may be more confident of the promotion of a female tradition of social innovation in the later asadora.

This brings us to *Oshin*, which was the first asadora to be both written and produced by women: the team of Okamoto Yukiko, the first female chief producer at NHK, and Hashida Sugako, arguably the most successful of all Japanese TV drama script writers. As a tribute to Hashida (and of course to exploit her popularity), the 1994 asadora beginning in October *Haru, Koi* is scripted by Hashida and based on her autobiography.

As can be seen from Figure 1.1, the general popularity of asadora had been declining since 1975. This was not necessarily due to a falling off of interest in the drama, since over the same period there was a tendency for morning television to be watched less. It was probably to be linked to an increase in the number of married working women during the period (Figure 1.3), for housewives had comprised the largest body of daytime viewers.[6]

It was to meet a possible drop in the popularity of asadora that *Oshin* was planned as a year-long drama. Since 1975 (commencing with *Mizu Iro no Toki*), the dramas had been six month serials, for the year-long schedule had been over-demanding on all involved, and was especially

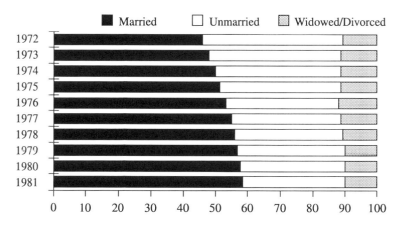

Figure 1.3 Breakdown of working women by marital status

(Adapted from Gotō et al. 1991:137)

85

draining on the writer.[7] Hashida produced 6,000 pages for *Oshin* before
and during the course of production over a period of eighteen months
(Hashida 1984:1; *Graf NHK* 1983 April, p.2). The decline in popularity
coincided suspiciously closely with the change to six month production.
Oshin was in part an attempt to recover the lost popularity of the late
sixties. But *Oshin* had other equally important agendas, and these are to
be glimpsed at the beginning of the 1980s in the reports of the NHK
Hōsō Bunka Kenkyūjo, whose work on public opinion and trends in
television viewing provides data available to producers of prospective
television programmes.

Background to Oshin

Nostalgia

In the late 1970s, NHK carried out a number of surveys to determine the
attitudes and interests of young people, and these surveys were reviewed
in an important article in *NHK Hōsō Bunka Kenkyū Nenpō* (Kazama
1981). The article was notable for the way it pointed up a moral slipping
in young people. It discussed the young people's 'subjects of thought
and attitudinal levels' as being 'diminished and shrunken' (English
synopsis: 258). NHK had carried out the survey as part of a general
concern that social standards with regard to modern youth were not as
high as they had been, and it highlighted a decrease in reading and a lack
of interest in politics compared to the 1960s. NHK's survey was provoked by a widespread concern that the so-called core Japanese values
had become eroded by the recent affluence Japan had achieved by the
end of the 1970s. Yoshino Kōsaku (1992:211–2) comments that for
some of the older generation at this time, such concern could be linked
directly to nationalist symbols: 'juvenile delinquency and the deterior-
ating standard of social manners among pupils were perceived in the
same context as the issues of such "old" nationalist symbols as the
"national" flag and anthem, and ethics courses'.

   In planning *Oshin*, it must have been decided to address this general
social concern with 'standards', so often a feature in the media of the
time. The beginning of *Oshin* was structured to appeal to this particular
nostalgia for a set of core values that predated postwar development with
its creation of a society in the late 1970s that was discouraged from
enjoying its newly-achieved affluence. At the beginning of the drama,
Oshin is presented to us as being impelled by a desire to review her life
and discover something which had been forgotten or lost, with the

specific purpose of *teaching the younger generation*. She travels north to Yamagata where she was born and is accompanied by Kei, her grandson, who was a listener and occasionally brash young pupil of the hardships that she experienced as the daughter of a tenant farmer (and who exemplifies a stereotypical modern youth in the casual way in which he addresses his grandmother). Kei is not in fact a blood relative, for his father was adopted by Oshin out of obligation to Kayo, the granddaughter of her former mistress who had taught her to read and write and enabled her to escape rural poverty.

By opening the drama in this way, Hashida Sugako is intimating that Oshin is a surrogate grandmother of all young Japanese, who are not related to her by blood. Indeed, Hashida admits as much, for it was her intention in *Oshin* to write 'a requiem for our mothers born in the Meiji period' (*Graf NHK* 1983:2–3; *Oshin: NHK Dorama Gaido* 1983:6–7). In writing her requiem (which is at the same time, of course, a praise song), Hashida is thus offering her own version of the debate on the decline in cultural values (at the heart of which is the sense of obligation to one's familial superior), whereby over-indulged modern youth has no idea of the sacrifices that older generations made on its behalf. This was highlighted at the very beginning of the drama when Oshin comments: 'We lived through hard times' (Episode 3, screened April 6, 1983). And the presentation of Oshin's children and grandchildren at the beginning of the drama as a group of people who fight amongst themselves and, in the case of the wife of her surviving eldest son, the open hostility shown to Oshin, her mother-in-law (which contrasts with Oshin herself later in the drama), are all indicators (but not unambiguous ones) that something has gone wrong. Social disharmony contrasts with the evident prosperity the family has achieved.

In Episode 4, the older Oshin stands in front of the house in which she was born and weeps: 'At that time [as a small child] I did not know we were poor'. The weight of this was to emphasise that other values were more important than single-minded materialistic motivation. In other words, the drama was promoting a particular nostalgic version of the past. But if it was lamenting the demise of traditional values, at the same time the drama promoted Oshin as an upwardly mobile Japanese, for, as Oshin reiterated throughout the drama, it was the experience of poverty and its distress that fired her with the desire to make money. This ambiguity, the nostalgia for past core values such as obligation to the family, and the single-minded dedication to one's own material improvement (which in Oshin's case meant *leaving* the family village), ran through the drama and makes it difficult to read the drama as either a purely nostalgic attempt to recuperate the past, or, as we shall see later with regard to its representation of women, as a radical text rewriting women's contribution to modern Japanese economic success. The drama in effect did a lot of different work at the same time, and it would be wrong to assume that the differing ideological streams cohere or even contradict: multiple readings are possible, depending on the social and cultural background that the Japanese viewer brings to the television screen.

The conservatively educative aspect to *Oshin* drawing on the appeal of nostalgia was taken up by Simul Press, which brought out a selection of 'wise sayings' from the drama, arranged in various categories such as 'husband and wife', 'parents and children', 'wife and mother in law' (Hashida 1984). This educative aspect to the drama, brought to a head in the name of Oshin herself (which we shall discuss later), was one of the factors responsible for the programme's huge popularity. But we would be wrong to characterise the drama as simply an exercise in cynical social conservatism, for Hashida (teamed with Okamoto) had a wider moral purpose, and the potent mixture that went to make up *Oshin* was to carry it far beyond Japan. This mixture was important. *Oshin* was not simply an accommodation to a nostalgia for traditional virtues, or for the morality attendant on the 'traditional Japanese woman'; nor was it a transition from an earlier ethic to an ethic of the 'modern independent woman'. Rather, it was something in between, a text that incorporated and mirrored social action with the multiplicity of its signposting, with women negotiating and twisting Japanese core values to produce a text that was both immensely popular and innovative with regard to women's role.

Women's history

Considering the structure of the beginning of *Oshin*, with the grandmother handing down precious wisdom to her grand*son*, we might of course consider that Muramatsu's criticisms had gone unheeded; but this seems not to have been the case. The knowledge that Oshin imparts to her *male* grandchild is that modern Japan was built with the sweat and suffering of Japanese women, and for that reason it is important for her male grandchild to be the listener. He must learn about and reflect on the sacrifices that were made by women like Oshin. In so doing, the enfeebled consciousness of modern youth will be reinvigorated. We can be certain that this is not a fanciful interpretation by simply looking at the back of the drama guide for *Oshin*, issued to publicise the drama (it was the first asadora guide and became a best-seller following the feverish popularity of *Oshin*).

At the back of the guide there is a section titled *Nihon kindai joseishi nenpyō/Dorama nenpyō* (A chronological table of the history of Japanese women/A table of the drama), in which the main events of Oshin's life are placed in a chart detailing important events in women's history in Japan (*Oshin: NHK Dorama Gaido*: 186–191). Okamoto Yukiko, in a symposium held in Tōkyō in February 1991, stressed that *Oshin* was significant as an intervention by women:

> Earlier, Dr. Surakhmad said that although this was a drama written and produced by women, there was a sense of universality to it. I, however, would like to stress the fact that this was a drama created by women . . . Watching *Oshin*, you understand that, behind all this, there are actually powerful women working extremely hard in what appears to be a male-dominated society. Ms. Hashida tried to portray that in the drama. I also worked hard to show that aspect; the actresses worked extremely hard.
>
> (NHK International 1991:67)

The fact that *Oshin* was understood by NHK to be a woman's production is attested to by the fact that, in the following drama *Romansu* (1984), there was no leading female while both protagonists were male, and that it was written and produced by men (*Asahi Shinbun* October 8, 1983, morning edition: 22). This does not imply that NHK abandoned the attempt to tell women's history through asadora (for *Hanekonma* 1986 did similar work as did *Inochi* 1988, using asadora techniques in the Sunday evening time slot), but rather that NHK needed to ring the changes. *Oshin* was strongly identified with the history of Japanese women. *Romansu*, however, was notably less popular.

Attitudes to the past war

In the early 1980s there was another important survey taken by NHK which was to have an influence on *Oshin*. This was conducted in the autumn of 1982, six months before *Oshin* began screening and a few months before filming began in Yamagata. The results of the survey were published at the same time as *Oshin* began screening in April 1983. Entitled '*Nihonjin no heiwakan*' (The Japanese outlook on peace), the survey was provoked by the criticisms levelled by Korea and China the previous summer regarding the contents of Japanese history schoolbooks. China made a formal protest on July 26. The controversy had gathered momentum since conservative proposals had been issued at the beginning of the 1980s, aimed at redressing what was described as a left-wing bias in high school history textbooks. The argument centred on the description of Japan's participation in the Pacific war simply as a war of 'advance' (*shinshutsu*), or as a war of 'aggression' (*shinryaku senso*) as alleged by China and Korea. Japanese history schoolbooks had been carefully reviewed by the Ministry of Education (*Monbushō*), and the past war euphemistically glossed. The criticisms provoked widespread social debate as to the legacy of the war, and involved high level visits to China and Korea by the Education Minister and leading members of the Liberal Democratic Party, the party in government at that time. Wakiya (1983:54) points out that there were very few Japanese who were unaware of the criticism. This led NHK to conduct a poll to assess attitudes to war and war guilt in the population as a whole and, in conducting this poll, it was careful not to align itself openly with either government or opposition, since on the subject of the past war, as the poll made clear, there were very clear attitudinal differences according to political affiliation, with the left of centre at ease with the statement that the past war was a war of aggression, and the right of centre more liable to emphasise the global pressures which led to Japanese expansion.[8]

Akiyama Toyoko's presentation of the survey and its results makes fascinating reading.[9] It may be a coincidence that it was published at the very time that *Oshin* began screening, but the relation between the two in terms of subject matter is not accidental at all, for Hashida herself emphasises the deliberate anti-war stance that she took in *Oshin*, and in the drama guide there is a section entitled 'Women at the time of war' (*Senso no naka de onna wa*) which recalls the war and emphasises the grief and privation experienced by Japanese women. This piece begins '*Chichi ya otto ga senso de korosareta*' (Both my father and husband were killed during the war) (*Oshin: NHK Dorama Gaido*: 145). Hashida herself recalled her own contribution to the war, and sense of guilt: 'I myself greatly cooperated in the War. Without really realizing what I was doing, I worked constructing switchboards for airplanes, believing that I was doing good . . . I now believe that all that can be looked upon as a war crime in a sense' (*Graf NHK* March 1984:30; *NHK International* 1991:72).

The survey attempts to produce a portrait of Japanese attitudes to the past war by asking key questions such as: 'Do you consider that in modern Japan remorse for the past war has been forgotten, and that we are now heading in a dangerous direction?' These were the years of

Nakasone as Prime Minister, Reagan as US President, and Thatcher as UK Prime Minister, and there was a perception that western allies (including, of course, Japan) were embarked on policies of military escalation. 50 per cent replied in the affirmative, and 36 per cent disagreed. NHK, by framing the question in such a way that it linked attitudes to the past war with present military policy, was in fact declaring a liberal stance, at odds with proposals to increase the military budget.[10]

The answers to this particular question are interesting for the difference in response between men and women (see Figure 1.4). It is a clear indication that women were more concerned than men about attitudes to the past war and present policy. Men were evenly divided on the issue (with an interesting reversal across the generations), and women were fairly consistent until the oldest group's results (who would have been in their 30s at the time of the war), which seems to suggest a reluctance to declare an opinion. Extrapolating simplistically from this graph, we might be able to state the rather obvious fact that, on an issue like this, the older male population is more likely to view the past war in a conservative fashion; that the younger male population is fairly liberal, as is the majority of the female population.

This may be tested against further data supplied by Akiyama. If the portrait produced by the first question might be considered anti-war in general, then a different portrait emerges from a later question which focuses specifically on perceptions of the past war, revealing an entrenched reluctance to describe the past war in a morally hostile manner (see Figure 1.5). If we examine the graph, we note that young men and women both share similar attitudes: those younger than 50 are more likely to describe the past in a critical manner. This holds with the data in Figure 1.4. This is reversed, as we might expect, with those who are in their fifties and beyond: these are the generations born before the war who are more likely to admit aggression, but mitigate this with the statement that aggressive militarism could not have been avoided. The most militaristic position has a much lower but steady level of support, rising with the generations in the case of Japanese men; but interestingly this rise is reversed to a decline in the case of women, indicating that there is a tendency towards assessing the militaristic past in a positive manner amongst younger women (and also to a lesser extent younger men). It is, of course, with regard to the youngest groups that the way Japan's history is described in the textbooks is of most importance. At about the age of 45, women begin to show an increased acceptance of the more extreme position, and share similar levels of support as the men.

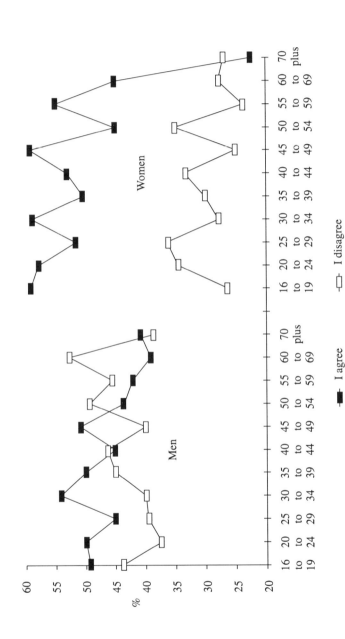

Figure 1.4 Japanese attitudes to the past war and present policy

Source: In answer to the statement: 'Modern Japan has abandoned remorse for the past war, and is now heading in a dangerous direction' (adapted from *NHK Hōsō Kenkyū to Chōsa* 1983 April, p.4)

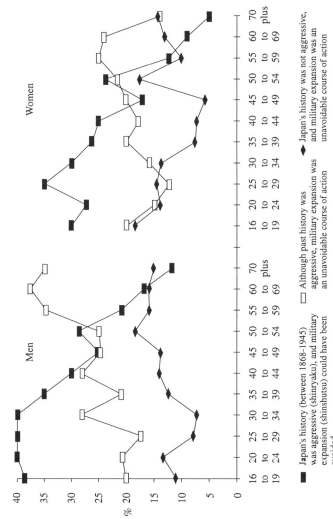

Figure 1.5 Japanese approval/disapproval of terms used to describe past history

Source: In answer to questions relating to approval/disapproval of terms used to describe Japan's aggressive militarism in the past (adapted from *NHK Hōsō Kenkyū to Chōsa* 1983 April, p.12)

We may compare Figures 1.4 and 1.5 with responses discussed by Wakiya in an article published in May 1983 based on the same poll taken the previous autumn (1983:54–63), and on data that emerged from a series of questions relating to the criticism of the history textbooks. The respondents were required to approve one of the following three statements:

1) Criticism levelled by both Korea and China is correct, that is to say: 'In recent textbooks the historical truth regarding Japan's militaristic aggression in the past has been distorted.' (12.5 per cent)

2) Since textbooks should not use morally loaded terminology (i.e. *shinryaku*) but should concentrate on objective presentation (i.e. opt for a less morally loaded term to describe Japan's expansion), China and Korea's criticisms are not appropriate. (10.9 per cent)

3) Every nation has the right to inform its citizens in the way that it thinks fit, so that foreign criticism on such matters is totally misplaced. (28.9 per cent)

Wakiya produced a graph based on these three results, in which he characterised 1) as positive (acceptance of the criticism) and 2) and 3) as negative (rejection) (see Figure 1.6).

When we examine this graph, we notice again that younger men and women are more inclined to accept the criticism, but that this differs across the generations. Whereas the decline in the male acceptance of the criticism might be expected from our experience of the other graphs, the sharp decrease in the female line is striking. In the case of the men, this is compensated for by an increase in the total rejection of the criticism; *but the women respond very differently*. As confident acceptance of the criticism declines, there is an increase in rejection (notably so between the ages of 40 and 50), but this tails off after 50 (those born before 1933), when there is a sharp decrease. But most significant is the higher level and sharp increase in the 'I don't know' responses (*wakaranai/mukaitō/kono koto o shiranai*). We would be wrong to accept this simply at face value for, as Wakiya points out, this was an issue with which all Japanese were familiar. It would seem to indicate once again an unwillingness, especially amongst the oldest generation, to state an opinion on such a socially divisive matter.

Considering these three graphs, it should now be possible to gauge whether *Oshin* was addressing the Japanese population in terms of their findings. Summarising the data: young men and women are generally

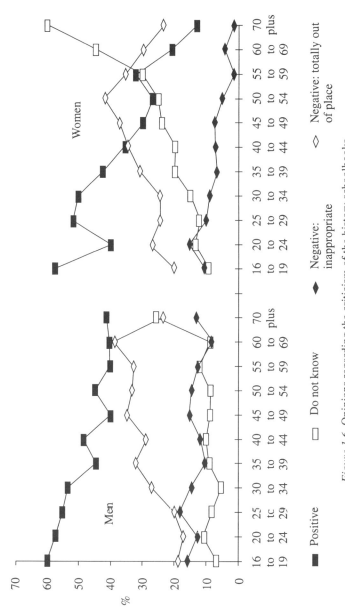

Figure 1.6 Opinions regarding the criticism of the history schoolbooks

Source: Adapted from *NHK Hōsō Kenkyū to Chōsa* 1983 May, p.55

happy with the admission that Japan had an aggressive militaristic past, and are able to accept criticism of the Ministry of Education's changes to the history textbooks. As a rule women are more likely to consider present action in terms of knowledge of past military aggression, and may therefore be said to be more anti-war. Older men and women are less likely to accept foreign criticism, and prefer to describe the past using more euphemistic terminology. But there were one or two surprises: there were significant levels of support from younger women for euphemistic descriptions of military aggression. And women in general displayed an unwillingness to commit themselves to an opinion regarding the criticism of the history schoolbooks. In a sense, there may be said to be an inherent contradiction here. If, as Figure 1.4 plainly shows, women are generally anti-militaristic, why then are sections of the female population content to whitewash militarism in the past? The answer to this must lie in the way the question regarding description of the past is posed. If it is posed in such a way as to have a bearing on action in the present, then an anti-war stance emerges. If it is posed as a choice between representing Japan's past in a hostile or favourable manner, then the favourable option will become a more likely choice, especially among younger women who have no personal recollection of the war years.

Oshin as history textbook

When we consider the work done at NHK assessing attitudes to the past war among the Japanese, and the not unexpected discovery that such attitudes were sharply delineated by generational difference, it then becomes possible to characterise *Oshin* as a response to that difference and also to the uncritical attitudes to the past war amongst younger Japanese (Yoshino 1992:208–15). In view of the fact that in 1982–3 discussion of education in Japan was dominated by controversy over the content of history textbooks, we may go even further and describe *Oshin* as an *alternative* national textbook, inculcating the post war liberal/left wing ideology of anti-militarism. At the conference held in 1991, Chinese reaction to *Oshin* reported that the 'programme was also a modern history of Japan'. *Oshin* addressed the Japanese population directly in terms of the questions posed by the above surveys, in ways that a Chinese audience could watch. In fact, when shown in China, the drama enjoyed a popularity as high as it had in Japan, and 'the portrayal of the Sino-Japanese war' was singled out as well treated (NHK International 1991:119). Throughout the drama, war and its impact on the protagonist was a major theme. In *Oshin*, Hashida and Okamoto juxta-posed militarism (the transformed Ryūzō) with pacifism (Shunsaku the army deserter; Kōta the communist). All three men were Oshin's part-ners, and her story is told in terms of her interaction with them. In so doing, *Oshin* sought to reexplain the difficult history of the century in terms of a single and approachable figure, Oshin, who herself, taught by Shunsaku at the outset, was consistently anti-war.

But the concern with the past war and militarism was not, of course, the only concern of the drama. Rather, by weaving the multiple educa-tive purposes together – in other words, a socially conservative desire to promote traditional values with the politically less conservative desire to encourage a hostile attitude towards past and present militarism – the drama was appealing to attitudes which spanned the generations. More-over, when we reconsider the broad anti-militarism expressed by all female age groups in Figure 1.4, we might go even further and suggest that Hashida and Okamoto were giving voice to the millions of Japanese women who – simply in their social roles as mothers, daughters and wives – would, like *Oshin*, have cursed war, wartime and mutual de-struction, just as Oshin did. *Oshin* was thus a history textbook written by women with a particular brief to declare a female anti-militarism. And this is why the drama guide for *Oshin* unambiguously focussed on Japanese women's experience of war and even included a section titled '*Oshin* and War' (p.156).

Generational difference

In the issues of *Bunken Geppō* in the years before *Oshin*, Makita Tetsuo and others collected data on the ratings for asadora according to sex and age. By comparing this data with the portrait that has emerged, we may consider how the attitudes noted above (in their generational aspect) apply to the generational spread of those who were watching asadora (Figure 1.7). If we consider Figure 1.7, it becomes immediately apparent that there is a notable increase in popularity as the viewer increases in age, and that this distribution is unchanged for the six dramas before *Oshin*. Men and women show a similar distribution, although the drama is clearly much more popular with women. There is also significant alteration between dramas, which suggests that this drama is not simply switched on because there is a clock in the corner of the TV screen (in other words: to tell the time, as is often said of asadora), but that the content of each drama will generate different levels of popularity. *Oshin*, for women over the age of 20 and men over the age of 60, achieved

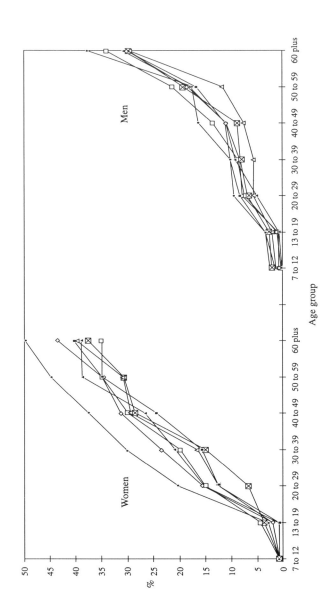

Figure 1.7 Ratings for Asadora taken by NHK 1980–1983

Source: Adapted from issues of *NHK Bunken Geppō* for the period

◇ Natchan 1980 June • Niji 1980 Nov △ Mansaku 1981 June ⊠ Honjitsu 1981 Nov • Haikara 1982 June □ Yoidon 1982 Nov • Oshin 1983 June

extraordinary success. We may now judge that Hashida and Okamoto, aware that asadora speaks most completely to the older Japanese, included in it a woman of a similar generation who was anti-war. In other words, *Oshin* addressed and persuaded those older Japanese to reflect on the history of the century, viewed through the eyes of Oshin, who loses her husband and her eldest son in the Pacific war. Asadora generally is not watched in any numbers by those less than 20; and this is for the good reason that most of them are already at school. They are also less popular with 20-year-olds, and this has been a common trait, although challenged recently by *Hirari* (1992), as Shiraishi Nobuko makes clear (1993). But what of those younger Japanese women who believed that Japan's history was not aggressive and military expansion was unavoidable? For women over 20, asadora (depending on the popularity of the individual drama which prior to *Oshin* oscillated between seven and fifteen per cent) may still be considered an effective medium. The same may be said for older male viewers.

But there was another aspect to the viewing pattern of *Oshin*, which addressed the problem of young Japanese holding to euphemistic descriptions of the military past. This was the brilliant move of employing a young girl (Kobayashi Ayako) to act out Oshin's childhood in Yamagata. This then gave *pre-school* children an added motivation for watching asadora. In other words, NHK was attempting to instill into the youngest children (before they got anywhere near the controversial textbooks) a sense of the terrible nature of war and of the loss and pain that it involves. At the same time, of course, it included the other socially conservative agenda of the traditional values (from, of course, a female perspective) that Oshin is offering her grandson – forbearance, family solidarity, and hard work. Indeed, the drama was so successful that from July 25 to August 17 a rerun was offered of the first 36 episodes (in which Kobayashi had starred) and the target audience was young children (though it was watched by all age groups) (*Asahi Shinbun* July 23, 1983, evening edition: p. 3). The ratings for this rerun, screened between 6:00 and 6:30 p.m., were on average 22.7 per cent for the three weeks – increasing over the period as word of mouth spread, to reach a remarkable high of 34.6 per cent on the last day (*Asahi Shinbun* August 24, 1983, evening edition: p. 11). Young children watched the rerun in significant numbers, as Miwa Tadashi (1983) makes clear, although he includes no data about the pre-school age group.

Naming in *Oshin*: *shinbō* (forbearance, patience, endurance)

Although we do not have space here to go through the whole of *Oshin* in detail, it is useful to focus on the way that naming operates in the drama, for this provides a key to the interpretation of the drama as a whole. We have discussed how *Oshin* intervenes socially in two particular ways: in a conservative mode whereby the younger generation is taught the value of hard work and forbearance; and in a less conservative anti-militaristic mode. But when we consider the way that naming operates in *Oshin* we must look for a broader category. And that category is the widest and most subscribed to, for it is nothing less than 'being Japanese'. *Oshin* operates as a meditation on and construction of what it means to be Japanese, and under what conditions key notions such as *shinbō* might have true currency.

This process of cultural formation and consensus may be seen in a simple structural manner. Oshin's mother is called Fuji: she is the source of Oshin's strength and (in contrast to Oshin's father) the source of the family unity. The bond between Oshin and her mother is strong and continues through the drama until Oshin finds herself in Ise in comparatively comfortable circumstances. The importance of this bond is reemphasised through the drama, as for example when Oshin walks from the home farm to Ginsan hot spring to say goodbye to her mother (who has to work as a geisha to feed her children), before she sets off once again into service in Sakata at the age of seven. Economic hardship necessitates separation between Oshin and her mother, and the bond between them is characterised as being strong enough to withstand such distance, because the bond itself, which is Oshin's tie to her family, is the reason for the separation in the first place. She goes into service as a maid at the age of seven so that her family will be given a bale of rice to fend off starvation.

Oshin's grandmother, Naka, is equally important to Oshin. Her mother teaches Oshin to be strong and to survive, but it is the grandmother who shows the most kindness to Oshin, and who gives her a symbolic 50 *sen* coin when she leaves for her first place of service (*hōkō saki*). The coin serves as a charm (*omamori*) and in effect acts as a receptacle of the familial warmth from which Oshin derives comfort in the hostile environment in which she works.

The names are strikingly allegorical. Fuji, of course, recalls immediately the sacred Mount Fuji; Naka has many possible meanings, the most obvious being an inwardness, implying that Oshin's grandmother represents (for Oshin) an internalised set of values. These would be the core values that a grandmother would, of course, be most likely to teach:

traditions, folk tales and family history. Her mother, on the other hand, is a source of spiritual and physical strength, and as such the use of the Fuji symbolism is clear. We may note also that Hashida is here constructing a female continuity (Naka to Fuji to Oshin) that adapts male nationalist symbols such as Mount Fuji. The male figures in *Oshin* (compared with the female figures) are less significant as influences: they exist most often as necessary impediments (Shunsaku is the greatest exception).

Oshin's father is a rough and brutal character who is violent to both Oshin and her mother. There is an implicit criticism of the father's lack of sexual restraint, brought into focus when Fuji stands in the Mogami river in mid-winter (when the water would be at freezing point) in order to provoke a miscarriage. But Oshin's father is not portrayed entirely unsympathetically, as we see in the poignant scene when Oshin floats away from home down the Mogami river to her first *hōkō saki*, and he stands with tears in his eyes calling after her. He is given a significant name: Sakuzō, composed of two characters which both mean 'making'. The idea is that creativity and spiritual strength form Oshin, who manifests both qualities.

When the 50 sen coin is taken from Oshin in her first place of work, she is unable to put up any longer with the treatment she receives and flees, intending to find her way home even though it is still midwinter. But it is too far, and she falls with exhaustion into a drift of snow, from which she is rescued by Shunsaku, a very important figure in the drama as a whole, despite the fact that he only appears in comparatively few episodes. Shunsaku is a deserter from the Japanese army. He had taken part in the war between Japan and Russia in 1905 (in which Japan destroyed the Russian Pacific fleet), and had become convinced of the moral superiority of pacifism, or, as he explains it, of not killing other people. Early in the drama, we are introduced to military police looking for him, so his appearance is not unexpected. He saves Oshin and takes her with him to his hideaway deep in the mountains, where he lives with an old woodsman who makes charcoal. Oshin spends the winter with him and he teaches her the rudiments of reading and writing (for which she had shown a passion), and most importantly imparts to her his philosophy that war is the greatest of all evils and can never be justified. There is an element of unreality in the seven-year-old Oshin absorbing such serious doctrine, but Kobayashi (the actress who is still fondly remembered for her role) somehow carried it off.

It is worth considering the timing of Oshin's leaving her first place of work and meeting with Shunsaku. It occurs on Saturday morning at the end of the *second week of viewing*: Episode 12 (April 16, 1983). This is a vital stage in establishing the popularity of asadora, since it is only the second weekend, and Saturday and Sunday provide valuable time for people to discuss the drama and communicate enthusiasm – important if the drama is to be popular. One of the key elements in a burgeoning popularity is *kuchikomi* (word of mouth), which is probably just as important as all the peripheral publicity. Shunsaku thus appears at the beginning of the third week. Beyond the expectations of the Oshin production team, the ratings in fact had already started their inexorable climb and would continue upward unabated for the next seven months.

The narrator describes Oshin's running away with a particular phrase, which is meaningful to both Oshin's name and her identity, and with which Shunsaku becomes inextricably linked: '*Oshin no shinbō no ito ga kireta*' (Oshin was no longer able to put up with it). Oshin's name itself, as discussed earlier, brings to mind the notion of *shinbō*: the initial o is diminutive, and *shin* carries the meaning of shinbō, amongst other meanings (as we shall see). And as if the viewer was not aware of this reading, it is insistently drummed in during the first two weeks. In Episode 7, Fuji uses it to encourage Oshin before she leaves home. She is told to *endure* (*omae shinbō shite na*!) when she arrives at the timber merchant's where she will be a maid and babysitter. When she goes to the local school (Episode 10) with the baby that she is looking after strapped to her back, she says to the teacher: *shinbō suru*! (I won't give up). It comes back again and again like a litany. But Hashida is in fact preparing the viewer for the point at which Oshin will reject *shinbō*, and this is where the drama departs from any simplistic nostalgic re-constuction of a past of unmerited suffering and merited reward. Oshin rejects shinbō when she is falsely accused of theft and when the symbolic coin (her grandmother's love – the core family values) is taken from her. For the audience it is a wonder that she did not run away earlier, for she was treated viciously by Tsune the housekeeper. There is much in common with the English serial novels of the 19th century (*Oliver Twist*, *Jane Eyre*) where the hero or heroine undergoes a childhood divorced from familial warmth, and this is a tradition that the asadora draws on.

Despite its apparently liberal orientation on the topic of war, however, *Oshin* was praised for its educative qualities by government ministers noted for their rightwing views. Makita discusses this briefly (1983: 24–5). Hashida herself publicly denounced the Education Minister who had given his approval to the drama in terms of the traditional values that it promoted (*Asahi Shinbun* no 9 May 19, 1983, morning edition: p. 22). Shinbō itself is a concept that is highly charged and capable of political manipulation. In fact, one could go further and suggest that it is a *political* concept, equivalent to selfsacrifice and endeavour on behalf of a community greater than oneself, be it the family (as with *Oshin*) or the nation. By promoting shinbō, *Oshin* could be seen to be inculcating values that were part of an earlier Japanese ethic, an ethic associated with the militaristic past, and with self-sacrifice on behalf of the Emperor. In the Shōwa Emperor's radio broadcast announcing defeat at the end of the Second World War, he made use of the concept of shinbō. And there is undoubtedly positive evaluation of shinbō in *Oshin*. We admire her for her ability to put up with difficulties and mistreatment, to forego food when her grandmother is ill, and later in the drama when Tanaka Yūko took over the part, her efforts to start a business in Ise, as well as her grim determination not to give in under the miserable treatment she receives from Kiyo (meaning purity), her mother-in-law. Oshin, in terms of the drama, has moral stature. Endurance as a virtue was also strongly in evidence in the making of *Oshin*, in which the actress Izumi Pinko, who played Fuji, was actually forced to undergo the hardship of standing in the icy Mogami river (Eguchi 1984:146–50).

Hashida was clearly aware of the controversial direction in which the promotion of such a concept might lead. For someone of her generation, the family and nation had been made equivalent in the recent past (Smith 1983:9–36). Hashida is therefore careful to circumscribe shinbō. Beyond a certain point forbearance, duty and self-sacrifice are shown to be impossible and not worth the effort. Oshin, though she is only a child, is pushed beyond endurance and runs away, even though by so doing she will bring shame on her family. But in the drama she is morally right. She is then saved by a *deserter from the army*. A direct parallel is being sketched: Shunsaku's desertion of duty as a soldier is as rational and rightminded as Oshin's running away. Hashida is making a subtle connection between the unreasonable self-sacrifice that a woman may be called upon to make for her family, and the folly of militarism and war for patriotic ends. We can be certain that the government minister (and Nakasone himself, who used the drama in one of his election speeches) failed to pick up this craftily placed but all-important connection. And by linking the two in this way, Hashida is also speaking indirectly to the trauma of the Second World War, when the general population endured appalling privations. It is a mark of her skill that she approaches such an explosive subject in such a way that she does not alienate her viewers, who held, as we have seen, a spectrum of opinions across different generations. We can be certain that this slipped by the government minister, but the population at large was more perceptive, for as Makita informs us, Shunsaku was the most popular of all the young men in the drama, even more so than the handsome Kōta, the man Oshin should have married (1983:27).

There is a key scene in Episode 14 while Oshin is staying with Shunsaku in his hideaway in the mountains. Shunsaku (whose name means exceeding intelligence joined with creativity) is musing on Oshin's name: "So your name is Oshin? It's a good name. The *shin* in your name must mean belief, the same one as in *shinnen* (faith) – *shin* can also mean mind/heart – of course the most important meaning must be shinbō – shin also means pith or core. It can also mean new, and truth, and of course, the word for god can also be read *shin*. You're lucky to have such a wonderful name!" (my translation). The presentation of this scene in visual terms is quite striking. Oshin tells Shunsaku her name as they stare into the fire in the centre of the cabin. The shot then dissolves from Oshin to the flames. In fact, Oshin literally dissolves into flames as she tells Shunsaku her name. The camera rests on the burning charcoal as we listen to Shunsaku intone the various readings for Oshin's name. As the speech comes to an end Shunsaku's face reappears through the flames. The visual effect underlines the impression that we have been given an important, almost spiritual, knowledge. Shunsaku is at this moment a kind of shaman, associated with fire and speaking through it (Blacker 1975:26, 93; also plates 20–23). And Shunsaku's link with a more spiritual kind of knowledge is emphasised by his final statement: *shin* is also a reading for god and signifies the folk religion of Japan, *Shintō* – though the way that Shunsaku presents the concept (*shin* as a reading for *kamisama*) also leaves open a Buddhist or even Christian reference.

Indeed, it is as though Shunsaku has in fact named Oshin. And her time with him is a ritualistic death and rebirth, a common feature in Shintō ritual. This is indicated by the fact that her mother even goes so far as to buy an *ihai* (Buddhist memorial tablet) for her because it is believed that she has perished and is buried under the snow. When Oshin returns home, she is a changed person: she has learnt to read and write the basic syllabary and has learnt by heart a poem taught her by Shunsaku in Episode 16 – a poem written by Yosano Akiko to her brother, when he was fighting in the war with Russia, and famous as an anti-war piece.

Shunsaku carries Oshin back down the mountain at the beginning of spring. It is a rash action, because once he has left the comparative security of the forest he is caught by the military police. He attempts to run (with Oshin still in his arms) and is shot in the back. It is a harsh moment, and underlines all the more strongly the moral superiority of Shunsaku's position. The camera then cuts to modern times, and Oshin as an old woman is reciting Yosano's poem as she recalls Shunsaku's death, with Kei her grandson listening. Thus, although the shinbō implied by Oshin's name has a conservative educative function, Hashida goes out of her way to rob the word of its most negative connotations. In a sense, she turns the apparent meaning of the word (in a context associated with war) – self-sacrifice on behalf of the nation – into the shinbō that Shunsaku exemplified by his refusal to fight.

After the episode with Shunsaku, Oshin returns home and, soon after, sets out for her second place of service. This is in Sakata, where she is taken under the wing of the third major female influence in her life, Kuni, who is the owner of a rice trading store and grandmother of Oshin's rival and friend. The name is again significant, meaning nation or native place. Kuni is responsible for Oshin developing into a capable and well-educated woman who masters the bridal arts, and learns some business skill. Kuni's name suggests national community, and by structuring the beginning in this way, Hashida is indicating a priority of loyalties: that the primary loyalty is to one's family (for that is why Oshin works at Kagaya), and a secondary loyalty is to the nation. This priority is, of course, the reverse of that emphasized in official propaganda before the war.

The parallel between Oshin's running away from her first place of service is thus made equivalent in the drama to the refusal of Shunsaku to bear arms, and this amounts to an inscribing of shinbō into non-militarism. But there is another key episode in the drama, alluded to in the plot outline at the beginning, which amounts to a rewriting of the notion of shinbō as it pertains to the traditional role of the Japanese wife. Exactly half way through the screening of the drama, Oshin, as a young mother and bride, was undergoing her second experience of persecution – once more by a woman placed in a position of power above her: Kiyo her mother-in-law. Her first persecutor had been Tsune, the house-keeper at the timber merchant's. The names of these two characters are again illustrative. *Tsune* means 'ordinary course of events', but also recalls the verb *tsuneru*, 'to pinch'. Tsune objectified the extreme poverty of Oshin and her family, and this was the main emphasis of the early episodes. Kiyo's role was rather different. Her name signifies 'purity' or even 'purify'. She represents the discipline to which the mother of the husband subjects the new bride on her arrival in the husband's home (Lebra 1984:36, 141–5). Kiyo rationalises her mistreatment of Oshin on the grounds that it is done in order to teach her how to become a 'good wife'. The other reason for the persecution lies in the fact that Ryūzō's mother opposed the marriage most strongly on class grounds.

The experience of persecution undergone by Oshin, and the way in which she reacted to that persecution (with saintly perseverance) struck a chord through Japanese society. But it was not so much the spectacle of suffering that Oshin presented, but the suspense generated by the knowledge that she would at some stage abandon her husband. This would have been known because the plot of *Oshin* was available in the guide which had gone on sale in March 1983, and the plot outline was given every week in TV guides and newspapers. It was evidenced by the ratings, which, after a dip during the trouble-free time spent in Tōkyō (Episodes 100–120), rose during the misery at Saga to the point at which Oshin made her announcement to leave (Episodes 121–144). This was especially marked in the Kansai region, where there was a growth of about eighteen per cent over this section to 49 per cent; while in the Kantō ratings grew by about fifteen per cent to 59 per cent. The difference of ten per cent between the Kansai and the Kantō was due to a tendency in the Kansai to watch less NHK. Overall, this section of the drama saw the ratings soar to their highest level since television began in Japan. After Oshin had made her announcement, the ratings began to drop away slightly: in the case of the Kansai there was a steady decline (Oshin leaving her husband was the peak rating for the Kansai); in Kantō there was a slight drop, followed by a maintained level of interest more or less until the end. The ratings indicate that Hashida and Okamoto had hit the right populist nerve, but the most arresting aspect to their treatment was that they led the audience to consider that Oshin's abandonment of husband and family was the right thing to do. This was borne out by the development of the drama itself: by leaving Saga, Oshin was able to find her independence in Ise and start her own business. The difference in the tendency of the ratings between the Kansai and Kantō regions is also instructive: Kansai is culturally more conservative than Kantō, and the experience Oshin undergoes as a bride entering her husband's house is of more interest than the sequence during which she sets up independently in Ise, though both achieved very high ratings. Thus although *Oshin* serves to inculcate the virtue of forbearance and endurance, it does so in a critical manner which bears on the role of the subordinate wife in a virilocal residence, and on the morality of bearing arms.

Oshin as Japan

When Oshin makes her announcement in Saga and sets off on her own, there is a further resonance to her departure which echoes through the drama. Her rejection of the traditional family and its constraints is a gesture towards modernity, and it was the drive towards modernity in this drama that was one of the keys to its popularity elsewhere in world. Translocation is, of course, part of the genre of asadora, as Makita pointed out, but in *Oshin* it has an especial importance. Oshin leaves Sakata (north) and moves to Tōkyō (capital), then from Saga (south) back to Tōkyō and Sakata, and finally to Ise (centre).

Oshin meets Ryūzō in Tōkyō and marries him there. In some respects they are ill matched. Indeed, if we consider his name, the first character being 'dragon' and the second being 'three' (since he is the third son), we might imagine that it bodes ill, since dragon suggests aggression. The name is also class specific and distinguishable from Oshin's father, Sakuzō, on that basis. The name of the man she should have married, Kōta, has more sympathetic connotations. The first character of his name signifies 'great flood', and the second simply 'large', perhaps together suggesting ocean. In the context of his work as a social reformer it implies his broad vision and sympathies, and also indicates the Pacific Ocean.

Oshin leaves Tōkyō with Ryūzō for Saga. After Saga she eventually finds her way to Ise (on the recommendation of Kōta). If we consider this movement structurally in terms of the geography of Japan, then Oshin, a woman of the far north, marries a man from the far south and eventually settles in the spiritual centre of Japan, Ise, which sits at the traditional division between east and west Japan. Ise is also known largely because it is the site of Ise Jingū, the most important of the Shintō shrines in Japan. The translocation of the drama, and its final siting in Ise, could not be more symbolic, for it is in Ise that Oshin achieves the dreamed-of prosperity, and by situating her there Hashida is ensuring that her commerical success gains a spiritual aura.

Oshin, as will by now be obvious, symbolises Japan, and the drama is a synecdoche for modern Japanese history. Her choice of partners is part of this: Ryūzō, apparently the open and liberal partner at first (representing the period of Taishō democracy in the 1920s), becomes a businessman supplying the war machine, and eventually destroys himself. Kōta, the social reformer, was the man that she should have married, but was too easily misled by Kayo – in itself a parable for the ineffectiveness of the left. The progression that she made through a variety of professions – rice farmer in the north and south, hairdresser and textile trader in Tōkyō, and finally fishmonger and supermarket owner in mid-Japan – is in itself a small parable about economic development from an agricultural base through to affluence. And the mobility that lay between the drama and its status as representative national fiction was perhaps the most cunning move that Hashida and Okamoto made. For by casting the drama in this way, they were able to appeal to an audience ripe for explanations of Japan's success, and by telling the story in the way they did, they were able to claim that in any evaluation of Japan's modern history, the story of Japanese women should be centre stage.

NOTES

The newspaper and magazine articles quoted from in this chapter include:

Graf NHK (precursor to Stera) articles relating to *Oshin*:

1983 Volume 24 (April) *'Hashida Sugako: 6000 mai ni tsuzuru hahatachi e no chinkonka'* (Hashida Sugako: a 6000 page requiem for mothers):2–3; *Shinbangumi: Oshin* (A New Drama: *Oshin*): 6–15.

1983 Volume 24 (October) *'Oshin: Shōwa no gekidō wo koe, Oshin wa anju no chi o motomete Isei ni: iseihen stāto* (*Oshin*: surviving the confusion of Showa, Oshin searching for a quiet place to live settles in Isei: the Isei section starts):10–15; *'Nikumare yaku ga namida nagashicha dame ne'* (You can't weep when you're playing the person everyone loves to hate):16–19.

1984 Volume 25 (March) *'Oshin wa watashi no messēji: Hashida Sugako, Okamoto Yūkiko [Producer of Oshin]'* (*Oshin* was my message):25–30.

NHK Weekly Sutera (Stera NHK Magazine). Special series commemorating the 50th anniversary of asadora: featuring a data file for each asadora published in five installments.

1993.10.01 issue *'Oboete imasuka anata no hiroin'*! (Do you remember your heroines?): 5–10.

1993.10.08 issue *'Asa wa yappari kore'* (This is what makes the morning [Discussion of the fiftieth asadora: *Karin*]): 5–16.

1993.10.15 issue *'Nihonjin no kokoro no furusato: mō ichido Oshin'* (The home of the Japanese heart: *Oshin* once again): 10–12.

1993.10.22 issue *'Aa, natsukashii Ohanahan'* (Fond memories of *Ohanahan* [1966–7]): 5–7.

1993.10.29 issue *'Dokusha no otayori'* (Letters from correspondents [concerned with asadora]): 86–7.

Asahi Shinbun: articles 1983–4 relating to *Oshin*.

1983 April 22, evening edition, p.9. *'Shinario no fukei: Oshin'* (Information about *Oshin* with section of script).

1983 May 19, morning edition, p.22. *'Bunso no shōsan wa meiwaku'* (Admiration [for *Oshin*] by the Minister for Justice causes problems).

1983 July 23, evening edition, p.3. *'Oshin naze konna ni ninki'* (Why is *Oshin* so popular?).

1983 August 15, morning edition, p.20. *'Mō hitori no Oshin'* (Other Oshins [programme screened 1983 August 15–20).

1983 August 24, evening edition, p.11. *'Tokei gawari de nai Oshin: denwa chosa de ninki o urazuke: Kokando 92 per cent, Shūchūdo 84 per cent'* (*Oshin* not just a means of telling the time [reference to the clock in the corner of the screen]: telephone provides corroboration: highest level of popularity 92 per cent, dedicated watching 84 per cent).

1983 August 26, evening edition, p.8. *'Oshin yaku no Kobayashi Ayako: minho renzoku dorama hatsushutsuen'* (Kobayashi Ayako who played *Oshin* takes on her first role in a commercial television serial drama).

1983 September 7, morning edition, p.22. *'Saga no imēji daun tai: Oshin ken kankōren ga NHK ni kogi'* (Saga's image is tarnished: the tourist association in *Oshin*-land criticises NHK).

1983 November 14, morning edition, p.22. *'Saga de koen kaijo wakasu: Okiyo no Takamorisan'* (Takamori, who plays Okiyo, enlivens a meeting in Saga).

1983 December 9, evening edition, p.8. *'Jukunen Oshin Tōjō: NHK toshiake kara Otowahen'* (Mature Oshin: from next year on NHK Otowa takes over).

1983 December 27, evening edition, p.13. *'Oshin mo jōei nitchu terebi sai: 18 nichi kara chūgoku san toshi de'* (*Oshin* will also be shown at a joint festival China/Japan: from the eighteenth in China in three cities).

1984 January 17, morning edition, p.24. *'Oshin ninki wa hoteishikidori'* (*Oshin*'s popularity goes according to the book).

1984 March 31, evening edition, p.13. *'Issen man en o kifu: Hashida Sugako'* (Hashida Sugako [author of *Oshin*] donates ten million yen).

1 *Oshin* in italics denotes the drama, and Oshin in plain type denotes the chief character in the drama.

I would like to thank my discussant, Jonathan Hall, at the *Women, Media and Consumption in Japan Workshop* at Hong Kong University November 1993 for making such a stimulating reading of my draft. I would also like to thank Makita Tetsuo and Shiraishi Nobuko for their kind assistance with this project. I would like to dedicate this to my fiancée with whom I rewatched the edited version of the drama, and shed a tear.

2 A practice called *kuchiberashi* – literally: reducing the number of mouths that must be fed.

3 The following brief discussion is indebted to both Makita and Muramatsu.

4 The fourth drama, *Uzushio* from 1964, was the first asadora to be written and scripted by women.

5 After a presentation on asadora given at the Nissan Institute, Oxford University, in January 1994, Dr Brian Powell commented that many of the elements that account for the popularity of asadora lie behind the popularity of both *Kabuki* and *Shingeki* drama.

6 Morning TV being watched less is attested to in the yearly television reports of *Bunken Geppō* (The NHK Report on Broadcast Research): see for

example Makita (1976:7). For information on housewives, see Saitō Kenji (1975:10–15).

7 This information and other similar comments derive from discussions with informants at NHK in Ōsaka and Tōkyō.

8 For a good example of a non-liberal position, see the article in *Asahi Shinbun* detailing the Education Minister's comments relating to the history textbooks (*Asahi Shinbun*, July 29, 1986, morning edition, p.2).

9 Akiyama makes this clear with a survey of different priorities between individuals of different political affiliations: those who voted Jimintō (Liberal Democrats, the party in government at the time) favoured, in order of priority: stability/order, economic strength, welfare, freedom/rights, and in fifth place pacifism; those who voted Shakaitō (Socialist) favoured: welfare, freedom/rights, economic strength, pacifism, and in fifth place stability/order; those who voted Kyōsantō (Communist) favoured: freedom/rights together with welfare joint first, pacifism in second place, order/stability, and economic strength fourth (1983:14).

10 Liberal is here defined as being broadly centre/left of centre.

2

READING JAPANESE IN KATEI GAHŌ: THE ART OF BEING AN UPPERCLASS WOMAN

Brian Moeran

The glossy monthly Japanese woman's magazine, *Katei Gahō* (House-hold Graphics), was launched in March 1958 (Figure 2.1). Aimed at the 40 year-old-woman who is well educated ('*intelli-san*'), lives in her own home, and whose husband's salary is in the higher income bracket, *Katei Gahō* is in fact read by a wide range of women, from some in their mid-twenties to others in their sixties.[1] In this respect, it addresses an older age group than do other Japanese magazines like *Classy* or *Clique*, and, like its nearest rivals *Sophia*, *Misses* and *Fujin Gahō*, is specifically targeted at married women whose children are at least in their teens. Like American *Vogue* in the way that it gives off an air of 'high cultural achievement', *Harper's Bazaar* for its dreams of exclusivity and unlimited spending power, *Family Circle* for its emphasis on food products, and *Options* with its slogan of 'Better food. Better homes. Better fashion', *Katei Gahō* combines and treats different themes in a way that makes it uniquely different from other women's magazines in contemporary Japan. At the same time, it is clear that it is read or looked through by all members of a household where it is taken and, unlike a number of other women's glossies, is frequently not thrown away but kept for some years. In other words, *Katei Gahō* is a high quality magazine which not only fulfills its promise of enjoyment of 'a splendid and delightful time' (*suteki na toki o tanoshimu*), but is seen to be well worth its monthly price of ¥1,000.[2]

During the course of its 35 years of publication, *Katei Gahō* has been through a number of stylistic, marketing and editorial changes. Nowadays, perhaps, it is hard to imagine that when the magazine was launched, there were no really visual magazines on the Japanese market and that its publisher, Sekai Bunkasha, was strongly influenced by the American magazine *Life*, although it wished to focus on domestic matters, rather than on news as such. In 1968, the publisher decided to adopt

Figure 2.1 Katei Gahō

its present modified B4 (*ōban*) size to set the magazine apart from its competitors; it is still the only woman's magazine in Japan – apart from *Miss Katei Gahō* – to make use of this unusually large format.

In the same year, a new sales policy was also adopted. At first, Sekai Bunkasha had made use of its already established network of door-to-door book salesmen to hawk the magazine to prospective women readers, and in this way had soon been able to build up a circulation of approximately 100,000 copies a month, before doubling that figure by the end of its first decade of publication. In 1968, however, it was decided to drop the door-to-door sales tactics and, instead, to sell *Katei*

Gahō to retail outlets through distributors. This enabled circulation to double once again to its present 400,000 copies a month, and its new policy in fact set a marketing precedent because most magazines in Japan are distributed to retail outlets on a 'sale or return' (*itaku hanbai*) basis.[3] As most advertisers have learned to their cost, the 'sale or return' method of retailing allows magazine publishers to make their circulations out to be greater than they actually are. By knowing precisely how many orders there are each month for each edition of its magazine, therefore, Sekai Bunkasha not only saves on printing costs, but also has accurate circulation figures which it can use to attract advertising for *Katei Gahō*. Consequently, up until the end of the 'bubble period' (1991), about 200 of the 430 or so pages that comprised each month's edition consisted of advertisements, although this figure has now dropped by about ten per cent owing to the current recession.

On the editorial side, the magazine started out by emphasizing 'lifestyle' (rather than '*Life*'!), but in about 1972 it was decided that cuisine should become the major focus of editorial and visual attention. The reasons for this shift were various. In the first place, given the fact that targeted readers of *Katei Gahō* were housewives aged somewhere around 40, food was an obvious area of their interest. Unlike today, there were then no other magazines on the market specializing in cuisine, so that this theme was selected in order to give *Katei Gahō* a competitive edge. It was also seen to mesh with the kind of luxury that people were becoming accustomed to as a result of Japan's high growth economy. Cuisine did not just mean 'food'; it meant a number of different ways of enjoying different kinds of food – in a Kyōto tea house or in an equally chic French restaurant in an exclusive part of Tōkyō. It also meant focussing on all the trappings that accompany the consumption of food – lacquerware, western-style china, cooking utensils, handcrafted pottery, and fitted kitchens, which together, of course, carried an aura of upperclass consumption and an ornamentation somewhat different from the glazed surfaces of *Elle* discussed by Barthes (1972), but unbridled beautification nonetheless.

Over the years, then, cuisine has been the central focus of the magazine's attention, and it is significant that this forms one of the three main sections, consisting of eight staff members, into which the Editorial Department is divided. The other two are 'Interior' (six members), and 'Fashion' (seven members).[4] In the so-called 'post bubble' period, following the stock market crash in mid-1991, editors have now shifted from a focus on 'things' (*mono*) *per se* to what they like to call '5W + 1H' (*where, why, who, what, when*, plus *how*) – probably best summed up as the 'contextualization' of themes. In other words, rather than focussing entirely on the cherry blossoms and foods associated therewith in its April edition, *Katei Gahō* now tries to contextualize this annual event within what its woman editor-in-chief calls 'Japan's good traditions', and thus to show its readers (who are seen as having time on their hands [*yutori no aru*] and being ready to enjoy life – especially those things which are 'spiritually uplifting' [*seishinteki ni yutaka*]) how best to enjoy such traditions for themselves.

The representation of Japanese traditions has been another important part of the magazine's development. In 1977, Sekai Bunkasha approached a number of top art designers in an attempt to upgrade the quality of *Katei Gahō*'s appearance, and it was from this time that the magazine took on its present luxurious format where all but a dozen or two of the 420 or more pages that grace each month's edition are of high-quality glossy paper on which are printed high-class colour photographs of food, fashion, and interior design, as well as advertisements (which are frequently created especially for *Katei Gahō* and are not used in any other magazine). The principle here is that one picture says more than a hundred pages of text and, to prove the point, the magazine's editors use specialist photographers for each of its different areas of interest in cuisine, interior and fashion.

The 'Face' of *Katei Gahō*

Before examining the contents of *Katei Gahō*, we should start by looking at its cover, since it is this which sells the magazine – both to readers and to advertisers – and thereby acts as an advertisement for itself (McCracken 1993:14) – a point made clear by the spoof on Japanese women's magazines found in *Crea* (February 1993) (Figure 2.2). It is the cover image and the 'sell lines' which frame what is to follow, create *genre* identity, and reveal where a magazine stands 'culturally' (Winship 1987:9; McCracken 1993:19–22). So, too, with *Katei Gahō* which can – and does – immediately establish itself as a *woman's* magazine, distinguishable from *other* women's magazines by its title, sell lines, photographic image, use of colours, and different fonts and scripts. Every *Katei Gahō* cover consists of the magazine's crimson red title in squared 'Gothic' Chinese characters at the top; a three quarter length photograph of a Japanese woman in her thirties or forties, smartly dressed in western style clothes and carrying a bunch of flowers under her left arm; and two sets of sell lines – one vertical (to the right), calling attention to the magazine's main feature of the month; the others horizontal

Figure 2.2 Spoof on *Katei Gahō* cover from *Crea*
(February 1993)

(to the left), announcing various features concerned with cuisine, fashion and accessories, and interior design. Title, headlines and photograph are always placed against a plain white background (Figure 2.3).

Let us start with the title of the magazine. Unlike most women's magazines, which make use of western (or western sounding) names written in Roman writing, *Katei Gahō* is a Japanese title written in Chinese characters. In this way, it immediately establishes itself culturally as a magazine for *Japanese* women, or rather for women who are concerned with being 'Japanese', as opposed to being 'western', thus

Figure 2.3 The face of *Katei Gahō*
(Courtesy of *Katei Gahō*)

connoting a youthful, independent, working lifestyle.[5] This image of Japaneseness is endorsed by the headlines which not only frequently refer to places or cuisine that are 'quintessentially' Japanese (Kyōto or *kaiseki* cuisine, for example), but are *always* written in a combination of Chinese characters and the two Japanese syllabaries, and *never* in Roman writing (which can only be found for the month of the year on the spine of the magazine, or for special acronyms like *TPO* [time, place, opportunity]). Moreover, one of the headlines is written vertically in the normal literary style, but infrequently found in other women's magazines.[6]

This reading of the title and headlines is supported by the photograph of the cover model. Generally, the adoption of certain types of hairstyle, neckline, facial and bodily poses for any cover model conveys certain information to a magazine's potential readers. For example, the cover images of European and American women's magazines like *Vogue*, *Elle* and *Marie Claire* (and, indeed, of their counterparts in Japan, as well as of Japanese publications like *with* and *25 ans*) affirm and sell such qualities as white (though often suntanned) skin, youth, beauty, physical charm, and sexuality as valuable attributes of *western* femininity (Winship 1987:9). *Katei Gahō*, too, affirms the importance of white skin, beauty and physical charm, but, by making frequent use of slightly older Japanese actress models, it also emphasizes 'Japaneseness', and a 'femininity' which is more specifically Japanese. This it does by presenting its cover model in a particular way: with invariably smiling mouth, red lipstick, luxuriant hair brushed back from a high forehead, tilted head, canted body cut off at the knees,[7] and bunch of flowers clasped somewhere between shoulder and hips. The cover model's clothes are designed to reinforce this sophisticated *Katei Gahō* 'face', for she is frequently dressed in a formal two-piece suit, whose skirt is cut off just above the knee (at the highest), and wears a high necked blouse that does not reveal any cleavage.

There are two points to be made here. Firstly, this sense of 'Japanese femininity' would appear not to be related to sexuality as such. Unlike that of cover models on the title pages of similar European or American magazines, or of some other Japanese magazines, the sexuality of the women portrayed on the covers of *Katei Gahō* is *not* brought out. We do *not* see a close-up of a young woman's face with full, open mouth and regular pearl white teeth (as we do, say, in *25 ans*); nor are we made unduly aware of the curves of her figure which, as we have seen, is always fully clothed, at least as far as her knees, where the photograph is cut off. Rather, the make-up, hair, occasional accessories (mainly earrings), and expensive clothes – together with the model's gaze and the fact that she carries flowers – help define the '*Katei Gahō* woman' as upperclass, sophisticated, upmarket, smooth-skinned, and immaculately groomed. Her face is photographed in a frontal position to reveal the 'T line' of nose and eye(brow)s, together with the oval jaw underlining (occasionally irregular) white teeth in a mouth rarely fully open. With the camera set round about thigh-height so that the model is always looking slightly downwards, the woman's gaze communicates more a sense of freshness and naturalness (assisted by the flowers), than the kind of overt sexuality found in many other women's magazines (both in Japan and elsewhere). Although it might be argued that Japanese magazines in general do not promote sexuality on their covers, I believe that, in the case of *Katei Gahō*, this absence of sexuality probably has less to do with a so-called Japanese *femininity*, than with the fact that the magazine's target readers are *middle-aged* housewives and mothers, for whom sexuality seems not to be an issue – either in terms of their own self image, or in the way that they relate to their husbands.

A second problem concerning my reading of 'Japaneseness' from the cover of *Katei Gahō* stems from the fact that cover models *always* wear *western* clothes. This problem is compounded by the fact that headlines do occasionally refer to non-Japanese features (such as *How to Enjoy Popular Italian Cuisine* [April 1992]). Here, the magazine finds itself trying to put forward more than a single message, since the *Katei Gahō* reader is expected to be 'Japanese', 'feminine' *and* sophisticated, and – as we shall have occasion to see – sophistication in contemporary Japanese society requires a middle-aged housewife to be acquainted with foreign, particularly western, customs and places, and to be able to look elegant when dressed in western-style clothing. Thus, the western clothes worn by the cover model represent a formal, public, neutral style (somewhat like the magazine's cover itself), which contrasts with the intimate, private, personal experience of being a Japanese woman at home, often in *kimono*, as represented in the inside pages of *Katei Gahō*.

Another defining characteristic of any magazine cover's image is the model's gaze. Both Winship (1987:11) and McCracken (1993:14) have followed Berger (1972) and argued that this gaze between model and potential reader in women's magazines marks a 'complicity' between women who see themselves reflected in an image defined by men, and that it indicates symbolically how women relate to one another through absent men. There is a sense in which this argument holds true for *Katei Gahō*. After all, like the magazine's contents which are mostly prepared by male senior editors, each cover is a cypher for men's skills. As the *Table of Contents* reveals, the cover model's photographer, designer, stylist, 'hair make' and couturiers are almost invariably men. Moreover, the way in which the title of the magazine is often emblazoned over the crown of each model's head subtly reminds us that the woman who epitomizes femininity, Japaneseness and sophistication is also a housewife and, by implication, mother: in other words, the *ryōsai kenbo*, 'good wife, wise mother' extolled by neo-Confucianists in Japan since the 17th century.

But is the cover model's gaze really defined by men when, as Winship points out, it is not a sexual look between woman and man, but 'the steady, self-contained, calm look of unruffled temper' (1987:12) that gazes back at potential women readers? Here we see 'the woman who can manage her emotions and her life. She is the woman whom "you" as reader can trust as friend; she looks as one woman to another speaking about what women share: the intimate knowledge of being a [Japanese] woman' (Winship 1987:12). In *Katei Gahō*, the model's gaze is both distant and slightly withdrawn, the gaze of one woman at another. That it is not more intimate or sexual is made clear by the fact that the model is depicted, not as a face, but as a *persona* expressed in her make-up, clothes, jewellery, flowers, body posture, and expression. In this context, the 'male' gaze is irrelevant, and the magazine's 'face' – the term used by western commentators – is in fact closer to the ideal of 'movement' (*ugoki*) aimed at by the staff of *Katei Gahō*.

There is something else about the cover models of *Katei Gahō*. They are selected for their overall *charm* (*kawairashisa*), rather than for their readily appreciable beauty or sexuality (however such qualities may be defined). Hence they tend to be actresses rather than (film, music, model) superstars, whose features are not necessarily perfect, and who thereby reassure readers that slightly irregular teeth, or over-dimpled cheeks, do not necessarily detract from their individual charm, which can be cultivated *within*. Inoue et al. (1989:149) have noted that the emphasis on womanly charm, rather than sexuality, is in fact a characteristic of other Japanese women's magazines such as *Shufu no Tomo* and *non-no* which, like *Katei Gahō*, differ from those American and European magazines which 'use glamorous women to represent physical perfection' and so 'rely on readers' personal sense of inferiority, especially about their physical appearance' (McCracken 1993:36). It is true that *Katei Gahō* implies that women's work in the home should somehow strive for the kind of ornamental perfection portrayed in the cover photo, but the model is definitely *not* chosen to sustain women readers' 'envy and feelings of insecurity', as McCracken argues.

This reading of the photographic image is supported by the magazine's sell lines which act as 'relay' texts (Barthes 1977), both to the photographic image and to the contents of each edition of *Katei Gahō*. As we have seen, these sell lines suggest that a woman's sophistication stems from an ability to appreciate and practice Japanese and international cuisine, to decorate tastefully the interior of her home, and to know how to dress well in a style that is – like the woman herself – totally 'coordinated'. At the same time, sell lines emphasize that women readers should appreciate literature (especially poetry) and art (in particular, ceramics), history and nature in Japan, and travel abroad. By providing a balance of topics that, on the one hand, are practical and part of readers' everyday lives, and, on the other, draw readers into a 'dream world' (*yume no sekai*), *Katei Gahō* aims to show its readers that everything is possible and that perfection lies in their own hands.[8]

The Japanese Dream

Much has been made of the 'dreams' to be found in 'women's advertising magazines' (McCracken 1993:4). In *Options*, for example, the ideology of femininity and individuality takes on the guise of 'Superwoman' (Winship 1983:45–6). Given that *Katei Gahō*'s editors talk openly of the 'dream world' to which they wish to attract their readers, we need to ask in what the *Katei Gahō* 'dream' consists, and how it is put across.

Briefly put, the magazine's dream concerns 'Japaneseness' (*wa*), and is imagined through such themes as nostalgia, nature and tradition. As we have seen, almost all readers are Japanese women, and, as the cover has already forewarned us, they are presented with a 'Japanese' lifestyle in the pages of *Katei Gahō*, even though – as editors will wryly admit – there is nothing these days all that Japanese about most people's everyday lives. By making use of a Japanese model on the cover and by refusing to use western models at any point in the magazine's feature articles, the magazine promotes as high 'cultural capital' (Bourdieu 1984) a dream which it then tries to connect to the reality of Japan's (sub)urban lifestyles, thereby fusing, rather than separating in some abstract sense, 'fantasy' and 'reality' (Winship 1983:45).

This the magazine achieves through *nostalgia*, in the sense that anyone in their forties is believed to have experienced some aspect of *wa* during their childhood. Thus 'summer', for example, will 'mean' to most readers the sound of windbells (*fūrin*) or a childhood recollection of scooping goldfish out of a bowl, while the New Year will bring instant memories of visiting a shrine and making rice cakes. In other words, wa means nostalgia for a past world that is generally no longer – a nostalgia epitomized, for example, by the series '(White radish, onion, bamboo shoot, water melon) and Yesterday', which opened each monthly edition of *Katei Gahō* in 1991, and which focussed on such events as a chance meeting between a boy on his way home from school through a giant radish field with a girl carrying a violin (January 1991), or a writer's mother and sister drinking water from a well near an onion field on their way home from his aunt's funeral in the local cemetery (February 1991).

Apart from this emphasis on the personal experience of childhood, *Katei Gahō* tries to present this sense of what it means to be 'Japanese' through photographs of the highest quality,[9] focussing on a lexicon of traditional images (carp banners fluttering in the May breeze, signifying Boys' Day; silver birches in the mountains, reminding readers of the potential coolness of summer; maples leaves dyed red against the back-drop of a mountain stream in autumn; bamboos weighed down by snow in winter; and so on), which can be seen ultimately to coalesce in the repeatedly used keyword *furusato* ('homeplace', May 1991, cf. Kelly 1990:68–70). In other words, nostalgia involves a rejection of the reader's present life, here and now, and posits instead a quiet, slightly unreal dreamworld, saturated with emotions from one's past life in which romance for the countryside is very strong.

These traditional images of 'Japaneseness' to a large extent form a second lexicon entitled *nature* (*shizen*). So far as those involved in the production of *Katei Gahō* are concerned, nature is a crucial part of wa which is interpreted as meaning 'together with nature, something Japanese' (*shizen to tomo ni, nihonteki na mono*). Hence, articles fre-quently relate aspects of nature directly to some aspect of Japanese culture. We find that sunrise at the New Year or cherry blossoms in spring, for example, will be linked to the 'Japanese people' and what it means to be 'Japanese' (January 1991, April 1993), summer fashion with summer greetings and a woman's 'heart' (*kokoro*, July 1991, cf. Moeran 1989), autumn flowers and moon viewing with classical Japanese literature (September 1991), and so on and so forth. Indeed, one year (1992), each month's edition of *Katei Gahō* – January, February, March – was referred to on the Table of Contents page by its classical Japanese name (*mitsugi, kisaragi, yayoi*), rather than by the more standard form (*ichigatsu, nigatsu, sangatsu*), each of which em-phasizes through its Chinese characters some aspect of nature (the moon, water, frost). In 1993, the month of April was similarly referred to by the standard literary appelation of 'flower clouds' (*hanagumori*, also used in certain ceramics advertisements), signifying where that month is located according to the poetic classification of nature adopted in Japanese classical (i.e. tenth century Heian) times.

This emphasis on nature and the seasons is by no means limited to feature articles and photo reportages. Much of the advertising that appears in *Katei Gahō* is also seasonal in content. This is most obvious in the use of a word like 'spring' or 'summer' to advertise fashions and cosmetics (Lapin Blanche and Kanebō's *Raphaie*), or food products (Lipton's tea and Itō ham), and in advertisements for Japanese sweet cake manufacturers, where monthly 'seasonality' is a crucial part of their production and consumption (for example, Toraya's *Arashiyama* cakes in 'season' between April 1 and April 10 [April 1993]). But we also find the seasons reflected in numerous other advertisements – for ceramics manufacturers like Noritake, which has different product ranges for different seasons, or Royal Doulton, which has different coloured tea cups and saucers for each season (green in spring, red in autumn) placed against different 'seasonal' backgrounds (moss, and a rock with maple leaves, respectively); for accessories, where Mikimoto will use a stag beetle in its summer campaign ad, Jesus Yanes contrasting seasonal colours, and Wakatsuki the more customary winter and summer 'collections' of its diamonds.

But ads go further in their reflection of the seasons. Some may consciously refer to important family events like Father's or Mother's Day (Morozoff, Wedgwood), mid-year and year-end gift giving seasons, Christmas, adults day, and so on (see Moeran and Skov 1993: 122–124). Parker, for example, advertises one of its fountain pens with the headline: '*Cherries blossom. Spring at eighteenth. Use this pen to congratulate yourself on and remember successfully passing your exams*' (*Sakura saku, jūhachi no haru. Gōkaku no oiwai ni, kono pen o kinen ni shite kudasai* [April 1993]), thereby neatly combining the flowering of youth with educational (hence social) success, *and* the annual rite of cherry blossom viewing. Other ads consciously make use of seasonal events – like an autumn sports day, or going back to the family home for the mid-summer return of the ancestors (*obon*, Morozoff) – in order to play on ideals of Japaneseness (in the latter case, involving family relations) that arise therefrom.

There is, then, constant reference in both features and advertisements in *Katei Gahō* to nature, the seasons, and tradition (*dentō*) – a reference which is very much a coherent part of its focus on 'Japaneseness'. Not only is this depiction of nature clearly nostalgic, in the sense that it evokes images which come from a period when Japan was not so highly urbanized or industrialized, and which thus belong to that indefinable period before nature was – it is said – 'destroyed' by the ills that accompany 'progress'. It also emphasizes such visual images by *textual* allusions to the heyday of Japanese literature. For example, a special feature on spring flowers (March 1991) is linked throughout to poetry from the *Manyōshū* eighth century collection of poems. In this respect, 'nature' is historical and – as the numerous photo-reportages of cuisine with their lacquerware and ceramics attest – an integral part of 'traditional' Japanese material culture.

Readers' attitudes towards, and relation with, the material culture that makes up their lives is also subtly influenced by *Katei Gahō*'s contents. Although the magazine's editorial staff do not believe they have the right to criticize their readers' ways of life, they are prepared to show them alternative modes of living – how to use use traditional methods of medical treatment (*kanpōyaku*), for example – so that readers can discover for themselves that there are better ways to appreciate things and more enjoyable things to do. Thus, by depicting 'beautiful nature' (*kirei na shizen*), *Katei Gahō* tries to make people think differently about why they need certain things. A new product, such as a pair of high class binoculars, for example, can come on the market and be used in any number of ways. Rather than letting them be sold 'straight', the magazine may feature them in an article on, say, bird watching and thereby link them with the natural environment. Similarly, all kinds of natural foods and ingredients, together with the best ways to serve them (by means of the best cooking utensils made from high quality steel, wrought iron, or bamboo) will also be put forward as alternative methods of preparing particular dishes for particular forms of cuisine.

This commodification of nature is by no means exceptional. Indeed, it merely emphasizes what has already been noted with regard to the advertisements that appear in the magazine. Perhaps what can be said here, however, is that – like many other Japanese women's magazines (Moeran and Skov 1995) – *Katei Gahō* takes this commodification of nature much further than similar publications, which themselves seem to be a good step ahead of women's magazines in Europe and the United States, where fashions and cosmetics may be the seasonal mainstays, but where publishers appear to have little grasp of the advertising sales potential generated by instituting a 'cultural predilection' for such seasonal and life-cycle events as Christmas, Valentine's Day, engagements, weddings, Mother's Day, Father's Day, and so on.[10] Moreover, in its emphases, too, *Katei Gahō* makes readers realize through its features on fashion, cuisine and interior decor that neither food nor materials in general are what they used to be, and that nature should not merely provide some kind of aesthetic pleasure to be savoured by the five senses, but should itself form the kernel of an overall Japanese lifestyle, and hence of readers' very being.

Seasonality

In *Katei Gahō*, the emphasis in all Japanese women's magazines on the temporal cycle of events that can be successfully marketed is taken one

123

step further. This point can be grasped more readily if we focus on food which, as we have seen, is the main theme in *Katei Gahō*. Although the magazine does feature articles on, for example, Italian cuisine (April 1991), or French wines (December 1992),[11] the magazine's primary emphasis is on Japanese cuisine and the ingredients – mainly vegetables and fish – which are used therein. The crucial keyword used by almost all Japanese magazines (Inoue et al. 1989:172) in such features is *shun*.

Shun constitutes the philosophy behind the choice of what is featured in each month's edition of *Katei Gahō*, and refers to a ten day period (or 'season') used to distinguish between beginning (*jōjun*), middle (*chūjun*), and end (*gejun*) of each month, as well as to 'seasonality' in Japanese cuisine. This raises a question of meaning, which is explained by one member of *Katei Gahō*'s Editorial Department in the following manner: on the one hand, shun can be interpreted as being the 'tastiest' time for a particular vegetable, fruit or fish; on the other, it can signify something 'just before its best' – a concept particularly favoured in the tea ceremony, as developed by Sen no Rikyū. In other words, in the tea ceremony a particular food is served just before coming into 'season' in order to make guests feel that they have eaten something special (because they have not eaten it before). This coincides with the much prized concept of 'first produce' (*hatsumono*) used to herald a new season – a concept adhered to in country farmhouses which still offer hatsumono to the ancestors before allowing living household members to consume it, and in such customs as that practised during the Edo Period, when fishermen on the Bōsō peninsula would vie with one another to deliver the first bonito fish of the season to the shōgun. Indeed, hatsumono used to be such a powerful idea that some Edo husbands are said to have pawned their wives in order to be able to partake of a newly in-season food! This passion for hatsumono also encouraged farmers to try to speed up the growth of their produce (by using 'night soil', for example, which emitted heat into the earth and so hastened the maturation of the vegetables growing there), since they stood to get much higher prices for it then than at normal harvesting times.

According to the canons of Japanese cuisine, Kyōto used to be the determining point of a particular food's shun, although different regions of Japan had, and still have, a slightly different season for the same vegetable or fish, and nowadays the Tōkyō-Ōsaka axis perhaps forms the basis for each food's seasonality. Just as the progress of the cherry blossoms or the monsoon front is reported regularly on Japanese television news programmes as each creeps gently northwards from Kagoshima in the south towards Hokkaidō in the north, so does the coming into 'season' of bamboo shoots in spring and *matsutake* mushrooms in autumn at slightly different times get reported to readers of *Katei Gahō*. This means, in effect, that each 'season' lasts from a month to a month and a half.

This lengthening of the concept of shun to take account of the whole of the Japanese archipelago (or, at least, of its four main islands) has its advantages for those working on each edition of *Katei Gahō*. One of the features of the magazine industry in Japan is that every magazine is put on sale at least one month, and sometimes five to six weeks, before its cover publication date. This means that the April edition will be in the bookshops on March 1 (and that the contents of the June edition will first be discussed on March 10). Since a majority of the readers of *Katei Gahō* live in the Kantō region, where each 'season' is comparatively late, editors can – like tea ceremony masters – use each shun somewhat in advance of normality. For example, in Tōkyō, matsutake mushrooms are available only from the very end of September until mid-November. They will, however, be included in the October edition which comes out on 1 September. In this way, the magazine serves its Kantō readers a visual delicacy three to four weeks before it comes into season in their real lives, and is still 'seasonal' enough for those living in Ōsaka, Shikoku or Kyūshū to the south.

Advertising

The fact that shun is used both as a marker of 'nature' and 'seasonality' in *Katei Gahō*'s discourse on 'Japaneseness', and as structuring principle, prompts me to turn to the relation between advertising and editorial matter. Advertising is intended – and seen by readers – to be an integral part of what both the Editorial and Advertising Departments call a textual and visual 'flow' (*nagare*) and, as McCracken has forcefully argued (1993, Chapters 2 and 3), is designed in most women's magazines to seem like 'a natural and logical extension of the editorial content' (1993:38). As we have seen, advertisements come to between 40 and 50 per cent of the total number of pages in each edition of *Katei Gahō*. What is advertised depends somewhat on the month of the year – June and December, for example, are popular with those selling accessories since it is in these months that people get their six-monthly bonuses, while cosmetics advertising is particularly heavy in spring and autumn.[12] In general, the Advertising Department regards *Katei Gahō*'s main advertisers as being in the categories of, first, fashion, next cosmetics, and then (Japanese) foods (particularly cakes).[13]

Advertising is, of course, very much part of a magazine's image so that *where* ads are placed is extremely important, both for editorial staff and for advertisers themselves.[14] The opening block of advertisements in every edition of *Katei Gahō* tends to be fixed each year, thereby facilitating an extension of the magazine's 'face'. From 1992 into 1993, for example, this 'face' consisted of an inside cover two-page advertisement for Kanebō *Raphaie*, with seasonal reference and visual and textual allusions to the refined arts of painting and classical music; two pages of ads for Chanel ready-to-wear; a double page spread, with seasonal reference, for Bulgari jewellery; an ad for Chanel perfume *No. 19*, a single page seasonal photograph of Mt Fuji and the Table of Contents, before the opening block was completed by an advertisement for Christian Dior's *Diorissimo*. The back cover was consistently taken out by Hasebe Seiko for its *Credor* watch, while the inside back cover was purchased by both interior (Sala Azabu) and cosmetics (Noevir) companies. In other words, the most important opening and closing advertisements were for cosmetics, fashion, accessories (and, to a lesser degree, interior), which invited readers to reflect upon their own potential beauty, sophistication and cultural talents.

As in many other Japanese women's magazines, advertisements are usually placed in blocks, usually of between eight and twelve pages, interspersed between editorial or photographic matter, and increasing in frequency in the latter half of each edition. In strong contrast to many American or European women's magazines which devote the large majority of their early pages to advertising, *Katei Gahō* does not interrupt its editorial matter with advertisements. For example, in May 1993, the Japanese magazine's main feature – following the four page *Editor's Report*, two page photo feature on Japanese baths, and eight page block of ads – consisted of 34 uninterrupted pages of text and photographs. It was followed by a four page block of advertisements, after which came a second uninterrupted feature of 22 pages. There were then two more pages of ads, a six page feature, and a block of twelve pages of advertising – giving a total of 34 pages of ads in the magazine's first 110 pages. Thus, in this edition of *Katei Gahō*, there were 68 pages of advertising in the first 200 printed pages, and a further 117 (including tie-ins) in the remaining 232.

The staff of the Advertising Department of *Katei Gahō* are particularly concerned with 'flow' when it comes to the placing of advertisements – a concern which ensures that advertising both harmonizes with editorial matter when placed opposite features and does *not* break up features. Adjacency is thus an important *aesthetic*, rather than merely commercial, principle in the structure of a magazine and can influence the relationship between advertising and editorial matter in several ways.

The first and most obvious form of this principle is through *product similarity*. Advertisements connected with food, for example, tend to be placed before or after an article on cuisine, and others for underwear fashion and jewellery in blocks either side of a feature on lingerie and accessories co-ordination (Figure 2.4). This kind of product placement can be more subtle, as when an advertisement for Givenchy depicts a model in green evening gown with gold bodice opposite a feature on how Japanese women should wear evening clothes and accessories (December 1992), or when a perfume known for its floral note is placed opposite a photograph of seasonal flowers.

A second form of harmonizing advertising and editorial matter is by means of *design*, in particular through the repetition of motifs found in the illustrations of both ad and feature on the page opposite. For example, an advertisement for Piaget with photograph of a man's fingers touching a woman's black gloved hand was placed opposite a 'tie-in' for Missoni Club which started with a photograph of three gloved hands grasping three golf clubs (April 1993). Similarly, a feature on how to take care of one's hands was preceded by an ad for a Hanai Yukiko watch by Citizen, where both had almost identical illustrations of three or four hands pointing vertically upwards (September 1992) (Figure 2.5). Alternatively, and more subtly, the image of a full moon not only graced the opening page of an article on autumn moon viewing, but could also be found on an octagonal dish by Fujimoto Nōdō used in an advertisement by Nakamuraya on the page opposite (September 1991) (Figure 2.6). This emphasis on design can also be found within blocks of advertisements where an ad for Comtesse accessories, for instance, was placed opposite another by Naigai for the *CB Collection*, because both made use of a visual of a woman's torso (April 1993); where facing ads for Concord watches and Tōkyū Hotels both featured a model with finger pointing to chin (November 1991); and a watch (Dior) and car (Jaguar) ads found themselves together primarily because of the way in which each product was photographed in the same manner diagonally across the page (Figure 2.7).

A third form of adjacency is *colour*. An advertisement for Jean Lassale *Thalassa* gold watches, with illuminated opera house framed by a starkly contrasting black and white background, was placed opposite the final page of a feature on house design, with its own sharply etched photograph in black, greys, white and gold of a house with its lights on

Figure 2.4 From body hugging teddy wear to a revival of the mini-slip. Product similarity in editorial and advertising matter (Courtesy of *Katei Gahō*)

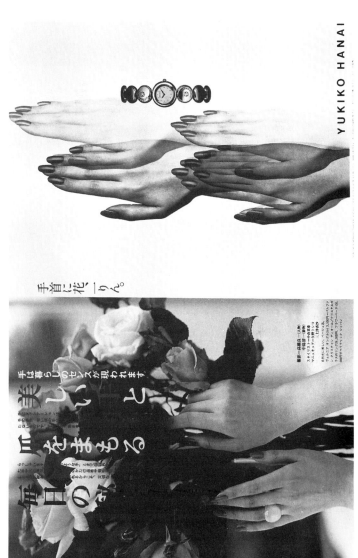

YUKIKO HANAI

手首に花一りん。

美しいと

毎日の出会う

花を買る

Figure 2.5 'A flower for the wrist'. Design aesthetics 1 (Courtesy of *Katei Gahō*)

Figure 2.6 Moon viewing in autumn. Design aesthetics 2 (Courtesy of *Katei Gahō*)

西洋の神秘、J。

Jaguar Japan Limited

JAGUAR

Christian Dior

Swiss made. Registered design.

Figure 2.7 'Treasures from the west'. Design aesthetics 3 (Courtesy of *Katei Gahō*).

at dusk (March 1991). Similarly, a feature on the tea ceremony and the Dolls' Festival (*hinamatsuri*, March 1992) had opposite it an advertisement for Toraya tea ceremony cakes, whose pink decoration perfectly matched the headline used for the photo-reportage.

Finally, adjacency can also be achieved through *language*. An advertisement for Hon Takasagoya cakes, for example, was placed opposite an article on deep fried dishes, not so much because they both made use of food in their visuals, but because the headlines in both advertisement and editorial referred to the word 'mother' (*haha, okāsan*) (February 1991). Similarly, an editorial page featuring special cakes for each of the four seasons (*shunka shūtō*) was matched by an advertisement for Toraya cakes whose headline referred to matching the seasons (*kisetsu*) (June 1991), while an advertisement for *Mariko Kohga art* was placed opposite a Pola Antique Gallery advertisement for an *art nouveau* glass exhibition (November 1991).

A Readerly Text

In the way it invites an essentially passive, receptive and disciplined readership which is prepared to accept the meanings of 'tradition', 'Japaneseness' and so on as depicted therein, *Katei Gahō* strikes me as being more a 'readerly' (Barthes 1975) than 'producerly' (Fiske 1989) text. It is true, as we shall see below, that readers *are* invited to create their own interpretations of, and to act in their own ways upon, certain visual images; true, too, that there are the occasional contradictory voices (as when a nun proclaims the vanity of materialism and luxury in an article enclosed by advertisements for expensive, fashionable clothes and jewellery [June 1991]); nevertheless meanings are for the most part closed. *Katei Gahō* remains in control of itself, and of its readers.

The closed nature of *Katei Gahō* is re-enforced by the kind of thematic correlation between (covert) advertising and editorial content outlined above, and described by McCracken (1993:38) as an exercise in 'pervasive homologous saturation' or 'subliminal synergism' (1993: 48), predisposing readers more favourably towards purchased advertisements. There is plenty of evidence in the magazine's structure to support this. For example, a feature on how best to coordinate watch and bracelet not only starts opposite an advertisement for Piaget (whose product, marketed by Heiwadō, appears in the reportage itself), but advertises watches and accessories by such regular clients as Seikō (Back Cover), Cartier, Bulgari, and Mikimoto, as well as fashion clothing by other advertisers like Chanel, Missoni, Ferragamo, Celine, and Ferre (the last of which is marketed by Ellebis, whose two page advertisement for Sonya Rykiel appears a little later on [April 1993]). Similarly, another feature in the same issue, this time on kitchen systems, recommends products by Kitchen House, which has a two page spread in the block of advertising preceeding the article, as well as those put out by other regular advertisers like INAX, ABC, SieMatic, and Matsushita Denkō. This kind of covert advertising, which is found in cosmetics, fashion, and accessories features in particular, can be taken to finer metonymical lengths – as when, for example, an advertisement for Oscar de la Renta's boutique in Mitsukoshi is placed opposite a fashion reportage in which the model is photographed standing in front of a cast-iron lion which – as every Japanese reader would immediately recognize – graces the entrance of that department store in Nihonbashi, Tōkyō.

In spite of the obvious attempt on the part of *Katei Gahō*'s Editorial and Advertising Departments to make advertising 'seem a natural and logical extension of the editorial content' (McCracken 1993:38), I cannot accept McCracken's patently anti-commercial bias in her study of American 'women's advertising magazines'. In the first place, as I have argued above, both editorial and advertising staff were clearly concerned with their magazine's overall *aesthetics of design*. It was primarily this, rather than a desparate attempt to match products with editorial matter in order to please advertisers, which determined what kind of advertisements they placed where.[15] This can be seen in a series of Chanel ads placed in *Katei Gahō* in 1991. For example, a feature on the 'boom' in high quality pearls with photograph of model in pearl necklace and earrings was matched by an adjacent advertisement for a Chanel watch with pearl strap (January, Figure 2.8), while a second feature on (eye) make-up in November was preceded by an advertise-ment for Chanel's *Eye Lift*. However, many of the products featured in this reportage (Yves Saint Laurent's *Teinte de Soie* line smoothing foundation, for example) were *not* advertised in the magazine, while others (like Cosme Decorte's *Multiple Plasma*) that were not featured, *were* advertised. Moreover, an article on home *esthétique* and skin care in August of the same year was preceded by an advertisement for Chanel, but for one of its watches (*Le Temps*) and not for either of the skin care products (*Lotion Douce* and *Gommage Vital*) featured in the editorial content.

In other words, both Editorial and Advertising Departments will try to create a match in advertising and editorial matter as and when it is possible to do so, but they do not go out of their way to order special advertisements for particular features. Rather, they make do with the ads

Figure 2.8 'Nonchalantly, high class pearls . . .' Design aesthetics 4 (Courtesy of *Katei Gahō*)

that they have on order and, although I have here picked out examples of various forms of adjacency, it should be stressed that they do not come up with aesthetically – and commercially – successful combinations all that frequently.

Secondly, *Katei Gahō* staff were patently aware of the fact that they had to please *two* audiences – their readers and their advertisers (Moeran 1993:86–91) – and they knew which of these two groups – their readers – was more important. In other words, they believed in editorial independence and strongly rejected the idea that the contents of their magazine should be determined by advertisers, in the manner suggested by McCracken for American magazines.

Thirdly, they also knew the characteristics of these readers: upper-class, sophisticated, middle-aged women who devoted a considerable amount of their time to the *aesthetics* of cuisine, make-up and clothing. In other words, they structured *Katei Gahō* according to certain canons of *taste*, rather than according to the whims and demands of capitalist enterprises, and such canons, they insisted, were as much their own and – more importantly – those of their readers, as they were those of their advertisers. From my inquiries into the *production*, rather than merely reception, point of view, therefore, I am unconvinced by the case for media 'conspiracy'.

Discussion and Conclusion

Let me conclude with a few remarks. First, *Katei Gahō* staff's understanding of its readership leads me to comment on the 'dream world' put forward by women's magazines all over the world. Winship (1987:55) has argued that 'women's enjoyment of fashion, food and furnishings is, in part, undoubtedly the enjoyment of a *fantasy of displacement*' (her italics), where the goals that readers cannot achieve in many areas of social life are displaced into areas where they *are* possible. This is certainly true of *Katei Gahō* which focusses on the 'experts' responsible for the appetizing food, floral designs, interior lay-outs and which, by photographing them in their homes, presents them as 'ordinary people' like the readers. This area of possibility is also kept open by a Confucian insistence that perfection can be achieved through study, and that ordinary women can in this way become perfect wives, mothers, cooks, hostesses, and practitioners of Japan's traditional arts. *Katei Gahō* is thus a 'how to' manual.

But it also acts as a 'work of art' at which readers can gaze and see themselves reflected. The point is that the 'dream world' put forward by the magazine's publishers is not just realizable, but realizable in all sorts of different ways. There is thus no great disjunction between the 'dream world' and the 'reality' of readers' everyday lives. For example, *Katei Gahō*'s editors make sure that they present material that is within the financial possibility of its women readers who *can* afford many of the luxuries presented in the magazine's pages. Here they carefully link the improbable with the probable. A feature titled '*How to live with art*' not only provides numerous photographs of wealthy 'Parisian madames' at home in their appartments, showing the ways in which they incorporate art objects into their lifestyles. It also provides hints about how Japanese women readers might wish to aestheticize their homes. Similarly, another feature – this time on summer foods – starts out by depicting a woman in kimono kneeling on the verandah of a beautiful old wooden house, set against a background of a spacious, wooded garden. Nearby are a vase of flowers, with displays of food on a long low wooden table, a glass statuette in one corner of the room, and a scroll hanging on the dried mud wall beside it. The house looks very Japanese, very beautiful, very special, very different from anything lived in by ordinary readers. Yet it *is* lived in by the woman in kimono in the photograph, and, although readers cannot live in this particular house, they *can* buy the glass statuette and so become part of the total scene that they see before them. Similarly, they *can* create their own small pond of water with its bamboo clapper (*shishi odoshi*) and they, too, can place all kinds of different beer bottles to cool in the water that gathers there. Thus, while the actual house and garden are undoubtedly beyond the means of most *Katei Gahō* readers, the elements that those living there incorporate into their lives can be imitated. In this respect, the world of *Katei Gahō* must be both real for someone and a world in which such dreams can in part be realized by everyone else. It thus cleverly combines the familiar (a particular seasonal dish with the Girls' Day dolls festival, for example) with the exotic (the cuisine comes from Kyōto, the dolls from a village in the far north of Japan) and, like other women's magazines all over the world, provides for 'those rhythms and routines of women's lives in which private time and space are precious, work and leisure merge, activities overlap, and dreams and escape often feed on a modest vocabulary of everyday possibilities' (Winship 1987:13).

Second, the 'dream world' of *Katei Gahō* totally *isolates* its women readers in a number of important ways. In the first place – and surprisingly, given the overall emphasis on family relationships – women are isolated at *home*. Readers are rarely given glimpses of more than one or two women together in a home at any one time (usually in articles featuring cooking and food); they never actually *see* other members of a woman's family, although these may be alluded to in the text of an article or advertisement (as we have seen with Morozoff). Instead, *Katei Gahō* depicts a Japanese home in which either the woman is alone, or she is herself the viewer of an – often absurdly spacious – empty room. In some respects, of course, this view realistically reflects that of the 40-year-old non-working mother whose husband is at work all day and whose children are at school. By emphasizing the isolated role of women in the privacy of their homes, and by portraying them almost invariably in either aprons or kimono, *Katei Gahō* appears to uphold, both visually and ideologically, the 'traditional' role of Japanese women. This isolation more or less prevents women themselves from communicating with one another, from realizing that they do in fact share problems that go beyond the aesthetic and culinary satisfaction of other members of their household.

This kind of social isolation is also to be found in *Katei Gahō*'s depiction of *nature*. Every bamboo grove, mountain plateau, or sea shore shown in the magazine's pages is totally devoid of people. In other words, women are obliged to commune with nature entirely on their own, rather like Zen Buddhist nuns in meditation. Moreover, in that nature in *Katei Gahō* is a central part of the dream of 'Japaneseness' (wa), readers find that, in order to achieve this dream, they must create a lifestyle in which they are totally *alone*.

Given the Confucian premises that define Japanese women in *relation* to others (fathers, husbands, sons), this is rather extraordinary. Moreover, when we remember the endless discussions of Japanese society as 'group' oriented, we may be excused, perhaps, for thinking that such an interpretation of *Katei Gahō* is beyond the sociological pale. However, what we should also realize is that different women's magazines perform different functions and that what is good for one magazine does not necessarily hold for another, nor will it necessarily be so for the same magazine over a long period of time. In other words, all women's magazines are extremely variable, both in themselves and as a media type. Unlike the impression given by McCracken in her critique of American women's advertising magazines, we are not dealing with 'high art' but with a popular cultural form. It is precisely because magazines *are* popular that they are always in the process of change.[16]

My reading of *Katei Gahō* as an isolating medium makes more sense when we realize that its feature articles and photo-reportages virtually ignore contemporary urban life – in that crowded streets, traffic, department stores, entertainment areas, and above all people (Berman 1988) are *very* selectively shown, if at all. A fashion model might, as we have seen, be posed in front of one of the lions at the entrance to Mitsukoshi. Readers may be given a glimpse of a smart restaurant in a secluded street in Kyōto. For the most part, however, all visuals in *Katei Gahō* deny the existence of modern urban life in Japan, and focus instead on quiet scenes in the countryside where neither traffic, bullet trains, department stores, convenience stores, pachinko parlours, video game centres, love (*avec*, or city) hotels, nor any other aspect of Japan's active consumer society is visible.

Again, this is odd, especially when we realize that in many other women's magazines the contradiction between 'nature' and 'city' has been reconciled according to the terms of the consumer economy. As Lise Skov and I have argued elsewhere (Moeran and Skov 1995), the way in which the *city* is emphasized in fashion reportages may allow married women, through consumption, to escape the confines of their home and workplace into the anonymity of the city. In this respect, the usual separation of private and public for housewives is reversed, since the city provides them with a personal, private space to which they can withdraw as well-dressed consumers when not fulfilling their public duties as wives and mothers. Much like Baudelaire (Wolff 1985), however, *Katei Gahō* renders the (sub)urban *flaneuse* 'invisible'.

In *Katei Gahō* a woman's personal, private space is very much in the (empty) home, where, dressed in Japanese kimono or a housewife's apron, she devotes herself to Japanese pursuits all on her own. The aesthetic staging, which elsewhere takes place in the city in front of others, is in *Katei Gahō* totally solitary and so private that it can be perceived by nobody. In this context, 'Japaneseness' becomes little more than an elusive idea, a daydream, which – by offering an extremely selective and adapted perspective of Japanese tradition – exists primarily as a consumer cultural lifestyle created for a particular segment of the market.

Everything about *Katei Gahō* points to that kind of effacement of boundaries between art and everyday life that has been seen by some to characterize postmodernism. Although it is becoming fashionable to talk of 'postmodernism' in Japan as one almost evolutionary step forwards from the previous 'recent' (or 'premodern', *kindai*) and 'present' (or 'modern', *gendai*) periods of modernity, it is equally clear that 'the aestheticization of everyday life' is not new, either in Japan – where the Heian Court initiated a long-running trend that has been variously continued by sixteenth century samurai warriors, eighteenth century Edo *chōnin* townsmen, and twentieth century folk craft *aficionados* (to name but three such 'cultural specialists') – or elsewhere (Featherstone 1991a:65–82). In many respects, *Katei Gahō* can be said to continue this lengthy tradition in Japan, both by turning life into a work of art and by inviting *women* to aestheticize their everyday lives. Japan's 'post-modernism' here harks back to the Heian period (794–1182), when women were for the most part isolated in remote parts of palace build-ings, and when a similar nostalgia for the past also prevailed. This suggests that we are indeed concerned with what John Clammer (1992: 205) has elsewhere referred to as the 'transmodern', rather than with the more denigrating 'non-modernism' suggested by Miyoshi and Harootunian (1989b:x).

With its aestheticization of everyday life, *Katei Gahō* also presents a much more conventional image of the housewife's liking for beautiful things – an image which, though also well known in the west, is largely ignored by those writing on (post)modernism. My argument here is that housewife aesthetics are both a product of – and provide a counter-image to – modern urban life. Interestingly, the magazine's major stylistic reform and present format were effected in 1977, at more or less that time when a so-called 'new breed' of young Japanese (*shinjinrui*) took to dancing in the streets of Harajuku, and to riding their motorbikes in cavalcades around the main roads of Tōkyō. In other words, the renewed aestheticization of an older generation's everyday lifestyle, and indeed of Japanese culture as a whole, has coincided with the perceived 'breakdown' of neo-Confucian ideals in Japanese society. Whereas *Katei Gahō* is certainly a stronghold of conservativism, it is also based on a collapse of the distinction between high (traditional) art and mass culture and reveals how the management of Japan's high cultural herit-age has been displaced into the hands of the media. The magazine may thus be read as a response to the kind of radical break seen to characterize postmodernism, and by aiming to control rather than decontrol emo-tions – as well as to provide through stylistic connotation (Jameson 1991:19) a connected rather than disconnected series of images in order to give stability to the subjectivism of modern life (Featherstone 1991a: 79) – adopts as *retro*-modernism the stuff of which its dreams are made.

NOTES

1 According to a *Reader's Profiles* (*sic*) put out by the publisher of *Katei Gahō*, actual readers range from young women in their early twenties (4.1 per cent) to older women in their late fifties and sixties (11.1 per cent). Women aged between 35 and 44 years amount to 40 per cent of the total

readership, and the average reader's age is 41.6 years. Furthermore, 59.5 per cent have received university or junior college education; 36.7 per cent are full-time housewives, while 52.9 per cent hold jobs of one sort or another; 83 per cent own their own homes; 51.5 per cent have a family income of over ¥10 million a year, and all but 1.8 per cent have been abroad at least once.

I would like to take this opportunity to thank the following people for their assistance in providing information and data to enable me to write this paper: Ōshima Sachiko, Nakano Shunichi, and Ishikawa Takanobu (Editorial Department); Kitoh Masashi and Shizawa Hiromitsu (Advertising Department); and Shimura Kazunobu (Design).

2 *Reader's Profiles* intimates that only 10.9 per cent of *Katei Gahō*'s readers keep the magazine to themselves. The 'pass along' readership ranges from two (26.6 per cent) to three (29.9 per cent), on the one hand, to more than ten readers (8.6 per cent), on the other. 20.9 per cent of readers keep *Katei Gahō* for an indefinite, long period, and 53.3 per cent for some time prior to disposal. Only 4.1 per cent replied to the March 1991 questionnaire that they disposed of the magazine every month.

3 It should be noted that only a few Japanese magazines make use of subscriptions as a source of sales (and reliable sales figures). *Katei Gahō*'s circulation figure is higher than – say – the 200,000 copies of the monthly *Fujin Kōron*, but considerably less than the one million plus of *Ie no Hikari*.

4 There is a fourth section for 'Special Themes' (three members). In addition, there are four (freely circulating) assistant editors, and the woman editor-in-chief. All in all, the Editorial Department consists of 29 persons.

5 We should recognize that the title format is never quite the same and that stylistic changes are rung from year to year. In 1991, for example, the words *Katei Gahō* were written in Roman writing beside the main title; in 1993, they had been replaced by the volume number.

It should be noted that a second magazine, *Miss Katei Gahō*, was launched by Sekai Bunkasha in August 1989. Aimed at nurturing younger women as potential readers of *Katei Gahō* when they become older, *Miss Katei Gahō* has made a concession to the 'western' lifestyles of younger women, in that the title *Miss* is always written in Roman writing beside the Chinese characters for *Katei Gahō*.

6 Inoue et al. (1989:210) have calculated that the overall use of Chinese characters is approximately 40 per cent, and of foreign words 30 per cent, in women's magazines, *vis-à-vis* more than 50 per cent and about 20 per cent respectively in men's magazines. They also show (1989:216–7) how the language used in *Shufu no Tomo*, addressed to older housewives, is generally more formal and puts more distance between magazine and reader than does the young women's magazine *non-no*.

7 The style cleverly avoids what editors and designers informed me was the Japanese woman's weak point: her legs.

8 A point also made by Winship in her discussion of women's magazines in England. She quotes an editor of *Vogue* as saying that, in her magazine, 'we are 60% selling a dream and 40% offering practical advice' (1987:13).

9 Almost all pages in *Katei Gahō* are glossy, and all photographs printed

thereon in colour. Clearly, there has long been a link between colour, women, and conspicuous consumption, which relates to men's (and working women's) leisure (Winship (1983:50; 1987:54–5), but the primary function in colour photography in *Katei Gahō* is to create a sense of high class 'luxury' (*yūga*) and 'extravagance' (*zeitaku*) – two words that are frequently found in the headlines of both feature articles and advertisements carried therein.

10 For a (belated) realization by the publisher of *Parents* of the lucrative potential of major life events like weddings and the birth of children, see McCracken (1993:268).

11 Even here, *Katei Gahō* usually features *Japanese* expertise in creating a particular European cuisine, or appreciating fine wines (see, for example, *'Caviar to foie gras'* – *chef 5 nin, seiya no kyōsaku*, December 1992).

12 Advertising figures for January and May 1993 editions were as follows:

	January 1993			May 1993	
1	jewellery	37 pp	1	fashion	55 pp
2=	cosmetics	35	2=	cosmetics	24
2=	food	35	2=	jewellery	24
4	other	30	4	food	20
5	fashion	22	5	other	13
6	bags & shoes	14	6	chinaware	11
7	interior	11	7	interior	10
8	chinaware	10	8	bags & shoes	6

13 About twenty years ago, the magazine was supported by the large famous food manufacturers like Kikkōman, Yukijirushi, and Ajinomoto, but with the launching in the 1980s of cheaper magazines like *Lettuce Club* and *Orange Page* targeted at working women, these companies shifted the bulk of their advertising to the new titles which, like *Options*, were busy creating the idea of their readers as 'superwomen' who could go out and work *and* make immediate feasts for their families with the help of Kikkōman sauce, or whatever. In this respect, *Katei Gahō* lost out because it did not go in for ready-made foods.

14 This is recognized in the price structure of *Katei Gahō*'s advertising rates, where (in December 1991) a four colour, offset printed, back cover cost ¥2.8 million, and a normal, full page, four colour ad ¥2 million. Japanese, like European and American, advertisers prefer to have their ads placed in the first, rather than second, half of a magazine (a fact reflected in a ¥100,000 surcharge on such ads), but on the left rather than right page since magazines are opened and read from right to left (see Moeran 1991). For the record, tie-ins cost ¥2.1 million per page (¥2 million for space charge and ¥100,000 for production costs).

15 Although editorial and advertising staff are employed by the same

141

company, Sekai Bunkasha, they do *not* do the same job. There is always a struggle between journalists, who regard editorial freedom as a professional right, and advertising men, whose professionalism is more concerned with meeting their clients' wishes (see Moeran 1991).

16 The generally favourable financial situation in which Japanese magazine publishers found themselves in the second half of the 80s and 1990–91 may have allowed them more editorial independence than is credited for equivalent magazines in Europe or the United States.

3

ANTIPHONAL PERFORMANCES?

Japanese Women's Magazines and Women's Voices

Nancy Rosenberger

In this chapter, I present young single women's perceptions of their own lives as seen through the prism of magazines targeted at them. Because these magazines offer ideas and images of independence and freedom, they represent an alternative to the dominant morality that is sympathetic to trends towards leisure activities before marriage, later marriage and later, less frequent childbirth.[1] The large number, popularity and accessibility of these magazines call for an exploration of what images and articles in the magazines attempt to convey to young single women. This is one aim of this chapter. However, young women participate in schools, families, and work situations that strongly encourage group cooperation and womanly nurturance. Thus women's perceptions are situated among contending ideas and practices. The question of what magazines attempt to communicate must be expanded to ask what the targeted women are thinking and doing. This chapter poses the question of the extent to which the images and ideas of young women's magazines fit with the lives of the women they address. Ultimately, I ask what positions young Japanese women take in relation to the often contradictory ideas and images through which they build their lives.

Theoretically, this study is based on several assumptions. First, these women's magazines are ideological symbolic forms that carry both meaning and power to their constituency (Thompson 1990:56). That is, the meanings and knowledge that they convey have the potential to enmesh women in a network of ideas and activities that they use to construct their self-images in a social field (Foucault 1980:94). Women's magazines have some power over the way women categorize themselves, their wishes for self-actualization and relationship, and their sexual desires. Second, the magazines establish a discourse of ideas and practices that, while not always coherent within itself, presents an alternative to the discourse of ideas and practices presented to young women by dominant institutions such as family, school and work. Thus, these magazines exist in a contested terrain and it is often at these points of contradiction that women gain agency, sometimes through taking multiple positions (McNay 1992:42). Third, media messages need to be understood according to their reception, not only their production, and thus I make an effort to understand 'how particular individuals, situated in specific circumstances, make sense of media messages and incorporate them into their daily lives' (Thompson 1990:306).

Japanese women's 'lifestyle' magazines have increased tremendously in number over the last two decades. In 1988, there were 61 women's magazines which had a circulation via bookstores of over 10,000; 45 of these have started publication since 1970, including almost all of those aimed at unmarried single women (Inoue et al. 1989: 19–21). I counted over 80 in 1992 in a leading Tōkyō bookstore. In the early 90s, the market niches are still increasing, both from the demand side as women's societal roles increase and from the supply side as publishing houses, advertisers, and product makers try to increase their markets.

In this chapter, I focus on magazines newly targetting the growing group of single women who delay marriage beyond the 'appropriate' age of 25.[2] In 1990, 40 per cent of women between 25 and 29 and fourteen per cent of women between 30 and 34 were single, compared with 21 per cent and six per cent respectively in 1975 (Keizai Kikakuchō 1992:26). Secondly, I focus on single women themselves, using 50 interviews done in 1993 with women between 25 and 39. My main questions are: what kind of performances do these magazines encourage their target audience to stage? How do the everyday lives of young women match images conveyed in these magazines?

The phrase 'antiphonal performances' indicates that magazines and audience respond to each other in public performances, but that the extent of communication is open to question. Magazines buy market research in which agencies standardize and package the views and actions of the targetted audience so that producers and publishers can easily grasp their needs and interests as 'consumers' (Moeran 1993). Some magazines have reader clubs and solicit letters or surveys from their readers; article writers do interview women, but they are usually well-educated Tōkyōites who form the standard image in these magazines.

The magazines' performances and the performances they recommend for women are fragmented and varied according to the context of reception. My research shows that women look over a variety of magazines irregularly, reading magazine contents and cover images on large ads suspended in subway cars or in newspapers, skimming articles while standing in bookstores, and often buying magazines only if headlines catch their interest. Magazine ideas also travel through informal discourse as women exchange magazines and views with friends, often reading them together. In urban areas most women see and are influenced to some extent by magazines' words and images.

Thus, antiphonal performances occur between magazines and women in response to both highly managed yet unpredictable images of each other. Sometimes just across the stage from each other and sometimes at far ends of the concert hall, even singing across oceans to each other, or whispering intimately in strange lands, the women and magazines put on a kaleidoscopic, Alice-in-Wonderland kind of antiphonal performance.

Like Alice, the young single women are in less powerful positions than the publishing houses and marketing/ad agencies who with the makers' blessings have the right to paint the roses red if that is the style. Targets of consumption throughout their formative years, potential readers have been disciplined to learn the language of consumer signs, to study magazine images and reflect them back on themselves. They have been taught a heightened self-consciousness of themselves as subjects being gazed upon by others, subjects who can refashion themselves in various images through ever-changing styles (Ewen 1988:76). Japanese women's magazines offer young women goods that carry images of freedom, independence, international sophistication, status and sexuality (Rosenberger 1991b). Advising on the scent, skin quality, make-up and clothes for everyday events, young women's magazines also counsel their readers on proper attitudes towards and selection of performance situations (marriage, work, dates).

Yet women retain individual agency, appropriating and integrating what they want (Thompson 1990:319; McNay 1992:23). Like Alice, they carry a common sense view from their everyday world, and use it to gauge the craziness of the magazines' tea parties. Young women interpret magazines' messages in relation to other voices of friends, parents, teachers, workmates and superiors, integrating the hum of current moral discourses, the 'modern culture of technology' as well as alternative discourses of individualism (Miyanaga 1991). Approaching 30, they increasingly interpolate magazine images via dominant ideas of maturity. Although young women cannot control the images directed their way, they can choose not to read or buy the magazines or to read selectively.

These rather distorted antiphonal performances between magazines and young women occur in a context of competing discourses. According to Stuart Hall's metaphor (1991), people in the late industrial age are both stitched and unstitched – stitched into place in a local, moral community, and yet unstitched as they participate in an elite global culture of consumption.[3] In the first situation, anchored or rooted in the constructions of Japan, work, school, and family, young women are called towards ideal images of socially mature housewives: modest, sensitive to others, nurturing, with appropriate language and manners, and remembrance of social obligations. In the second situation, unrooted from these local concerns, women are invited to pay attention only to themselves and their same-age friends, to indulge individualistic desires for leisure, travel and goods, and to create a sexually-appealing, sophisticated style that has status in the world-wide circuit of consumption.

These two positions shoot through both sides of these antiphonal performances, bringing tension to women's perceptions about their own lives and plurality to magazines' discourses. While in general women tend towards rootedness, and the magazines bend towards a globalized culture, I argue that the tension between the two positions is the dynamic that binds them together. The centrifugal force of being unstitched and the centripetal force of being stitched in place result in excitement and confusion that magazines play on and women meet with curiosity and anxiety, making them keen to read the magazines. The degree of tension varies, however: differences in education, region and socio-economic status among the women result in diverse experiences of the local/global tension.

Magazines

The magazines considered in this study are: *Chere*, *Classy*, *Clique*, *Cosmopolitan*, *Elle Japon*, *Frau*, *Nikkei Woman* and *Oggi* (Figure 3.1). This does not exhaust the lifestyle magazines designed for this age group, but represents a number of different publishers who are active in this market niche.

Although *Chere* is not a strong contender in this group, its special survey on 27-year-old single OL or office ladies conveys a standardized magazine image of this group: glamorized secretaries with good incomes but no promotion, who socially and psychologically are unmoored.

> We don't understand love, but it is not that we don't know it. We are not amateurs at work, but we can't be called pros. There are times when our selves can be seen, but still times when people don't see them. 27 is a season when we are neither here nor there. We live in a free age, but sometimes we get swallowed by the

Figure 3.1 Magazine covers: *Cosmopolitan*, *Oggi*,
Classy, and *Frau*

waves of that freedom and lose sight of everything. I would like to
find a silhouette of the future at least until thirty. Now one more
time I want to face this strange age.

(*Chere*, 1993: 4)

Magazines construct women's anxieties, presenting them as unsure and
struggling, enjoying their freedom and the development of their 'selves',
yet unable to gain recognition or acceptance as independent, single
women.

147

Chere idealizes and standardizes a young woman who has delayed marriage to enjoy a life rich with goods, leisure and travel, together with horizontal relationships of friendship and heterosexuality. The description is in selective terms: money and possessions, bodies, sexuality, work and their residence. The average 27-year-old has a yearly income of ¥3,290,000 and savings of ¥2,080,000. She owns nine jackets, sixteen skirts, 23 dresses, eight rings and three watches. In fashion she wants color and 'something like herself'. Half of them spend more than US$100 per month on lessons of some kind. The average OL worries about her body: eighteen per cent think their bust is too small and 21 per cent think their rear is too big. 46 per cent have a boyfriend and report having sex 2.5 times per month; the rest wish they did. 40 per cent of these young women have gone abroad more than four times. Experiencing some freedom, the young single woman wants more. Although 83 per cent live with parents, 45 per cent would like to try living on their own.

Chere presents young women's attitude towards work as ambivalent. About 60 per cent are satisfied with their work and 29 per cent want to get promotions, but 92 per cent have wanted to quit work. Being a woman at work is advantageous because their work is light and they are judged easily, but it is disadvantageous because salaries are low and their opinions are made light of. Almost all have been bothered by the question: 'Aren't you married yet?' but this standardized OL would like to marry by the age of 30.8 and have her first child by 31.6 years of age (*Chere*, 1993:7–54).

In short, the magazine's ideal has light attachments in a young woman's hierarchical spheres of work and family. She wants respect, but not the obligation that goes with it. Her focus is on herself, her sexuality and independence expressed in terms of consumer taste. Marriage and children float on the horizon in the shape of the ideal nuclear family minus cross-generational or cross-gender problems.

This average profile is similar to performances suggested by other magazines for this group. Attention on self through body care and adornment dominates, especially in contrast with magazines for young, married women. Yet there is less emphasis on body care and fashion in these magazines than in those for younger women which carry many how-to articles on make-up and fashion. Gone are the fashion catalogs and what is left are fewer expensive, foreign brands that offer elite sophistication. The magazines invite single women to continue their postponement of marriage and to participate in a high-class global culture (Hannerz 1991). With information from the magazines, readers can imagine themselves as cosmopolitan elites, appealing in the world centers. The elite, cosmopolitan culture that takes shape in these magazines is overwhelmingly western, presented with many English loan words. Several of the magazines for this age group originate in other elite countries with some original articles – *Cosmopolitan* from the U.S., *Elle Japon* from France, and *Oggi* from Italy. The vast majority of models are first-world Caucasians. Japanese single women read interviews with Madonna and Whoopi Goldberg in *Cosmopolitan*. In *Frau* they view Princess Diana in pearls and Jodi Foster in very little. In *Classy* they study Venetian glass.

Magazines teach single women to be actors adept on a varied global stage, travelling with discretion. The magazines even go beyond descriptions of Parisian shops or Mediterranean islands to advice on intimate relations with the people. A Japanese essayist in *Cosmopolitan* (1993:7) characterizes various European men: English men are easy for lunch, but be careful if you marry them – they may turn into Charles; for Greeks, just add olive oil and they'll eat anything; Italian men are hard to care for – meticulous in their dress with mother complexes. *Classy* (1993:36) gives advice on how to act in European pools – to be 'individualistic', but not to take off tops to tan evenly. In *Frau* (1993: 82), a male foreigner warns that 'Japanese women are said to be too serious, but there is safety and manners you can't buy with money' and goes on to caution against thieves, drugs and being mistaken for a whore.

Magazines push an elite global culture with stories and pictures of 'international' single women, both Japanese and foreign. They show Japanese women living, working and studying abroad: a Japanese studying in Paris for a year, her husband left behind; a designer working for Polo Ralph Lauren Japan in New York; an NGO worker in Nepal (*Nikkei Woman* 1993:76, 8). These personal stories are represented as individual agency: having the strength to turn one's life around and start again. The focus is usually on the USA or Europe, but recently articles on the ease of working in trendy Asian cities have also started to appear (Figure 3.2).

Oggi (1993:34–9) weaves a common culture with other single women in the elite cosmopolitan set through pictures of young Parisian and New York City women made familiar with names, ages, and occupations. Japanese women can imagine themselves in a personal metropolis without boundaries as these young women share their clothes and hairstyles, their apartments and their problems at work. In the back pages of the same magazine, world elites of the so-called peripheries also share 'global careers': an airline stewardess from Taiwan, a DJ

Figure 3.2 Elite cosmopolitans
(Courtesy of Singapore Airlines)

from Bangkok, a fashion designer from Seoul. Their hobbies of horseback-riding, golfing, and gourmet-eating match the high-status, western leisure which magazines recommend for Japanese women (*Oggi* 1993:209–219).

The individualized, appealing body is the springboard to catapult women out of their places and groups of enculturation into an elite global culture. A young woman can literally embody signs of global status by buying brand name international goods that affect her 'atmosphere': her appearance, her smell, the feel of her skin. Communication occurs through the adorned body embedded in the international circuit of commodity signs. It can expand into shared entertainment as magazines educate their readers in western movies and music.

In magazines for older single women, the construction of intimate entertainment in an individualized interior becomes part of the search for personal style. Articles on goods such as Venetian glass, or skills such as French cooking, help older single women navigate their ways into a global/personal lifestyle. In the creation of living spaces, more creative hybridization (Hannerz 1991:124) appears with, for example, a triangular-shaped low table with pillows around it on a wooden floor, or a sofa without legs for Japanese-style comfort (see Rosenberger 1992b). The 'exotic' (read inferior) also appears. Young women are shown decorating their low Japanese-style warming tables (*kotatsu*) with batik from Bali or hand-woven cloth from India. Thus, personal identities take shape through the appropriation of foreign goods within a carefully measured understanding of Japan's delicate position between the west, who once conquered Japan, and Asia, whom Japan once conquered.

As part of a safely homogenized global culture, Japanese styles can re-enter as a controlled difference equal to other differences, and refined by foreign users. The origins of products and models become intermixed; Shiseidō cosmetics uses a western model and The Gap chooses a Japanese model. Japanese designers with international reputations are listed in ad-articles with Italian or French designers. In interior decoration magazines in which foreign styles such as Art Deco or Baroque are lined up, Japanesque is often included as well. Thus, the local identity is not lost in this particular formulation of global culture, but it is re-interpreted and narrowly defined, given a stamp of approval within a global system of signs.

The global images of these magazines pose a double movement: firstly, towards engagement with other elite cosmopolitans by developing an individualized, sexualized identity (Evans 1993) and secondly, towards disengagement from older local folk who prefer an identity appropriate to Japanese common sense and hierarchical social relation-ships. For those vested in the local point of view, these movements are potentially destabilizing in a moral sense and decenter the Japanese national identity. Magazines implicitly urge young women to 'unstitch' their desires from the group-oriented social relations of school, work and family and attach them to self-oriented relations with other cosmopolitan elite people. For the culture-makers of the media, these movements shape people whose unrooted, malleable identities respond quickly to the ever-changing looks and meanings of style (Ewen 1988).

An article in *Frau* (1993:86) depicts the spirit of this movement nicely: 'How to have manners to be re-born as a real international person'. An ad in *Cosmopolitan* (1993:33) introduces Espo Inter-national College in Tōkyō where a woman can become 'stylish, natural and well-bred' by studying hair, make-up, western etiquette and cloth-ing style. *Classy* (1993:74) suggests joining a hotel's 'staff system salon' to learn western-style cooking and bed-making; 'change your heart' from a traditional Japanese girl to a global (read western) individual.

One important aspect of becoming unstitched from the local context is the process of becoming sexualized in one's public fashion perform-ance by adorning and adjusting one's body to embody a generalized sexual desire. This desire is ambiguous, attached to self, to the goods that fashion the sexuality, and to the imagined other gazing at self.

Magazines surround their readers with the idea of female sexuality: underplayed, yet undeniably present. Rarely do we see Japanese women in suggestive poses; but foreign models portray sexuality in scant clothing and passionate embraces with men. Foreign-born magazines feature sex in cover articles. For example, *Elle* (1993:18–44) centered on 'Love and sex: the presentiment of a sexy love' with pictures from western movies and reports on sex in Japan, England, France, Germany, Brazil and Korea, in that order. AIDS also gets attention. In contrast, Japanese publishers bury frank talks about sex in the back, less glossy pages of the magazine with manuals on penis education and letters from both sexes on fellatio or orgasms, usually with black-and-white car-toons, the form of much of Japan's pornography. This active interest in sex is frank but contextualized, buried under a glossy front of innocence (Figure 3.3).

Japanese magazines for single women usually avoid showing Japanese women and foreign men together. The occasional men accompanying Japanese models are non-agressive Japanese males posing as escorts. This fosters the image of Japanese young women as independent, but it leaves the international sphere open to sexual fantasy. Becoming

THERE'S NOTHING
LIKE THIS

あなたのキスと
ゴードンジンさえあれば、
あとは何もいらない。

SEX

各国ELLE読者アンケートによる
セックス・リポート

「あなたはセックスをどうとらえていますか」——エル・ジャポンは、
'92年11月5日号の誌上で、他の9カ国のELLEと共に読者アンケートを投げかけた。
これに対し予想をはるかに上回る回答率と反響の数々。
セックスに関する生まなタブーがなくなる一方、エイズの危機が声高に叫ばれる現代、
女性たちは、セックスに対してどのように考え、またどんな悩みを抱えているのか——
各国ELLEのアンケート結果も交え、"現代女性のセックス観"を探ってみた。

Figure 3.3 *Elle* sex report: strategic placement of alcohol ad opposite feature on sex habits around the world
(*Elle Japon*, July 5, 1993)

unstitched as a global-level consumer becomes imbued with sexual desire.

This near-taboo on the representation of Japanese women with foreign men suggests an opposite movement in these magazines, stitching Japanese women back into place. Through an ongoing debate on marriage, magazines maintain single women's anxiety about being independent cosmopolitans who might get shut out of close relations within the Japanese community. In its Japanese version *Cosmopolitan* (1993) asks:

> The marriage slid into before 30 – can you be happy? Marriage is in the air with Masako's wedding. Thinking about the appropriate marriage age. Compromise is unpleasant. People your age are gradually taken care of. What is the marriage period that can make you happy?

The article presents methods to figure out your own marriage time as well as your favorite man's by use of horoscopes. *Frau* (1993:94) suggests to readers that marriage will bring them into the 'elegance' of Japanese history and ritual as it has Masako (the new wife of the Emperor's eldest son) in her private tutoring to enter the Imperial household. Inviting common Japanese women to model themselves after this elite woman, the writers intone: 'Career isn't enough; one needs a sense of beauty and manners . . . It's more than upbringing, it's refinement'. Masako embodies the life cycle for women idealized by these magazines; until 29 she was a highly-educated, independent single with the income and English to cover the world. Yet at 29 she gave it all up for marriage and country, becoming the symbol of proper Japanese femininity as she submitted to the confining traditions of the Emperor's household. As her finery around the wedding time showed, she will continue to be a high-level consumer with an adjusted set of 'needs'.

Classy (1993:36) attempts to offer a middle way between elite cosmopolitan identity and Japanese identity through 'new marriage lifestyles'. Have an 'adult-like style' by studying abroad together in New York. Bring your overseas life into your apartment in Japan with a souvenir-decorated interior. Or, reclaim your pride as a Japanese by decorating in a 'positive Japanese style'. Even *Nikkei Woman* (1993:45) for working women interviews a lovelorn woman who assures readers that 'if you heighten your self, a high quality man will appear'.

Magazines targeting Japanese single women delaying marriage ride on this tension between being individualized, sexualized consumers of the global elite and being Japanese wives and mothers, enmeshed in social relations of enduring emotion and obligation. One of the main themes of 1993 magazines was the enticing independence of living alone, but magazines subtly maintain the theme of loneliness. *Clique* (1993:20–51) features women's residences, showing young women sitting in their rented apartments and advising on floor plans, loan applications, and negotiations.

> Marriage is okay, but I can't give up this ease. I can return anytime, eat anything, no-one complains – this freedom! Sometimes it is lonely, but if I put out energy . . . the song of living alone.

> (*Clique*, 1993:98)

Nikkei Woman (1993:56) advises women that they should 'buy their own place while in their thirties' with a 33-year-old college professor smiling from her resort home porch as proof. Elsewhere, *Nikkei Woman* (1993:102) encourages women emotionally: 'Sad if good weather on Sunday and all alone? Weekend syndrome prescription: find ways of being alone. Get ready for tomorrow. Don't just watch TV, shop, telephone, and sleep. Get used to being alone'.

Articles on work also sustain the ambivalence between identities embedded in company hierarchies and the individual glamour of being an independent working woman. On the one hand, young single women are represented as successful workers in lucrative, if not always high status, positions. Short interviews with women who have started their own company or work out of their home are frequent fillers towards the back of many of these magazines. *Nikkei Woman* invites readers to learn business strategies to climb the corporate ladder. On the other hand, in an addendum to a U.S. article on bad bosses in *Cosmopolitan* (1993:82), the demands of the Japanese hierarchy emerge. Examples of the worst Japanese bosses include one who demanded that his female employees wear mini skirts and another who made his secretary buy train tickets at 5am for his son.

The underside of the bid for independence and individuality emerges when the topics of marriage and work meet. *Chere* (1993:32) sums it up in the word *yokubari*, or greed, that describes the woman who wants both work and marriage. The idea that work becomes a selfish pursuit once one marries and has children lurks behind the scenes. Thus, the tension between being local or global emerges as young women are represented both as fashionable workers and as women with responsibility to raise children.

The push towards re-stitching elite, self-oriented consumers into mainstream other-oriented morality is clear in a lead article in *Frau*

(1993). Middle-aged Japanese intellectuals advise young Japanese women on manners. For example, a woman author complains of young women's long flowing hair that blows into others' faces on the trains. 'They all wear make-up now just like in foreign countries, so you can't tell the difference between students, OL, hostesses and mistresses . . . Young women today simply blame others and don't reflect on themselves.' She suggests that married men cheat on their wives with glamorous OL, but don't divorce because, ultimately, they prefer their wives who can cook and who talk gently (p.16). A male author complains that young women use language that shows lack of knowledge and upbringing. He notes that Masako's friends, interviewed on TV the day of the royal wedding, did not use such language (p.14).

Not only the conservative elite of Japan, but foreigners, too, are held up as paragons to bring wandering Japanese women back into the fold, however. Another male author accuses young Japanese of selfishness because they cling to their lovers even when the lover wants to leave. 'In the individualism of the west, you care for yourself and for the other', recognize the self of your partner and in so doing maintain your own 'self' (p.18). Even oft-maligned Koreans are brought in, made fun of and yet held up for a moral lesson. A male author tells of seeing Koreans eat toast with a knife and fork in Paris; while it was wrong, they didn't make a noise like Japanese girls do when they eat (p.12). The same internationalism that acts as a centrifugal force towards independence and freedom also acts as a centripetal force towards the local moral community. Even the use of Caucasian models distances the sexualized, individualized ideal, making it easier to spurn in the long run.

Young women stand in the nexus of this dynamic tension between invitations to perform as cosmopolitan sophisticates and subtle warnings to return to the Japanese sphere of proper social relations. Indeed, I would propose that it is this very tension and anxiety that magazines play on to sustain their attraction to young single women. As we will see below, young women may approach these magazines with mixed feelings, but because they feel the anxiety of 'being neither here nor there', the tensions raised in the magazines appeal to them. Magazines reproduce and magnify these young women's questions about love, marriage, work, maturity, and freedom.

Specific women get no precise answers. One ultimate question, 'what is right for me?', never will be answered in this medium, for very few women are the 'average' wealthy, highly educated cosmopolitans represented in these magazines. Neither will the other ultimate question, 'why do young women in Japan have these struggles?', be answered because the analysis stops with the ideal, standard individual. Magazines ignore larger answers that require a close look at both local history and the global political economy.

Such an analysis would expose the links between the tensions mentioned above and the contradictions for women in late capitalism. As Evans (1993) suggests, young women are a contested terrain within consumer capitalism. Late twentieth century capitalism calls on women of all classes to take on expanded roles as wage laborers and as consumers. This combination harbors a contradiction because women are first-class citizens as consumers, but usually second class citizens as workers. Furthermore, the roles of procreator and housewife remain proscribed for women by society, usually with heavy state support (Rosenberger 1991a).

> Female sexuality has . . . been the focus of diverse, often contradictory, discourses which contest the residue of procreation and domesticity within a consumer capitalism no longer content with such restricted definitions . . . Still severely proscribed by femininity, female sexuality has nevertheless become active, recreational, material independent, consumerist and consumed, a key site of conflict, resistance and division.
>
> (Evans 1993:41)

In short, magazines capitalize on tensions which they help create through their making of consumer culture, through their own and their sponsors' use of women's cheap labor, and through their compromises with Japanese ruling elders' concern for birth and childraising. Women are vulnerable subjects because they struggle with these contradictions in their everyday lives.

What Are Young Single Women Saying?

In the summer of 1993, I interviewed 56 single women between the ages of 25 and 39.[4] Even in this non-random sample, obtained through introductions from friends and acquaintances, much more variation emerged than in the standard images of women's magazines. They varied by age, region of the country, education, and socio-economic level. Approximately half were from Tōkyō and half from a provincial city in the north. Slightly over half were graduates of four-year universities or had some graduate education, while slightly under half had graduated from high school, vocational school or junior college. They varied in monthly take-home pay from approximately ¥90,000 per month to

¥360,000 per month. Although five were unemployed or in school, of the rest, half got take-home pay of between ¥170,000 and ¥230,000, a quarter got between ¥90,000 and ¥160,000, and a quarter got between ¥250,000 and ¥360,000. The diversity among these women soon de-centers the images propounded by the magazines.

As interviewer, I influenced the presentations of self offered by the interviewees. They knew that I was a Caucasian, American woman in Japan on research, older than they by 10–20 years, a married professional with children. I calculate my effect on their interview performances as pushing them on the one hand towards magazine images of independence and international sophistication, yet also towards images of settled life within a home as well.

Reading magazines

Do these women even read magazines? About half did read fashion or lifestyle magazines, even if only occasionally or when standing in a bookstore, a practice of which Japanese store-owners are quite tolerant. Ten people said they never read magazines at all. Cooking magazines were the next most popular type of magazine, with ten people reading them. After this came weekly news or gossip magazines (seven), work-related magazines (six), interior design magazines (three), news magazines (three), hobby magazines (two) and travel magazines (two) respectively.

Within the sphere of fashion and lifestyle magazines, the women interviewed did not always prefer those targetting single women between 25 and 35. They often stayed with those they had read at younger ages. Among the interviewees, magazines targetting them were mentioned 29 times.[5] However, fashion and lifestyle magazines targetting younger single women were mentioned 31 times.[6] These magazines are comparatively new and not as available in the provincial city as in large urban areas; the majority of women reading magazines for the younger set were from the provinces. The interviewees read popular cooking magazines such as *Orange Page* or *Lettuce Club* designed to appeal to women under 35, but they did not read lifestyle magazines aimed at married women of the same age. Lead articles in the latter magazines such as 'Getting confidence in raising children' (*Mine* 1991), or 'Finding work convenient for a housewife' (*Suteki na Okusan* 1993), address women who have shifted their consumer images towards the localized sphere of family and are enticed towards individuality through home decorating (Rosenberger 1992b).

Most women felt that no appropriate women's magazines existed for them. A 33-year-old Tōkyōite said: 'Not many magazines target women of my age'. A 32-year-old from the provincial city stated: 'I don't read fashion magazines anymore. I did a lot until 23 or 24, but from 30, I stopped buying them. The magazines targetting women in their thirties are for mothers, and the younger ones show campus fashion . . . to get a man.' In contrast, a 30-year-old Tōkyōite who had migrated from the provinces found lifestyle magazines for various ages helpful. 'Sometimes I read *non-no* and *an-an*. I can see women's ways of living. I can improve. I look at *Cosmopolitan* and think "Ah! Women can do this . . ."' A friend sitting nearby, however, simply responded: 'I'm satisfied with life'.

Other women felt no need for fashion or lifestyle magazines. A 29-year-old Tōkyō woman who was quite fashionably dressed, was a high-level consumer, but was searching for a more unique look than magazines offered. She asserted,

> I don't read fashion magazines. I look at people as I walk around town and see who looks cool and find the same kind of clothes. In magazines, everthing has the same look, like uniforms. I want to find things that are like me (*jibun nari*).

A 32-year-old Tōkyō school teacher, who in her dress and words seem to care little for fashion, refused them because she rejected consumerism: 'All the magazines seem alike. It isn't information I want . . . I sew my own clothes in the summer and buy a few suits at bonus time.' Others found themselves wearing either work uniforms or T-shirts, or had lost interest in magazines because they no longer read them with friends.

In sum, not a high proportion of women read the magazines targetting this delayed-marriage group. Very few were enthusiastic about the magazines, though many felt an ambiguous attraction to them.

Travel

In relation to the emphasis on western places and items in the women's magazines, the interviewees found travel appealing, but had travelled less than the magazine images. A full one-third of them had never travelled overseas, compared with thirteen per cent in the *Chere* profile; this had a regional bent as only six of them were from Tōkyō, but level of education was not important. Another third had travelled overseas once. While in the *Chere* profile 40 per cent had travelled abroad more than four times, only seven of my interviewees had.

Interviewees' perceptions of destinations conformed to the hierarchical images projected in magazines, travel ads and brochures (Rosenberger 1993). They preferred elite western countries of the center for serious travel, though they used the Pacific islands or Asia for relaxation and cheap shopping. Europe was the most popular destination, Pacific islands next, with the U.S. and the four Tigers tying for third.[7] The Pacific islands, Japan's backyard, are for relaxation and fun with friends. The four Tigers and the U.S. are for buying name brand goods. The eating is good in Hong Kong and Singapore. Europe is for culture, going to art museums and seeing the villages, the more experienced travellers extolling the characteristics of the people as models for their lives. Interviewees described Italians as 'proud . . . even the old people look good. They are individualistic, fashionable, and they enjoy life.'

Although the U.S. is a frightening place to go because of crime, many idolized its image of emancipation and individualism. A 31-year-old lab assistant from the provincial city admired the fashion in the U.S., using it as a way to criticize Japanese conformity to high-class fashion.

> In San Francisco I was amazed at how roughly the people dressed. It looked cool. I thought this is really individualistic. I would like to dress like that rather than following Japanese brand fads. It made me feel empty – here, what is there? Japanese are all twisted one way and don't look at their own country's things. Like in Hawaii, I felt, 'Are there only Japanese here?' They were all dressed in the same form.

Although a few admitted to shopping – 'we are women, so if there is shopping, we will do it' – many argued that art museums, sightseeing or beach relaxation were their purposes in travel. The interviewees wanted to actually grasp the international flavor and images, rather than the goods themselves.

Interviewees perceived their Japanese companions as important in their travel experiences, something receiving little comment in magazines highlighting international goods and sights. A third of the interviewees travelled with friends or to see friends, and five with work friends on company funds. One 34-year-old from the provinces had travelled abroad seven times as 'goal-in' bonuses from Recruit Co., owner of the golf and ski resort where she worked. Two older singles (37 and 39) from Tōkyō went to Italy almost every year on their own or with family members, and were both trying to learn Italian. Eight women had journeyed abroad more independently for extended study or homestays, but for the most part, the international adventure was one that simultaneously rooted them more deeply in horizontal connections within Japanese society.

Aligning more closely with the magazine's images, some interviewees used travel to gain independence, even to resist their parents' ideas. Three women used their savings against their parents' wishes and studied abroad: English in England, piano in Switzerland and conservative religion in New York. The nurse who went to England said: 'I wouldn't be the self I am if I hadn't gone. It helped me mature.' A 29-year-old woman from Tōkyō resisted her mother's advice on a joint trip to Hong Kong when she bought a deep purple jacket she wore during the interview. Her mother, who lived in the provinces, had said: 'It's so loud. You shouldn't walk around in it. Please don't buy that, at least that.'

Despite the magazine image of a standard consumer with extra money to spend, low incomes stopped many interviewees from travelling as they wished. A 30-year-old secretary from Tōkyō said: 'I yearn for travel. I want to take it easy, but I don't have any money. Travel is an escape from present reality. I want to go but I can't.' A 27-year-old secretary in the provincial city making US$1000 a month studied Spanish once per week, but had no possibility of going to Spain. A telephone operator of 32 in the City Hall up north said shortly: 'I have neither free time nor money to travel. I go to see my sister in Saitama.' In short, most interviewees had acquired the desire to participate in the cosmopolitan images of travel, but achievement of that reality remained a dream in many of their lives.

Marriage

Discussions of marriage bring tension into the magazine discourses; did the interviewees show a similar tension between independence and marriage? In response to whether they wanted to marry or not, the overwhelming response was affirmative; they wanted and expected to marry. Marriage with the right partner was attractive: 'it'll be enjoyable'; 'having a husband and children is good for a woman'; 'it's a natural thing you should do'. If left single, many worry about being alone when sick or old. About a quarter of the women responded with a 'yes, but' answer, however, indicating that the marriage decision was not easy for them. They added conditions such as 'if there is a good person', 'if I have an *en* (special connection) with someone', or 'if I can continue my work'.

Although there is little mention of children in lifestyle magazines for this single age group, many were more enthusiastic about having children than marrying. Only four said they definitely did not want children, either because they wanted to work or because they were older. Another four were not too positive about children, but felt that if their husbands wanted a child, they would cooperate. Thus most expected to marry and have children, much like the standard OL in the *Chere* profile. Yet their unwillingness to compromise should not be ignored because in Japan, the introduction (*omiai*) system allows anyone to meet and marry someone if they simply want to marry.

The world of boyfriends was farther away for this group than the standardized profile. Only a third had boyfriends as compared with half in *Chere*. Most said that the relationship had not gotten to the point of talk about marriage yet. Like the *Chere* OL, most wished they had a boyfriend. In that sense their lives reverberated with the atmosphere of fantasized desire for sexuality in magazines. A difference for many was that they were not working so hard to be sexually attractive in appearances, conveying a neat but modest appearance.

Tension existed around marriage and centered on two areas: worry about withdrawing from work and 'society', and anxiety about finding an appropriate marriage partner. Because marriage usually occurs with the intent of having children soon after, the question of continuing work after marriage and childbirth loomed large. A little over a quarter said they wanted to continue working no matter what, and had to find a man who would agree. This group included a mixture of regions and educational levels. About half hedged: seven would change to less demanding work; six felt it would be difficult with children; five said it would depend on the husband's transfers and wishes; six had decided it would not be necessary to continue to work. In short, the majority of women were willing to compromise on this point, although very few wanted to disappear into a household.

These women were very similar to the *Chere* image in the percentage of those who were satisfied with their work – 60 per cent in the magazine were well-satisfied and 57 per cent in my sample found meaning (*yarigai*) in their work. Among the interviewees, their meaning in work stemmed from connection with other people: 'I feel useful to people', or 'I meet various people'. A remark of one 25-year-old OL was telling, however, when she said: 'Work would have a different meaning to us if we knew we would get promotions like men.'

All the women saw marriage as a turning point that would change their working lives. A 29-year-old university graduate looking for work in Tōkyō said: 'It's scary to think of being in the house not knowing the movements of society. My friends seem happy at home but . . . ' A 28-year-old supervisor in a grocery store in Tōkyō concentrated more on her future role: 'I would like to work some, but maybe not full-time. I want to be a good wife.' A 29-year-old conference planner in Tōkyō felt she had little choice:

> I would quit when the kids were little. I can't do this work and put them in full time day care . . . even if I do get fulfillment. I want to care for children until three or four years of age. After that if I can return, I will. It would be too busy; my body and heart would collapse.

This future plan influenced her to stretch pre-marriage years of hard work and hard play – in this case, diving in Okinawa and Bali.

A 33-year-old dentist from northern Hokkaidō studying in Tōkyō worried about the prospects of continuing her career:

> My male friends say it's okay if the wife works, but you must take care of the home. It isn't just economics. Men dentists who are practicing come home and they want lights on. Men want their own wives to cut the vegetables. They want their wife making a life.

Many of the women saw marriage and children as a cut-off point after which they would change their pace and find a different job that would replace status and money with personal meaning. The work they imagined usually was oriented towards serving other people. For example, a 32-year-old who worked in a bank in Tōkyō hoped to switch to art therapy with her own studio. Several wanted to work with the handicapped. These women looked forward to this chance to change their careers; a few older ones had already changed or were actively looking for more satisfying work without waiting for the economic support of a husband. They did not enjoy jobs with little responsibility or personal meaning, nor did they like late hours. Some had quit because of difficulties with superiors.

This job change linked with the idea voiced by some that women mature 'as women' after marriage and children, meaning that they become less selfish and more nurturing. A 32-year-old high school teacher commented: 'From outside, you aren't mature if you aren't married. It seems natural if you marry. The students think so, too. They even offer to introduce me to men sometimes.' They did not wish to become like women superiors, judged by them or others as narrow and unbending, intent on details. Thus, most conceived of marriage as a decisive break that would stitch them more firmly into the dominant Japanese expectations for women. They accepted this, though some with regrets. As we have seen, magazines reinforce both the the regrets and the expectations.

Overwhelmingly, interviewees believed that their own money would decrease with marriage, except those who planned to continue working and those with little income now. As housewives, however, some pointed out that they would control more money, except that it would be used for different purposes. They thought that free time, too, would decrease. Most presented a neutral front about this; three were depressed at this prospect, suggesting they might delay marriage even farther, and seven looked forward to more time with their partners or children.

A second source of tension was whether an appropriate marriage partner could be found. These women did not want a 'husband' (*shujin* or *danna*) with connotations of master; they wanted a partner (*patonā*). In the *Chere* magazine survey, the preferred traits in a husband were kind, honest, interesting, masculine and reliable, in that order. Interviewees' responses were more complicated, emphasizing husbands' emotional investment. A 29-year-old elementary teacher in the provincial city described it well: 'I want us to be able to respect each other. I don't like people who want to be indulged. I want us to stimulate each other. I want him to understand my work and I will respect his work.' About 40 per cent mentioned some form of mutual support in which wives received as well as gave understanding, respect and care. About 20 per cent preferred someone with whom they could relax and another 20 per cent wanted a person who was not dependent and had his own goals. A few mentioned that they did not want someone who was a 'straight worker', always busy and gone. Several of the poorer women remarked on economic security and four wanted 'someone they could depend on'. In sum, the majority of women were looking for a companion who held up his end of the relationship.

The conclusion is ambiguous. Women do carry tension around their worries about work and partners, tallying closely with tensions carried by magazines. Marriage was a topic that most interviewees wanted to talk about and, if anything, they downplayed their worries. A cloud would come over their faces, or a quick remark such as 'this is my biggest worry', and then a positive face reemerged. Yet overall, the interviewees did not communicate as high a degree of anxiety about marriage as the magazine articles would indicate. Women were firm in their resolutions to live life fully before marriage and to wait for the right person. Most expected that they would marry one day, and counselled themselves to let life take its course.

Interviewees were conscious that a sizable portion of the tension around marriage came from outside, especially up to 30 or 31 years of age. Almost half of the women felt pressure from their parents to marry and many felt some from relatives and neighbors. This is an aspect not dwelt upon by magazines, where family members are generally absent. Some parents were quite frank, telling their daughters: 'Think of your age! How old do you think you are?' 'Why don't you marry?' 'Isn't there anyone?' Other parents expressed the wish 'to see our grandchild's face' and hoped that their daughter would have the happiness of a husband and family. One woman in the provincial city had become 'a little mother-in-law' to her brother's new wife who had joined the family and felt that she should marry soon because she was a burden. A 30-year-old in the provinces had refused several introductions, but was thinking she might give up her teaching job for the next one. A 31-year-old OL at a large company reported resisting her mother's pressure: 'It's my life, so let me alone.' Her mother cried and said: 'Though I worked so hard to bring you up!' Most tried to avoid the subject at home, but such pressure increased the tension for women, even if they were satisfied with their lives.

The tension about marriage seemed less keen for many over 31 years of age. Pressures and expectations from parents and relatives had lightened as women became resigned, so that older single women could define their ideas about marriage at a more personal level. Although a few had actively spurned marriage, most simply had not met the right man yet. Some were in a hurry because they wanted to have children, but even those who mentioned that they would like to marry tomorrow philosophized that if they felt too rushed (*aseru*), it wouldn't work, so they were going at their 'own pace'.

Just as most had not chosen a career, most had also not chosen a single life, but having fallen into a career and a freer lifestyle, they saw its value. Seven of the women, all 32 years old or above, had become somewhat indifferent: 'I don't not want to marry, but it doesn't matter that much if I don't.' A 32-year-old translator in Tōkyō had passed an era of intense introductions (*omiai*) with prospective mates, and now said: 'I've proven my capabilities and am interested in my work. I am testing what I can do as a person.' A 38-year-old free-lance magazine writer in Tōkyō had been delighted at the feeling of freedom when she decided not to marry at 27. She had dived into her work with relish. Now she said: 'I mustn't forget that feeling of emancipation. It was a shock.

Then I realized I was 32. I didn't decide to be unmarried. It just happened. So now if I have a chance . . . I would particularly like to know what it feels like to be pregnant.' As I left her office however, she said she was leaving to do a story on Club Med in the south Pacific. 'With this work, will I ever be able to commit myself to marriage?', she laughed.

Only two of the interviewees were no longer interested in the marriage debate. A 37-year-old woman who had gotten promoted in an advertising agency in the provincial city said clearly: 'I don't care if I marry. I am making lots of women friends who are quite close. My friends and I talk of making a home together when we are old. My mother still calls with profiles of men to introduce me to, but I say, "Just give it up, mother."' The other woman was a 37-year-old from Tōkyō. 'I have always felt doubts about the marriage system in Japan. The idea that the woman always makes dinners . . . My mother never says good things about marriage.' In sum, these older women appeared to be thinking through marriage on their own terms and were less vulnerable to magazines' agitations. Those considering non-marriage no longer fit the magazines' norm.

Lastly, women carry with them externally imposed conditions for marriage that rarely get recognition in magazines, but nonetheless maintain tensions that magazines can play on. A full quarter of the women needed to consider caring for their parents in old age because they were only children or one of several sisters. Because parents often receive care sometime in their lives in the home of one child, this responsibility would not allow marriage to a first son with similar responsibilities. The field of men was significantly narrowed even though, in most cases, the woman's parents did not expect to formally adopt her husband as an heir with their name as in the past. These pressures to care for parents in old age relate to deep emotional relationships as well as obligations; they are not so easily brushed aside as magazine images pretend. Many women delay introducing their boyfriends to parents until they have determined to marry, because they feel parents will interfere if conditions are not right and know persistence may be difficult. In one case, a 32-year-old telephone operator in the provinces had several difficult conditions: her parents wanted to formally adopt in her husband as an heir; she wanted to continue work without transferring for a husband; and her hands were somewhat crippled. Such a woman does not appear in the magazines.

In sum, women were quite aware of the demands that marriage would make upon them as women. Their words revealed both doubts and hopes around marriage, much like the tensions the magazines played on. But most foresaw a long-term resolution of that tension in the next stage of life. Many gave merit to the characteristics of feminine maturity that were associated with marriage and children. The vast majority of them did not express any wish to change the demands of marriage, but felt they must be resigned to them. Their resistance lay not in trying to change the institution of marriage, but in having a long time to enjoy themselves and work before marriage. In this sense, their attitude was quite similar to that implied in the magazines: make an individual adjustment, but do not challenge the basic structures of society.

Conclusion

How, then, do we characterize the antiphonal performances of women's magazines and young women in their everyday lives? In some ways the performances do reverberate and communicate with each other. First, magazines and young women exchange similar concerns with independent cosmopolitan sophistication. Young women want to escape being stitched into place, if only temporarily, as much as the magazines want to support that escape. Second, performances on both sides express tensions around the expected transition from present enjoyment of single life and future commitment to married life. The questions and uncertainties of these Alice-like women vibrate with the never-ending debates of the Wonderland-like magazines. The exchange of performances as global elites takes place as if aware of itself as a story inside a story; both women and magazines know the storyline will return to 'real life', even as the drama of shape-changing styles seems to overwhelm past or future. Even the magazines know that, ultimately, they owe their existence to the modern culture of technology and the social system that supports it.

Yet for all the excitement of being unstitched in magazines' Wonderland, women's performances ultimately take place above ground where sisters, mothers and future children await. The magazines respond only to selective aspects of young women's lives, reducing them to individualized bodies much like Alice. The lives of real women are more complicated – emotionally intertwined with social relations that magazines can conveniently ignore. Although magazines mainly emphasize ties with selves, friends and boyfriends, women continue to relate to parents, work superiors, and past teachers and mentors who live on within them. On the one hand, the tension is less than the magazines suggest, because at some level most are sympathetic to the dominant, other-oriented social system to which they became habituated as they grew up. Young women also have groups of friends with whom they share their leisured single life and dream of or dread the years to come.

On the other hand, the tension is keenly felt by women, while magazines only flirt with the tension to nurture consumers. Sooner or later, women will either have children or not, satisfy parents or not, be perceived as mature or not, care for elders or not. Furthermore, the choice is not so clear-cut as I have drawn it in this chapter, a text that also has reduced young women's experiences. A multiplicity of discourses surrounds women, and the contradictions described here come not only from magazines, but from government, family and friends, too. Even if they decide to marry, the contradictions between playing leading and supporting roles of housewife, worker, and consumer continue to demand tension-filled performances.

Although young women take on the roles of elite, leisure-minded consumers when they can, they always compromise. Some do so because they do not have the incomes of the standard OL or because they live in the provinces. Miyanaga (1991) suggests that Japanese young people integrate the discourses of individualism and mainstream collectivism into a middle way of 'passive individualism' in which they do not completely commit themselves to institutional groups, but keep themselves protected within small groups of friends. They do not bring individuality into institutions, but neither do they fully integrate into institutional groups. I would add that this requires compartmentalization of life, a conscious contextualization in which most Japanese are well-trained (Tobin 1992a, Rosenberger 1992a). This indicates, as do my findings, that Japanese young women commit fully neither to individualized, sexualized consumerism, nor to the institutions of work or family. Even in the future, they may not be as devoted to family as their mothers were. Many of these women will shape their lives with multiple positions, shifting between practices and ideas of the dominant morality and of the 'selfish' world described in the magazines. The magazines discussed here also produce in a paradoxical or multiple manner; although they will live or die with the investment of consumers in changing global tastes, they must also integrate the discourses of Japanese culture with western-born consumerism. The middle way of contextualization works for both of them through the dividing up of the life cycle into stages, with different sets of relationships and different styles of individualism and consumerism in each. Their antiphonal performances work, then, to a point, as their tensions build on each other. Yet, while magazines ultimately depend on Alice wandering with open curiosity through Wonderland, women seem to know they will finally rely on people like Alice's sister sitting by the tree. The question is, what is she reading?

NOTES

This chapter has been based on the following magazines:

Chere 1993 July, Tōkyō: PHP Kenkyū.
Classy 1993 August, Tōkyō: Kōbunsha.
Clique 1993 June 20, Tōkyō: Magazine House.
Cosmopolitan 1993 July 20, Tōkyō: Shūeisha.
Elle Japon 1993 July, Tōkyō.
Frau 1993 June 22, Tōkyō: Kōdansha.
Mine 1991 May 10, Tōkyō: Kōdansha.
Nikkei Woman 1993 July, Tōkyō: Nihon Keizai Shinbunsha.
Oggi 1993 July, Tōkyō: Shōgakukan
Suteki na Okusan 1993 July, Tōkyō: Shufu to Seikatsusha.

1 While in 1970, 65 per cent of women married in the first half of their twenties, 26 per cent in the second half, and four per cent in their thirties, in 1989, 41 per cent married in the first half of their twenties, 44 per cent married in the second half and ten per cent in their thirties. In 1990, 40.8 per cent of women travelling abroad were in their twenties. In 1990, the birth rate was 1.54; 44 per cent had one child, while 37 per cent had two children (Bando 1992:6, 81, 60).
2 In the 90s, with the marriage of Princess Masako at 29 and the widespread knowledge that the average marriage age is rising, this ideal age for marriage has loosened somewhat.
3 A globalized culture would include many more aspects, most particularly integration in a division of labor that is global in scope, with service workers and managers in countries of the center and assemblers and low-level service workers in peripheral countries. Located in the center, these women are part of the elite side of a globalized culture, able to choose from a selection of high-priced goods, to work in 'clean' jobs, and to maintain control over their sexuality.
4 24 women were between 25 and 29; 27 women between 30 and 34, and five were between 35 and 39. 26 were from Tōkyō and 30 from the northern city. 32 had graduated from a four-year university or had some graduate education (five) and 24 had graduated from high school, vocational school or junior college.
5 These magazines included: *Cosmopolitan, 25 Ans, Classy, Nikkei Woman, Le Coeur, Hanako, Crea, Frau, Clique, Elle Japon, Marie Claire, Ryūkō Tsūshin*, ranked from most to least mentioned.
6 These magazines included *With, More, an-an, JJ, non-no, CanCam. With* and *More*, which target the 22 to 25 age group, were mentioned by far the most often.
7 Pacific islands include Bali and Hawaii; the four Tigers include Hong Kong, Singapore, Taiwan and Korea, with Hong Kong and Singapore as the more popular destinations.

4

ENVIRONMENTALISM SEEN THROUGH JAPANESE WOMEN'S MAGAZINES

Lise Skov

'Women's magazines are a mirror reflecting women's culture,' says Inoue Teruko in one of her studies of Japanese women's magazines (1985:80). It is, of course, only a qualified truth, but here I will leave aside a possible critique and take the statement as my starting point for an exploration of, firstly, the way in which this women's culture is transformed through a flow of commercial trends and, secondly, the way in which women's culture relates to the wider culture of which it is a part. In this I am inspired by Ulf Hannerz's discussion of cultural complexity (1992), and, following him, I use the term subculture to describe women's culture not necessarily to imply a marginal or subordinate culture, but simply a segment of a larger Japanese culture.

I will present a reading of the way in which young women's magazines have dealt with the issue of environmentalism in advertising, editorials and advertorials. Magazines will be analyzed in the light of recent political debates over the environment in order to produce a holistic view of the various, often contradictory, factors that have contributed to the increased interest for environmentalism in women's media in recent years. The focus is on magazines for young unmarried women from their teens to their late twenties, and I have read through most of the widely available magazines for these age groups which were published in 1990 when environmentalism made a hit in women's magazines, and the years following the phenomenon which the Japanese press named an 'ecology boom'.

Given the heightened media attention to the issue, it is hardly surprising to find that often there was a discrepancy between the image of environmental care which certain institutions sought to promote, on the one hand, and any actual steps taken to protect the environment, on the other. The Ministry of Construction, for example, displayed its devotion to nature by sponsoring the International Flower and Greenery Exposition

170

(abbreviated *Hanahaku*) in Ōsaka, at the same time as planning the construction of an airport on Ishigaki Island which would lead to the destruction of one of the last healthy coral reefs in Okinawa (Holliman 1990:284). For their part, women's magazines, and to a lesser extent men's magazines, featured headlines such as 'Ecological summer' (Figure 4.1) and 'We love the Mother Earth', but references to actual environmental politics were few and far between. Rather, ecology excelled as a style, apparently detached from the problems that had given birth to the trend.

The translation of environmental concern into consumer culture has by no means been exclusive to Japan. In late 1989, for example, a number of Paris high fashion designers devoted their spring-summer 90 collections to the environment – either literally, in the titles of the collections, or in colour and style. From then until today, men's and women's magazines from various countries have taken up issues of environmentalism, and designers of different nationalities have not only donated parts of their income to environmental movements, but also worked to develop less polluting production methods and explore the possibilities of recycling. The diffusion of environmentalism into consumer culture is thus something close to a global process.

We may note in passing that this seems to be perfectly complemented by some environmental movements' gradual mutation into profit-making organisations. Greenpeace, in particular, with its keen attention to media effects, seems to be more similar to a transnational corporation than to our notion of a social movement, and *Der Spiegel* (38/1991) has even described Greenpeace as a 'money machine', dubbing the movement 'The McDonald's of the environmental scene'.

What makes Japan outstanding in this global process of consumer cultural change seems to be no more than the fact that environmental concern was adopted by the media in a very immediate and thorough manner, thereby creating an ecology *boom*. Whereas parallel changes in most western countries were on their way for a long time, starting as understated displacements in the margins of consumer culture and gradually moving to popular brands such as Esprit and the Body Shop, environmentalism in Japan was embraced by the commercial media as early as April 1990, when the department store Marui wrote 'ecology' in enormous letters down the front of its multi-storeyed building in Shinjuku, in central Tōkyō.

April 22 1990 was the first 'Earth Day', organised by an association of American environmental movements as a global commemoration of the environmental crisis. But whereas Earth Day in most western coun-

Figure 4.1 Elle Japon intoning the trend of the season
(May 1990)

tries was marked by environmental demonstrations, in Japan it was celebrated by the launching of a torrent of so-called ecology products, many of which had little or no positive impact on the environment. An example of this is Suntory brewery's Earth Beer, on the earth-coloured labels of whose bottles was written 'Suntory is thinking about the earth'. In terms of sales, the new product was successful, in spite of the fact that neither bottles nor cans were recyclable. Nor were labels, in spite of their frayed eco look, made of recycled paper. Actually nothing was recycled or recyclable in the big ecology tent in downtown Tōkyō that Suntory had put up to serve Earth Beer and snacks in order to celebrate Earth Day. So, while Suntory supposedly was thinking about the earth, we might ask what this *Bier und Boden* thinking was really about.

Upon closer inspection, it turned out that the only environmental measure in the whole Earth Beer campaign was the change of the metal ring to a so-called pop-top used to open a beer can. Previously, a Japanese beer can had been opened by pulling a little ring attached to a triangular piece of metal which was then torn out of the can to make a hole through which the beer could pour. The novelty was that the ring now would press down a little piece of metal, still attached to the lid, into the can to make a hole. The ring of the Earth Beer could thus not be thrown away separately from the can. The reason why Suntory promoted this as environmentalism was that small pieces of metal, thrown away in the gutter, were washed from the sewers into the rivers where – it was known – fishes would die if they swallowed them. Without going into a detailed criticism of this particular campaign, we can say that there is a problem of scale between the 'save a fish today' approach to environmentalism and the huge media promotion that accompanied it. 'The image that shows that you are aware of the environment is more important than the awareness itself', stated an ambivalent headline in the *Japan Economic Journal* (1990a) in the early months on the boom, when market analysts took the opportunity to calm potential advertisers in the industry by assuring them that all this talk about ecology would not undermine the consumer market.

In order to understand the ecology boom, we must look at the complex interplay of factors which went into its making. Some of these factors have to do with the way in which Japanese media persistently seek to stage and control consumer culture, whereas others are related to environmental politics at both national and international levels. During the late 80s and early 90s, the need to protect the environment became a key issue for a number of government institutions and large industrial corporations, as well as, of course, for environmental movements operating in Japan.

Most of these background factors, however, were hardly visible in women's magazines at the time when features on global warming, animal testing or other environmental issues were most notable for their absence. While presenting ecology as the theme of the season, magazines stuck to their well-tried formulae of personal issues among which ecology was a name given to a new style for women to shape their appearance. The genealogy of the ecology boom *was* carefully scrutinized, but primarily in terms of its connection to previous trends, as is clear from *Elle Japon*'s depiction of ecology as a tree, accompanying a lengthy analytical editorial (Figure 4.2).

In this chapter I will scratch the glossy surfaces of women's magazines to catch a glimpse of what was behind the ecology boom. In this, I will attempt to create a coherence of layers of meaning under layers of meaning, in order to trace the delicate conditioning of political and economic trends in the realm of Japanese women's consumption.

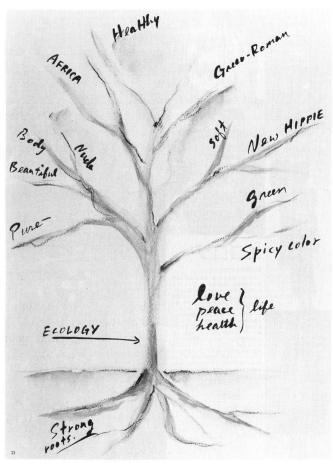

Figure 4.2 The genealogy of ecology
(*Elle Japon*, May 1990)

A 'Boom-based Society'

The first question to be asked here is why the blending of consumption and environmentalism turned into an ecology boom in Japan when, in most western consumer societies, they merged in a much more gradual process? In order to answer this we must examine the term boom (*būmu*), which in Japanese is a popular loanword used to describe economic as well as cultural trends.

Japanese consumer culture of the 1980s and early 90s has been characterized by a rapid successive turnover of trends. Advertising designs, fashion colours, styles of consumer goods have been replaced regularly with new designs, colours and styles – leaving a carefully co-ordinated imprint, not only on the media, but also, for example, on uniforms worn by supermarket shop assistants and petrol station attendants, pencil cases bought by high school students, and dishes consumed in coffee shops. The fashionable Japanese wears clothes that are brand-new, impeccably clean, carefully ironed; and whole wardrobes have been discarded when the basic colour in fashion changed from blue to black to brown, or back again. The abrupt and all-encompassing cycle of Japanese fashions thus provides us with a model of the boom.

This was certainly the trajectory of the ecology boom. During the late spring and summer of 1990, a wide variety of consumer goods from cosmetics and fashion garments to shoes and jewellery, by way of detergents, cars, cordless telephones and Kodak film, were advertised with reference to the environment. This changed towards the beginning of 1991 when environmental movements had manifested their criticism of a number of products which had employed gratuitous references to environmental protection, and when environmental problems were increasingly being addressed as a political issue. At that time the trend was both revived and rechannelled so that ecology became a favourite theme of, surprisingly, Japanese finance. In the following years mountain rivers, wild forests, and tropical fishes were used repeatedly both in domestic and international advertising for Japanese investment banks. In the same period women's magazines continued to present ecology features, but in contrast to the previous all-encompassing adoption of ecology for just about everything, these tended to deal with gardening or outdoor wear.

One side-effect of successive booms is the creation of a strong sense of the here-and-now – which, at least to some extent, dispenses with the content and causality of what happens to be in style in a particular year. Indeed, the Japanese word boom refers to more than consumer trends:

environmental problems, economic fluctuations, political issues, cultural debates – along with television series, writers and models – have been popularized and then forgotten according to the same temporal logic. This has led one scholar to go so far as to argue that Japan is in fact a 'boom-based society' (Yoshimoto 1989:9).

According to Yoshimoto (1989:9), 'the boom artificially creates a new difference, which is exploited through the process of massive commodification, and is over when mass commodification makes it impossible for that particular difference to function as difference any longer. It is followed by another boom then, but this new boom based on a different kind of difference has to be over soon, too'. The temporal structure of the boom pushes trend-setters (in the widest sense of the term) to choose among an indefinite variety of potential 'differences' to single out one 'difference', such as the global environmental crisis, exaggerate it, and project it back onto society. When Yoshimoto talks about artificial differences, I do not take it to refer to something that does not exist, but to the fact that differences are intentionally frozen, packaged and marketed.

Yoshimoto's article deals with the way in which scholarship in Japan is subsumed into intellectual mass fashions. He is particularly concerned with the way in which, in the late 80s, the concept of postmodernism boomed and disappeared without even leaving an analysis of what the postmodern condition might mean in a Japanese context. Yoshimoto regrets the absence of barriers between consumer culture and academic culture when, in the west, academic culture tends to contain a more or less pronounced element of anti-commercialism, enabling it to treasure its relative autonomy vis-à-vis consumer trends. The relatively unhindered flow between subcultures in Japan is also characteristic of the way in which environmental issues spread from international politics and environmental movements to consumer culture.

A similar point is made by Moeran concerning the use of keywords in Japanese popular culture. Keywords are defined as conceptually dense and lexically predictable terms used pervasively in specific cultural domains (Moeran 1989:55–75). In his analysis of certain Japanese keywords such as *seishin* (spirit) and *kokoro* (heart), Moeran finds that, in contrast to England where subcultures of arts, sports or nationalism tend to use sets of relatively exclusive keywords, in Japan the same relatively large number of core keywords are used in many different contexts from media coverage of high school baseball to art markets, by way of anthropological debates over Japanese culture. According to him, such semantic condensation bespeaks cultural integration. It thus seems that we are dealing with a kind of cultural homogeneity in the sense that keywords spread evenly throughout Japan. Of course, keywords such as ecology or postmodernism do not belong to the core of keywords. At the height of their respective booms, they may pervade large segments of Japanese culture for a short period, but they then begin to recede into more specific uses, signifying that the trend is on its wane. In this way, pervasive consumer trends apparently support the idea that Japan is a mass society organized according to a temporal logic.

But upon closer inspection, the ecology boom also seems to contradict the notion of cultural homogeneity, for even though women's magazines featured headlines on ecology, they inscribed the keyword in a discourse totally different from those of environmental movements and national politics. Hence the eco boom also delivers a corrective counter-image of pervasive cultural compartmentalization in contemporary Japan – in which women's consumer culture has a particularly ambivalent status. While women are largely excluded from issues of politics and power, they act as an avantgarde intoning new issues which the whole of society will have to face in the future. As discussed in the Introduction to this book, this was discovered in Japanese market surveys, conducted in the 80s, which found that women were 'ahead' of men in practically all cultural matters (HILL 1987:9–15). But whether women's position as trend-setters was accompanied by increased influence on society remains a moot point.

It is important to note also that the ambivalent homogeneity-cum-compartmentalization of a 'boom-based society' is not synonymous with consensus. On the contrary, the ongoing competition to define significant keywords is in itself an arena for cultural struggles over contested meanings, struggles which may well further fuel the popularity of the word. To illustrate this point with an example from the political arena, we can go back to the time leading up to the 1992 UN conference on Environment and Development in Rio de Janeiro, also known as the Earth Summit. At that time it was clear that the Japanese government intended to invest heavily in environmental support for third world countries (with the prospect of getting substantial returns), and government institutions were competing to put out environment programmes so that they would be rewarded with increased funds. Key players in this were, on the one hand, the Ministry for International Trade and Industry (MITI) – hoping that the environment would provide the vehicle for it to get back into the central position it had occupied in staging Japanese economic development in the 70s – and on the other, the Ministry of Finance, which had tabled a bill for green taxes as a

LISE SKOV

means of increasing its own funds in a way that would go down well with the Japanese public. Other government institutions which used the concern for ecology to promote themselves were: Japan's Overseas Economic Co-operation, the main agency for approving loan aid which was criticized for not monitoring the environmental impact of projects as it was supposed to; and the Environment Agency, which had been marginalized throughout the 80s after its controlling functions had been taken away from it. Former Prime Minister Takeshita took an unexpected interest in the environment, and even suggested that the Environment Agency be upgraded to a ministry. Rumour had it that this was a plot on his part to get back into power – but if that was his plan, he certainly was not successful (Rosario 1992b).

The struggles over the meaning of ecology that went on in young women's media were, however, far removed from such political intrigues. Such magazines as *non-no*, *Elle Japon*, *More*, *Classy* and *Spur*, which promoted the ecology theme from 1990 onwards, gradually began to present the issue of political action, but mainly through suggestions for saving water by skipping the early morning shower (*asashan*), or by discussions of whether or not to wear fur – in other words, by focussing on individual readers' responsibility to exercise the right consumer choices. Even though (as we shall see) environmental movements certainly influenced what we might call commodity aesthetics, women's magazines did not lend them a voice. On the backdrop of the seemingly homogenizing effect of the ecology boom, the boundaries between politics and women's culture were thus simultaneously crossed and reinforced.

Ecology Boom 1990

Commercial events, such as a high fashion collection or the Ōsaka Flower Expo (*Hanahaku*), are usually produced in a process that begins two to three years before the event actually takes place. The same goes for media trends, which are designed to coordinate product development and advertising campaigns into what is to become the current 'mood'. Preparations for the ecology boom thus point back in time to the way in which the environment had increasingly become a political issue during the 1980s.

In the latter half of the decade especially, it had become clear that deforestation, desertification, unsustainable agricultural practices, air and water pollution, global warming, and ozone depletion were environmental problems which were globally linked, and which had to be

178

addressed through internationally coordinated efforts. During that period, a number of international conferences had been held in order to create international consensus over these issues. It was, however, also clear that environmental problems were – and are – so serious that potentially they bring into question the very notion of economic growth and development which had created them. The media have reported global environmental issues with some confusion, often resulting in either apocalyptic anxiety or total scepticism. This reflects both the complexity of causal links between any single sources of pollution and the destruction of the environment, and the fact that the sciences that deliver data for this debate themselves have vested interests in sustained economic development.

The discovery of the so-called hole in the ozone layer over the Antarctic in 1985, however, generated a widespread sense of urgency, which eventually resulted in the 'Montreal Protocol on Substances that Deplete the Ozone Layer' of 1987, under the United Nations Environment Programme – an international agreement to phase out the worldwide production and consumption of cloroflourocarbons (CFCs) (Morisette 1991). Japan joined the Montreal Protocol in September 1988, at which time Japanese companies using or producing CFCs had already seized the opportunity to develop industrial processes that did not include the harmful CFCs. In this they were successful; they managed to increase their market share on a global scale, even though the US companies are still the largest in the field (Johnstone 1990).

The most direct effect that the ozone problem had on the Japanese consumer market had to do with self-protection: the toiletries market benefited directly from anxiety over the destruction of the ozone layer through increased sales of skin care products that screen out ultraviolet light (Dentsū 1991:85). This, of course, went well with the widespread liking for pale skin in Japan, and for the toiletries industry there was no contradiction between the increased sales of sun blockers and skin bleach. But the ecology boom also carried other traces of the problem – as, for example, in a new line in young women's clothing, with 60s inspired flared trousers and striped tanks, which was introduced under the brand name 'Ozone Community'.

Other terms from environmental debates appeared in brand names and advertisements, often in Latin letters or Japanese *katakana* syllabary. 'Ecology', rather than 'environment' acted as the English language keyword of the trend – like Earth Day, it was adapted from the United States. The company Goodman launched new casual wear with the inscription 'Ecology Movement from Tōkyō Japan – Earth Day Memorial', while Jean-Charles de Castelbajac, textile and garment importer, advertised that 'support nature is pure' and 'save the nature is always in style', written among drawings of people, wild animals and trees. Frequent use of English words such as 'nature', 'earth', 'friend' and 'communication' did, indeed, anchor ecology within the horizons of Japanese consumer culture. Supposedly endangered animals, such as seals and whales, were drawn like *manga* figures, and they even spoke in English. One shopping bag suggested this: 'We are all part of our Mother Earth. Save our nature. Treat Animals kindly. Be Friendly to animals. Try to communicate with them.'

Imagine a photograph of deep blue sky above deep blue sea in which, in the foreground, an enormous humpback whale dives so that the camera lens can catch the delicate curves of water splashing and the broad fluke of the mammal frozen in dynamic movement. This kind of visual appeared in the summer of 1990 in numerous versions and for different purposes. Immediately recognizable as propaganda material for WWF, Greenpeace and other environmental organizations which have chosen the saving of whales as a means towards their *own* survival, it also appeared as an advertisement for Suntory beer[1] and for Seibu Department Store, as well as in the form of a framed photo on sale in many of Tōkyō's small art galleries as part of their seasonal nature photo exhibitions.

The colour associated with environmentalism was not green, but brown, which in April 1990 was dubbed 'earth' or 'ecology colour'. As the colour of the season, it was promoted in numerous photo-reportages in a wide range of young women's magazines which practically presented everything from underwear to cosmetics in ecology colours, thereby suggesting an alternative to the previously ubiquitous pink. Some magazines revelled in colour impressions related to natural phenomena, like *La Seine*'s (April 1990) photo reportage from a beach featuring monotonous sand colours – poetically stating that 'beige (is) the colour of the sand on desert dunes . . .', or *Marie Claire*'s safari reportage from Africa – where the model appeared like a wild cat in a leopard spotted unitard, startledly escaping across the savannah. Other magazines incorporated earth colours into the ever-present typologies, which contrast different current styles to each other, as in *non-no*'s (May 20, 1990) reportage on three types of underwear: after the 'romantic' pinks in floral patterns, and the 'white and lace' classics, the third category featured 'ecology colour' underwear, brown and burnt red tricots, presented by models wearing mustard-coloured socks, playing with brown oil colours on a palette in an artist's studio.

Along with the earth colours came the so-called animal prints. The magazine *25 ans* (May 1990) even offered its readers several styles with prints in its lengthy 'Summer colour romance' feature, including the 'spicy elegance' of carrot-coloured knitwear in a zebra pattern, and the 'primitive casual' in a burnt yellow blouse with giraffe design and straw hat. During the summer of 1990, Tōkyō looked as if a whole zoo had been let loose to wander across the city crowds, leaving paw prints on everyone. Fabrics and jersey were printed to look like the skins of wild animals, and the streets thronged with zebra stripes, snake blotches, and the ubiquitous spots of the leopard.

At that time, ecology goods seemed to be a magical mediator between environmental care and increased consumption – as when Mitsukoshi Department Store, for example, launched its eco tag for goods that the Japan Environment Foundation had approved as 'helpful to the environment' (Hyodo 1991:73). Another aspect of the eco boom was the increased sales of second-hand clothes, especially from the 60s' United States. Imported from America were also old English-language newspapers which were used as a trendy form of wrapping in some shops, in contrast to Mitsukoshi's unsuccessful attempt to cut down on wrapping. Finally, ecology credit cards came into use for consumers who wanted to donate 0.5 per cent of each purchase they made to the Wild Bird Society, Japan's largest environmental movement (Holliman 1990:286).

To the purist, it would seem that all substantial environmentalism was taken out and replaced by environmentally *un*friendly consumerism in disguise. It would be crude, however, to overlook the fact that *some* business people, designers and environmentalists joined the eco trend with a genuine concern for the environment which was taken into consideration at a profound level in the production (but frequently not the distribution) process. But in spite of the sense of responsibility to the environment, such a strategy is not unproblematic either. The development of a market for environmentally friendly goods tends to be facilitated by, and dependent on, polluting and wasteful consumer industries and retailing chains – witness, for example, Mitsukoshi's eco tag, or Marui's attempt, thereafter, to set up a whole ecology floor in its Shibuya store. The popularity of second-hand clothes imported from the United States – sold at high prices in Tōkyō and Yokohama – similarly seems to question the notion of sustainability.[2] Indeed, if the global environmental crisis has called economic growth into question, the ecology boom points to the difficulties in finding an alternative.

Global Images

One symbol that more than any other contained the contradictions of the eco boom was the globe, which came into frequent use in advertising graphics in 1990. Gone was the aura of seriousness which the globe once signified as the visual introduction to NHK's news broadcasts. With it went the rarity and the promise of exploration conveyed by the first photos from space. Instead, inflatable blue-green earth balloons now appeared as the popular sign of the global environmental crisis, tangible for everyone – whether in an IGIN formalwear's advertisement where a model dressed in black barely manages to hold on to an earth balloon almost bigger than herself, or on the front cover of *Clique*, a women's magazine (April 5, 1990), whose smiling cover model holds a globe out towards the camera (Figure 4.3).

The international debate over the ozone layer in the late 80s had generated images of the globe accompanied by a sense of the earth not as unlimited resources, but in need of protection. In Japanese advertisements and magazines, the vulnerable globe was presented in a multiplicity of appearances, most of which had no immediate links to the ozone layer. An example is an advertisement for Kubota which 'visually expressed how the Earth has been harmed by placing adhesive plaster over a model of it to emphasize a sense of crisis towards environmental destruction' (Hyodo 1991:79). In a similar vein, Mitsukoshi's eco tag was a clever circular design which showed the earth embraced by big arms. Represented in these ways, the globe fulfills the criteria of the cute object so typical of Japanese consumer culture in the 80s (as discussed elsewhere in this volume by Sharon Kinsella). It is round, immobile, and cuddly, and in its vulnerability the earth is endlessly pitiable.

Another example from 1990 was an ad for NTT Data Communications showing a photo of the globe taken from space, accompanied by the headline, 'Have you talked to the Earth today?' (Hyodo 1991:77). The copy text went on to say that the aim of the corporation was to 'make use of our wisdom to provide the best balance between man and the Earth'. Whereas the advertisement places itself within the ecology trend, which speaks of nearness to nature, its ability to talk to the earth is based on long-distance telecommunications. The relation between man and his environment is not simply one of co-existence, but of separation and distance that can only be overcome through technological dominance. The sad beauty of science fiction-like loneliness is reinstated by communication technology, strangely at odds with the image of togetherness that the eco boom for the most part promoted.

Figure 4.3 Cute and cuddly globe (*Clique*, April 1990)

1990 marked just the beginning of the popularity of the earth in Japanese media. The frequency with which it appeared reached a climax at the time of the Earth Summit in 1992. At that time, the globe was not only used to advertise an exhibition of *Art for the Earth* and a book by Nonaka Tomoyo titled *We Earthlings*, but also Menicon contact lenses which visually linked the earth, protected by the ozone layer to the spherical shape of the eyeball, aided by a contact lens. Other visuals of the globe included an ad for Thierry Mugler fashion, which claimed it was 'for the man who just can't wait until the year 2000', and another of a rosy earth which took the publisher Kadokawa Bunko into 'the New

Age', while models from Fiorucci were photographed pumping up blue-green ballons with bicycle pumps.

In such advertisements, the globe indirectly drew attention to the fact that environmental issues are international – both because pollution tends to spread beyond national borders, and because multinational corporations in developing areas frequently endanger the human and natural environment through their large-scale projects and their limited concern for local communities. This certainly holds true of the Japanese forestry companies working in Southeast Asia and in Latin America, and often funded by official development assistance (ODA), although criticism of such involvement has largely been ignored by the Japanese press. At the Tōkyō Conference on Global Environment and Human Response to Sustainable Development in 1989, Japanese environmental groups were even banned from the official programme, in spite of the fact that the Japanese government had called 1989 the 'Year of Environmental Diplomacy'. Instead, environmental groups managed to set up alternative venues where they met with representatives of indigenous populations in Thailand, Indonesia and Brazil whose lives are severely affected by Japanese companies' activities in those areas. During the euphoria of the eco boom, few realized that a number of environmental movements, including Friends of the Earth, had simultaneously labelled 1990 the 'Ban Japan from the Rain Forest' year (Holliman 1990:288).

To the film buff, there is one more disturbing connotation of the balloon globe – the Great Dictator alone in his office performing a power-lecherous dance with the sphere because it is *his*. This sense of unlimited power seems to clash with the cuteness of the eco boom, but *this* globe shares some features in common with the dictator's dance balloon: it is controllable, foreseeable and manageable. Whereas Charlie Chaplin's vision of global power functioned as a concerned call against fascism in the 1930s, the ecology globe seems to dissolve the contradictions between humanism and dominance, as consumer culture, environmental care and the expansion of the Japanese economy were seen to follow one another in never-ending rotations. When the outlines of the world's landmasses are distinguishable in these globe images – which frequently they are not – we find ourselves gazing at the Pacific Ocean, highlighting Japan and its immediate neighbours.

There are historical reasons for the Japanese to consider themselves to be in a privileged situation when it comes to combining environmental politics with economic growth. Japan's industrial development in the 60s led to serious pollution problems, and it was not until the oil shock in 1973 that the government began to address the pollution problem, or at least one aspect of it, by introducing strict controls on emission gases in urban and industrial areas, at the same time as it rewarded the development of energy-efficient industrial processes (Delfs 1992). In this way, the Japanese government has managed to limit the emission of gases, especially sulphur dioxide which is known to acidify rain, although the average concentration of nitrogen oxides has not been brought down (*Economist* 1993). The actual effects of measures taken to stop air pollution have thus been limited, and after the designated control areas were abolished in 1986, air pollution has been on the increase again (Johnstone 1991; Kirkpatrick 1992).[3]

The reduction of sulphur dioxide in the air has been so well publicized that many Japanese consider their environmental problems to have been successfully solved. At the same time, it is also widely recognized that the anti-pollution policy was part of a successful government strategy to overcome the threat posed by the oil crisis, and hence it gave rise to further technological and economic development (Kirkpatrick 1992). The former head of international development of finance for Japan's Finance Ministry expressed his pride in Japan's economic achievements in one sentence: 'When a country gets rich enough, it can afford pollution control' (Poole 1988). The line of thought behind such a statement is that once a certain level of industrial capitalism is reached, pollution control can lead to sustained economic growth. Japan's anti-pollution measures are thus seen as a function of its affluence – notwithstanding the fact that Japan, along with western countries, has contributed to environmental problems in the developing countries by moving parts of its heavy industry to areas where only the poor are affected by pollution.

In the early 90s, however, the Japanese government and industry viewed global environmental problems with certain optimistic expectations. The problem of the ozone layer had already given Japanese industry an impetus for technological development, and the country's experience in pollution control had been turned into a crucial factor in its official development assistance (ODA). Pollution problems in the developing countries in Asia in particular have been optimistically interpreted as an opportunity for Japan to expand its economic activities in the region.[4]

When the image of the globe appeared on magazine covers and in corporate advertising, it contained all these contradictory elements – from the attractive cuddliness of the helpless to Japan's international economic expansion by way of pollution controlling technology and a science fiction-like fascination with electronics. All this came together in an apparent reconciliation of the global environmental crisis through the advancement and so-called internationalization of the Japanese economy, with the aid of government-supported research and development aimed at enabling Japanese companies to gain market shares from American industry, and selling environmental care to developing countries. The image was strangely harmonious and optimistic – as if economic growth and environmental care went hand in hand, the best of friends.

Japan's largest advertising agency, Dentsū, also adopted an optimistic view on the eco boom from a global perspective. In its *Japan Marketing and Advertising Yearbook 1992* (published in 1991, and presenting 1990 marketing data), in a chapter devoted to ecology as the style of the 90s, it says: 'When it comes to handling environmental issues, Japan is well behind Europe and the U.S., but concerning advertising communication, some strong positive trends have been seen recently' (Hyodo 1991:70). Here Dentsū implies that even though little has been done in Japan in terms of environmental protection, the success of the eco boom – and indirectly that of the advertising agency behind it – nevertheless secures Japan a good place on the global eco hitlists.

Environmental Movements and Women

So far, I have shown how contradictory political messages influenced the way in which the ecology boom was presented in women's magazines in spite of the fact that environmental issues were only rarely articulated there. It is now time to look at one potential source of resistance to the government's and industry's optimistic approach to environmental problems – social movements which have made the environment their key issue. I will look especially at the role women play in them.

There are about 3,000 active environmental movements in Japan, but they tend to be rather small and focussed on local issues. National coalitions such as The Japan Union for Nature Conservation (*Zenkoku Shizen Hogo Rengō*) and Nature Conservation Society of Japan (*Nihon Shizen Hogo Kyōkai*), the latter of which has 14,000 individual members, are small compared to western-based movements such as Friends of the Earth, the National Wildlife Federation and Greenpeace (Holliman 1990:285). In general, Japanese environmental movements have not managed to establish themselves as pressure groups to be reckoned with at the national level.

During the 60s and early 70s, so-called anti-pollution movements emerged around particular local problems, such as *Jishu Kōza* which diagnosed and publicized the Minamata disease – caused by mercury waste dumped by a chemical factory in the Minamata area (Ui 1985: 271). Another famous example is the *Sanrizuka* movement's ongoing resistance to the international airport in Narita. When the construction of the airport began in the late 60s, only one old woman among the affected land owners resisted expropriation and refused to move. Soon a popular symbol of resistance, Ōki Yone kept working on her plot of land at the runway site, until 1971 when her house was raided by riot police. She fought back, was beaten and broke three teeth before she was carried off the site on a police shield (Apter and Sawa 1984:180–2). After that, local farm women and women student activists followed her example when they chained themselves to trees that were to be cut down to stop the work of the bulldozers (Apter and Sawa 1984:86).

The founders and members of most of Japanese environmental movements have tended to perceive themselves as the victims of a specific form of pollution. In their work they have aimed to eliminate the sources of this pollution through political activity directed primarily at prefectural and local authorities. Even when some such movements have been successful, they have not provided the basis for turning the environment into a general issue which could capture the nation's interests (Pierce et al. 1990:56). Instead, it seems that the conflict between small-scale, on the one hand, and large-scale industrial use of natural resources, on the other, has been fought out by those directly involved. Even though the Sanrizuka movement was supported by a group of student activists, and hence was not entirely locally based, the thrust of its criticism was the government's obsession with economic growth through industrial development – a development which was in the process of undermining the social and economic basis of farming communities. During the confrontations with the police, women student activists even dressed like farm women to signal that they were fighting for the threatened community.

Today, environmental concern still tends to be limited to very specific areas of immediate value to those involved. This holds true also of Japan's largest environmental movement in terms of membership, the Wild Bird Society of Japan (*Nihon Yachō no Kai*) with 30,000 members (Holliman 1990:285). Here, the involvement with nature blends with a well-established use of nature as a pastime. Even though there are cases when the Wild Bird Society has been mobilised to preserve threatened wetlands, its direct involvement in protecting the environment is secondary to its main purpose of organizing 'bird watching' hikes, joined mainly by middle-aged women equipped with thermoses and binoculars.

In general, women are the main activists in Japanese environmental groups – hardly surprising in a society marked by pervasive gender segregation and full employment with long daily working hours for practically all men (Holliman 1990:287).[5] Iwao (1993:243) estimates that approximately ten per cent of the married, suburban women who do not hold any employment are involved in a social movement – frequently one focussing on consumer issues such as eliminating pesticides and chemical additives in food, avoiding pollution by synthetic detergents, or promoting recycling. Iwao's concern, however, is limited to the social structure of the movements (which she describes as horizontal and preferable to the vertical structure typical of Japanese corporations) and to the possibilities they offer for women to find a satisfactory way to spend time, thereby leaving aside the question of whether environmental movements managed by women activists are successful in obtaining their goals. Her therapeutic perspective on 'fulfillment through activism' (1993:242) may arise from the fact that the environmental groups have not been so successful, not just because a lot of women activists are primarily concerned with improving their own life (Iwao 1993:247), but also because consumer movements in general have met with strong resistance.

The largest among them is Seikatsu Club Consumers' Cooperative (*Seikatsu Club Seikyō*) with a membership of 170,000 housewives (Holliman 1990:286). Since the early 80s they have run their own candidates for election to local governments, and all their candidates are women in their thirties and forties, full-time housewives with children (Iwao 1993:248). Other important consumer movements include Japan Recycling Citizen's Center (*Nippon Recycling Undō Shimin no Kai*) with 40,000 supporters, and the Consumers' Union of Japan (*Nihon Shōhisha Renmei*) with 2,500 members (Holliman 1990:285–6). In a few cases, the concerns of consumer movements have been taken up by women's magazines, as when a writer for *Shufu no Tomo* along with other women started a catering service for homemade foods with no additives (Iwao 1993:176). But generally, the media have been hostile towards environmental movements and have certainly not helped them be heard. For example, Konishi Akiyuki, general manager and editor of the Mainichi newspaper, describes the silencing of a consumer group in his defence of what he calls the 'impartiality' of the Japanese press, something which he explicitly sees as an 'expression of [its] commercialism'. Even though his statement was made ten years ago, there is little reason to believe that such suppression is not still taking place. The general manager and editor says:

We may decide, for example, not to print a story about some chemical detergent being criticized by housewives and environmentalists, and I can't deny that we have been approached by the soap companies – which are naturally very anxious to have the story suppressed. But this sort of pressure from interest groups doesn't really have much influence now on the actual editorial decision; we kill the story because we think the environmentalists have a weak position – it doesn't meet the standards of scientific accuracy and thoroughness of the specialists on the staff who are covering the story. What we might do instead is to invite a representative of the soap company to debate the environmentalists, or to put the company's position in an advertisement; in this way we can turn our defensive impartiality into something more positive.

(Konishi 1983:17)

The positive element mentioned by Konishi seems to be the newspaper's own rewards in terms of more advertising and closer ties with the soap company. Not only does he silence the environmentalists without second thought; he turns the soap company's fear of criticism to the newspaper's financial advantage – which, presumably, is why he describes 'impartiality' as commercialism.

One long-term effect of this kind of news reporting may be read in a 1989 UN survey which revealed that Japanese policymakers and public had the lowest level of awareness of environmental issues among fourteen countries surveyed. It was also found that Japan had the lowest proportion of people who believed that they should contribute time and money to environmental groups (Holliman 1990:286). Whereas the ecology boom did enhance the general awareness of environmental problems in Japan, it did not convince consumers to pay more for environmentally friendly goods (*Japan Economic Journal* 1990b). The imagery of environmental movements certainly influenced the media in 1990, but this influence came from western, rather than local movements. Furthermore, while most of the activists in Japanese environmental movements are middle-aged housewives, the target readers of the magazines which were the most active in promoting the trend were young, unmarried women.

At the Eco Demo in Leopard Spots

An example of the way in which western environmental movements made up a source for Japanese women's magazines can be found in the

189

fashion photo reportage 'The influence of the Ecology Boom. Fashion information by Nishiyama Eiko' (Figure 4.4), in the monthly women's magazine *Classy* (July 1990). The fashion editorial opens with a visual of a couple, the woman fitting the stereotype of a Caucasian woman model, long and slender, straight legs, blond hair, and a toothy smile, whereas the man, also a Caucasian, is rather indefineable. Not only is he much shorter than the woman, he also lacks the self-conscious skills of

Figure 4.4 At the eco demo in leopard spots
(*Classy*, July 1990)

calmly controlling his appearance – which the woman model masters to some professional perfection. His presence adds a random touch to the fashion visual, as if he has simply emerged out of the crowd.

In contrast, the woman's clothes are carefully presented: a blouse with an imaginative pattern of leopard spots and gold chains (illustrating, perhaps, the wild beastie on a leash?), a beige-green suede skirt, and a green leather purse. And of course, the copy text lists prices and shops where these can be bought by interested readers. The setting is urban. We see wet asphalt – always a good background for fashion photography – and just behind the couple we sense a crowd of people with umbrellas. The man is also holding an umbrella over the couple's heads, and with the other hand displays a poster with a baby seal in its white fur with the English words handwritten at the top of the poster 'please save me'. The man and the woman are staged as if they are in the middle of an environmental demonstration, protesting in the streets against the destruction of wildlife.

In fashion history, artificial leopard spots and tiger stripes have gone through a fascinating transition since the 1940s when they first became popular. At the time real wild cats' fur was associated with Hollywood film actresses and other spectacular stars – both because of its price and exclusivity, and of its symbolic connotations in terms of wildness, big feline animals, and tropical heat. Being a real postwar fashion, man-made leopard spots were *second best*, on the one hand indicating class differences by imitating the real thing, on the other being democratically available to working and middleclass women who aspired to the irresistable look of the stars.

The element of kitsch in such pretention secured imitation leopard spots a glamorous place in punk in the late 70s when they were put on display exactly as vulgar and showy sexuality. As part of the aesthetics of bad taste which punks cultivated, nylon wildcats were freely combined with black leather and – the until then so classical – tartan prints. For what were punks other than contradictory urban indians who – like fake leopard spots themselves – staged a man-made wildness? Because of this popular aestheticization, imitation leopard lost its pretence of looking like real fur and became, instead, its counterpart.

As such, leopard spots re-emerged on the fashion scene in 1990 in a perfect match with the earth colour spectrum, but now they had taken on a new significance as the visible sign that the wearer was *against* real fur. Man-made nature had become a feature on the side of the animals in the ongoing environmental debate, at the same time as previous connotations of wildness and sexuality were still present, albeit weakened. In an article accompanying the *Classy* editorial, Nishiyama Eiko encouraged her women readers to try out leopard spots for themselves, now that they were stripped of their 'bad' connotations. In a curious manner the *Classy* model matched the eco demo dressed, as she is, in natural colours and leopard spots.

Along with this displacement in the politics of style, it should also be noted that the *Classy* model is very different from earlier Japanese women (for though embodying a western figure, she is essentially a Japanese woman) depicted in a fight for the environment – from Ōki Yone, for example, the old illiterate woman who battled against land expropriation. When riot police harrassed *her*, she startled them 'by saying that if they wanted to remove her from her house they would have to put their police sticks up her vagina, and then she flipped up her kimono. The police fled' (Apter and Sawa 1984:181). As presented in women's magazines, the eco boom did not teach women how to fend off riot police, but it did not present women as stereotypically close to nature either. The figure of the leopard-spotted model hardly suggests an endangered animal-like creature, craving to be saved. The seal is a cutie; and the small red-faced man leaning against her is possibly one of her cute gadgets, too. But she herself is not cute; her own appearance is one of detached mimicry, knowingly remaking nature so that fake leopard spots support her political point of view. One more layer is added to the visual because it is, after all, part of a fashion reportage, and the eco demo that it presents has never taken place. Whereas the effects of this particular happening are thus undermined, the use of political protest as a fashion setting is in itself a sign of displacement in the dream world of women's magazines, whereby the relation between political action, attitudes and personal consumption is put on the agenda – something which, given the overall hostile media treatment of environmentalism in Japan, should not be dismissed out of hand.

My argument is further that this stylistic mixture, in fact, reflects a problem which is quite real: that the reference to nature itself has become uncertain. In fashion, for example, cotton still holds a special position as the cheapest and most popular natural material, and is at the same time a long-term favourite with Japanese high fashion designers such as Yohji Yamamoto and Rei Kawakubo. But contrary to the widespread notion, wearing cotton is not in itself 'environmentally correct'. In Central and East Asia, cotton production has led to extreme monoculture, with the use of vast amounts of chemical fertilizer and consequent incalculable environmental damage to soil and subsoil water. And environmental costs do not stop when the raw material is brought within reach of the garment industries: processes of dyeing and finishing cotton produce considerable quantities of chemical waste, far more than does the dyeing of man-made fibres. This is especially true of dark shades like indigo which, though itself natural, needs chemical treatment before it can meet contemporary consumer demands for lasting colours. Thus, the popularity of blue jeans, which twenty years ago were the emblem of anti-fashion's built-in critique of the superfluous waste of capitalist consumerism, is today in the process of becoming one of the greatest environmental problems for the fashion industry.

When environmental care does not exist unless based on industrial technology, and when natural materials and environmentalism may be mutually exclusive, it is hard to criticize new polyester garments introduced as ecology goods, or indeed as 'man-made ecology' (Figure 4.5). That would be to ignore the fact that aesthetics is a dominant parameter, according to which even the designer who wants to work in natural fibres has to justify herself.

Conclusion

Whereas the ecology boom did not change the ongoing negotiations of female gender identity in terms of consumption in women's magazines (which, of course, is hardly surprising), it *did* introduce a new parameter into advertising which essentially makes the producers and advertisers more vulnerable to criticism. The Dentsū *Japan Marketing and Advertising Yearbook 1992* concludes its section on environmentalism with a warning:

> [I]t would be a mistake, and possibly damaging to the company's image, to take environmental problems lightly as a fad, vogue or fashion, since such advertising could point toward the conflicting interests of arguing for resolution of environmental problems while contributing to the expansion of industries that cause such problems.

> (Hyodo 1991:79)

The selling point of ecology is precisely that it is more than 'just a fashion'. It encourages potential consumers to look behind the appearances of media images to see whether commodities are produced in an environmentally sound way, to know in what direction product development is going, and to check whether companies donate money towards the protection of the environment. Even though the relationship between the 'image' and the 'awareness' – as the *Japan Economic Journal*

193

Figure 4.5 Man-made ecology (*Spur*, June 1990)

(1990a) headline had it – is rarely straight-forward, this relationship itself is questioned, and a company which advertises its care for nature runs the risk of losing more than its credibility if it is revealed that there is no action behind the environmental image.

By renouncing the sheen of advertising in its own limited, and often ambivalent, ways, the ecology boom was, in fact, going against the *detachment* of images and meanings which sociologists as different as Norbert Elias (1976) and Jean Baudrillard (1993) have analyzed as characteristic of contemporary society. Of course, this is in itself not a criticism of the general theories; my point here is simply that the field of consumer culture is so complex that it is impossible to condense it into a single overall trend without significant counter movements.

A product of the last year of the so-called bubble period of economic growth, the ecology boom looked both backwards to the exalted consumerism and fast turnover of trends of the 80s, and forwards to more subdued spending during the economic crisis of the 90s. It shows that consumer cultural change was on its way even before it was brought about by necessity in the form of the economic slow-down beginning in 1991.

In 1992, when the enthusiasm of 1990 seemed long gone, the magazine *non-no* put the question to its readers, 'Where did ecology go?'. Answers, which were analyzed in a short article on the *non-no fax friend* page, showed that out of 83 of the magazine's readers, 38 considered themselves to have a high level of ecological consciousness, whereas 45 did not. But exactly what this meant appeared rather vague. According to the survey, the most important lasting effect of ecology among these young women readers was that 53 out of 83 had stopped taking a shower and washing their hair in the morning (*asashan*), and thus only showered once a day instead of twice. A similar image is outlined in so-called 'eco life' surveys (Seikatsu Shikkihō 1992) which suggest that young women are more worried about the environment than any other age or gender group in Japan, at the same time as they also feel that they can *do* very little to stop the destruction of the environment.

Finally, in answer to the initial question of how Japanese women's culture relates to the wider culture of which it is a part, we have found contradictory links which place women at the forefront of changes in the cultural realm, but find them out on a limb when it comes to political and economic moves to integrate these changes into society as a whole. They are, in one sentence, both central and marginal. These contradictions, strongly felt by young women, are the basis for the ambivalent representations of environmentalism in women's magazines.

NOTES

1 In fact, Suntory had already used children's drawings of whales in its advertising posters in the late 1980s (Kalland and Moeran 1992: plate 27).
   An earlier version of this chapter has been published in Danish as 'Økologi på mode: Japanske billeder' in *Tendens: Tidsskrift for Kultursociologi* 1993 (6)2. I would like to thank Hazel Clark, Lars Kjærulf, Brian Moeran and Teddy Wulff for valuable comments at various stages of my work with this paper.
2 Clark (1994) puts forward a similar argument in relation to western-based fashion companies such as Helen Storey, Scrap Scrap and Esprit's Ecollection.
3 While Japan's real GNP has increased by 93 percent since the oil shock, its industrial energy consumption in 1990 was lower than in 1973 – partly due to the transfer of energy intensive industries (such as aluminium smelting) to countries with lower energy costs. Relative to GNP, Japan is the most energy efficient country in the world, with an annual per capita energy consumption in 1989 slightly lower than that of most Western European countries, and only 45 per cent of that of the United States (Delfs 1992).
4 Since 1987, there has been an increase in Japan's environment-related aid, mainly devoted to improving urban water supplies and waste disposal systems. The Japanese government has also helped establish a research centre for the environment in Thailand, and environmental monitoring stations in China (Rosario 1992).
5 As another reason why Japanese environmental movements are obliged to rely on housewives as volunteers, Holliman (1990:287) lists the absence of national service which in the United States, at least, has produced a regular stream of objectors who are assigned to social movements for a limited period to work for the public good. A contradictory alliance, indeed, between the environmentalists and the armed forces.

5

CONSUMING BODIES:

Constructing and Representing the Female Body in Contemporary Japanese Print Media

John Clammer

Open almost any of the widely circulated magazines that appear in abundance in every bookshop, convenience store or railway station kiosk in Japan and images of the human body appear. In some cases these images are simply photographs of people in the news, but in many they are in the form of advertisements – which in many of the over 2,000 magazine titles currently published in Japan constitute 50 percent or more of the total content (Moeran 1991) – or of posed figures placed there precisely to receive the gaze of the reader or viewer. A high proportion of these images (usually photographs, but – in the case of the tabloid newspaper and *manga* or comics published independently or as part of magazines – also drawings) are of the female body. In the case of women's magazines, these images are largely to promote consumption – of fashion, appliances, food, travel or cosmetics especially; in men's magazines, the image is itself consumed – by the male gaze (Figure 5.1).

Japan has often been represented as a society saturated with images (most famously or infamously by Roland Barthes [1970]). Whether or not this is strictly true, the sheer size and power of the Japanese media, and of advertising within the media, make it central to understanding cultural processes in contemporary Japan. This chapter will take only one aspect of the whole, but one which, it can be argued, illuminates many aspects of the functioning of that whole – the way in which the human body, and in this context specifically the female body, is constructed, represented and, as image, consumed in those media.

This subject would at first sight seem to be a straightforward example of visual ethnography. But, in fact, behind it or within it is a plethora of questions which goes to the heart of cultural theory and to the reasons for the emergence of interest in the body as a major theme in contemporary western social thought, too (Turner 1984, 1992; Shilling 1993). Certainly, most societies evidence concern with the presentation of the

197

Figure 5.1 'Beautiful nudity' – front cover of *an-an*
(October 2, 1992)

body, and the work of Erving Goffman (1965) should suggest that even in the United States presentation of the self and presentation of the body are closely related in ways not so dissimilar from those found in Japan (Kondo 1990). Concern with the body in society, then, necessarily raises philosophical and psychological questions (the issue of selfhood), while also raising questions of aesthetics (what is beautiful?), and of the mechanics of social interaction (body 'language' – posture and gesture – and, in Japan, an acute preoccupation with presentation). While western sociology of the body has transformed our understanding of social action and of the operation of specific institutions within society such as prisons or the medical system, it mostly lacks a comparative angle – being in many ways ethnocentric in its philosophical assumptions and range of examples. The study of the body in Japanese culture provides, perhaps, the perfect comparative counterpoint: an industrialized society with highly developed media, but with a distinct and autonomous culture formed by philosophical and religious forces very different from those of Europe and North America. One thing, however, certainly unites east and west: the common devotion to consumption as a way of life. In fact, an important theoretical development in the sociology of the body in the west has been the recognition that, of the many social spaces in which bodies interact, consumption is the site of many of the most intensive and meaningful of these (Featherstone 1991b; Shields 1992).

Here we are addressing the question of the handling by the Japanese media, and specifically print media, of the representation of the body. And generally the body, especially the female body, is presented either to promote the consumption of services or material objects – banks, clothes, cars, household appliances, for example – or to be consumed itself, most commonly as an image, by the gaze of the beholder, but occasionally – as in magazines promoting 'soaplands' or massage parlours – quite literally and physically, subsequent to a reading of the magazine by those who seek out the proffered services. The media are firstly not simply concerned with the pure aesthetics of the body, but with the exploitation of what is indeed an aesthetic canon for largely commercial ends (however elegantly disguised). In other words, the female form is presented within the realm of commodity aesthetics. The second consequence is that, however much the concern of theorists in the sociology of the body is for a full and rounded understanding of the embodied subject, the active and experiencing *self*, the concern of the print media and advertising is with the *presentation of the image*.

But, first, some observations about methodology, the delineation of the field, and the problem of the 'representation' or even 'construction' of the body. All forms of media present images of the body – even radio with its use of voice as an indicator of femininity/masculinity, youth/age, social status, ethnicity and other physical features expected to be inferred from aural information alone. But clearly film, television and the print media have the advantage of being able to present direct images in the form of pictures. This chapter will only concern itself with a segment of this total media world – the print media, and within the print media specifically the magazine. The field is thus much smaller than the total media, but still large, given the enormous number of magazines published and their very large total readership.

Here I will concentrate on a small number of titles drawn from three categories: magazines targeted at women, news and current affairs magazines of mass circulation which are read by both sexes, and magazines targeted at men. The body concerned will be that of the adult woman, as depicted primarily through photography, and the magazines selected are all of large circulation and easily available. The ones selected here, while by no means the only ones, are intended to supplement the analyses by Moeran of the upperclass housewives magazine *Katei Gahō*, by Rosenberger in her discussion of 'elite cosmopolitans', and by White in hers of adolescent-targeted media elsewhere in this volume.

While there is, of course, such a thing as a biological body (as espoused by the foundationalists), this biological body is at all times presented through clothing, decoration, posture, location in spatial relation to other bodies, and is constantly interpreted. It is this interpretation that constitutes the social construction of the body – through, for example, penal, sexual or medical practices, as shown by Foucault. This social construction is an ongoing *project*, not an accomplished state, and is constantly effected by factors such as ageing (biologically unavoidable, but managed in different ways individually and culturally), and by the constant redefining of the canons of appearance and presentation. It is here that the media play a major role in almost all contemporary societies, and most certainly in Japan.

Reading Japanese Magazines

Any general bookshop, most supermarkets and every convenience store, as well as many small general stores and all railway station kiosks (of which there is almost always more than one, even at the smallest suburban station), contain racks of magazines, often quite literally stacks of them, together with a large range of comic titles. Most are visually attractive with high quality advertising, graphics, layout, and paper. The fact that most magazines are bought directly from newsstands rather than by subscription, as is often the case in the west, is attributed at least in part to this visual and indeed even tactile appeal (Moeran 1991:1). Magazines are also commodities themselves and are commodities with a short shelf-life, mostly demanding only a very short attention span, so that they are generally looked at and browsed in, rather than *read* in the sense that a novel might be.

A characteristic of much of the Japanese periodical press is its mixing of genres, with text, advertisements, visuals and comics all in the same publication. The body is presented multiply through these forms: the ritualized pose of pin ups, the idealized pose of the fashion model, the stylized portraiture of the comic; and through textual discourses on diet, health care, body decoration and maintenance. The magazine medium has the further advantage of being able to create an interplay between written content, advertising and photographic or graphic content, which all add to its aesthetic appeal and to the strategic relationship between advertising and text – a matter of great concern to advertisers who appear to have distinct beliefs about the effectiveness of their advertisements in relation to their placing within a magazine. Out of the vast field of Japanese magazines so widely read in this most literate (and perhaps also visual) of cultures, only a tiny selection of magazines has been sampled for the purposes of this essay. In the first group are a few women's magazines: *CanCam*, a middle-market fashion magazine with a great deal of visual material; *Caz*, a magazine for white collar working women and younger housewives and containing materials not only on fashion, but on food, travel, make-up, health and similar matters; *Fujin Gahō*, an up-market, long-established and quite expensive fashion and lifestyle magazine for older housewives; and, by way of contrast, *Hanako*, a popular and very widely available magazine for young professional women, well-informed housewives and university students, which, while not containing nearly so much visual material as the others (which are saturated with it), does through its text provide a guide to what Foucault has aptly termed 'techniques of the body' – diet, make-up, medicine, deportment, etiquette and food.

In the second group are two men's magazines: *Urecco*, and the mass circulated *Weekly Playboy* which not only contains advertising, but actively advertises itself – especially on commuter trains. Many other men's magazines are interesting because of the *absence* of depictions of women in their pages: widely available examples such as *Popeye* or *Fine Boys* are full of pictures of very fashionable young men, but virtually no women, not even as accessories to the young men. For this reason, they have been left out of this sample.

The third category explored as a background phenomenon for the purposes of this chapter, are the three rival mass circulation weekly news, gossip, personality and comment magazines – *Friday*, *Focus*, and *Flash*. They are included here principally because of their high photographic content, low levels of advertising, and inevitable spread of visuals of nude or semi-nude women.

Caz evidently has as its target audience 'office ladies' and

JOHN CLAMMER

fashion-conscious younger women, all of whom travel a lot. Its content includes horoscopes, TV, movie, books, art and theatre information, articles on clothes, AIDS, parks in Tōkyō, and a range of reports on new consumer items. A high proportion of the magazine is related to travel and airport information, English conversation tips, travel insurance, money, shopping tips in places like Hong Kong, Bali, Guam and Hawaii, and domestic travel suggestions, for example for holidays in Okinawa. It has more visual advertising than *Hanako*, concentrating on face products, tea, new entertainment spots, sports gear, hi-fi equipment and trendily designed telephones. The female body image presented throughout, whether in articles or in advertisements, is of well-dressed, but rather girlish-looking women, many with crooked teeth, and all young with the exception of one very well-dressed middle-aged woman of calm and serious appearance who appears to recommend moisture lotions and face-creams with a great air of (in the text 'scientific') authority and jargon. In this magazine, non-Japanese models are not used so frequently, but they do appear in a context which soon becomes recognizable as a pattern: adverts relating to body hair, breast-firming devices and underwear usually feature foreigners. In these polite middle-brow magazines, Japanese women almost never appear undressed; nor do they ever seem to have a 'problem' with body hair, although it is obviously Japanese women who buy the products advertised. A discourse of race as class/income enters very obviously into the visual language of advertising – revealing the foreigner as exotic, yet as having distinct problems with being or becoming attractive. The general body shape of western women appears as attractive (longer legged, bigger-breasted), but the details (body hair, skin) are not. Revealingly, almost no black or non-Japanese Asian models are to be found in the adverts in the specifically Japanese media, although a kind of ambiguous-looking Eurasian type is quite popular (Figure 5.2). But where they do appear (in *Hanako*), pushing useful household appliances, like many Japanese models, they do so in enormous empty rooms of European design, bearing very little resemblance to the reality of the typical Japanese urban interior.

The body image in *CanCam* is even more revealing semiotically. Here we have a magazine explicitly devoted to fashion – its articles, advertisements and the photo-spreads which take up most of its pages are all about fashion, make-up or diet – except for a tiny number of ads devoted to cars (a fashion accessory?), and gossipy articles on interesting 'boys' in the media and entertainment worlds. Certain images stand out: elegant but conservative; either very dressed-up, or looking

202

Figure 5.2 A rare example of a black model in *Elle Japon* (July 5, 1993)

'natural' with the help of substantial amounts of make-up and carefully chosen clothing; a very standardized physical shape that looks good in tweeds and woolens; dressing appropriately by the season of the year; classical or European settings; and what in Europe would be considered distinctly upper-middle class accessories – pearls and handbags. Casual in *Cancam* means a studied but simple elegance. Many of these traits are heightened to an even greater degree in *Fujin Gahō*. Here elegant models of distinctly wealthy appearance and often of middle age disport themselves in kimono or very smart western-style clothes, in spacious interiors or outdoors. The advertisements which focus on up-market fashion also relate to fine china, jewels, and art works, while articles deal with fine and traditional arts, elegant hotels or *onsen* (hot springs), 'society' news, Japanese foods and holidays in good resorts. The inevitable consumer guides are a feature, too, but of similar up-market nature. The models are either Japanese of distinctly 'upperclass looks', or very elegant Europeans. All are fully dressed and the body is presented as groomed – very carefully made-up, wrapped with expensive simplicity. 'Good taste' and 'sensitivity' are hallmarks of the style presented. The world of embassy parties, receptions and society weddings fills these pages, even though in reality they are read by many 'ordinary' housewives and working women.

Hanako, in common with most Japanese mass circulation magazines, is actually primarily a guide to consumption, and has a general content not that different from many of its rivals – a mixture of brief articles on travel, movies, restaurants, skiing and other sports, plays, books, and a heavy weightage towards news and views on make-up, beauty tips, exercise, weight control, and interestingly – I would argue – household appliances, as well as tips on storage and organization in the notoriously small Japanese homes, doubtlessly dwelt in by many of *Hanako*'s readers. Much of this information is overt or disguised advertising (presenting itself as information about new products), and in some cases the boundary between the two is very indistinct. One recent issue (#234, February 1993, for instance) contains a lengthy feature of six pages on, separated by one page from a full page advertisement for, Tōkyō Beauty Center, complete with a questionnaire to help the reader assess whether she needs anything (or rather what she needs) from the range of services provided. Two things in particular stand out. The first is that relatively little of the material actually depicts bodies (there are pictures of products, but not of people), but that almost all of the text is about body management – make-up, diet, weight and exercise primarily, with additional material on fashion, travel and accessories. In *Hanako*, the text is written and it is the sub-text that is visual. Virtually the sole theme of the text is that one's primary concern is to care for the body, which should be young, smooth, with no visible hair except on the top of the head, well-dressed, but not in a distinctive way, and of average size and shape. In all the adverts which do directly depict women, more than half are not Japanese. Young fresh-faced Japanese models are used to promote products as diverse as handbags, banks and facewashes. Foreign models, however, are in the numerical majority (generally of a vaguely Italian appearance), and promote foods, fashions, bags and cars (Japanese, but with Italianate names). Only one of the Japanese models is what would conventionally be described as glamorous; all the others are again 'average' in appearance, which is perhaps appropriate as they are pushing drinks and banks, while the glamorous one is promoting a Shiseidō lipstick.

Men's magazines might be expected to depict the female body in a different way. But this is not the case, despite the fact that here the emphasis moves from depiction through advertising to 'direct' depiction in the form of photos – specifically of clothed, bathing-suited, or nude/ semi-nude women – always Japanese and usually young, often very young. In fact, the type of woman featured differs little from the average fashion model, except in posture (typically highlighting breasts or buttocks) and facial expression. Here there is a tendency for men's magazines to emphasize, in particular, the direct gaze and the pout. It is not that these expressions are completely absent from women's maga- zines: fashion models look and smile, but rarely gaze. In other words, gaze and a heightened sexuality seem to go together. Similarly with the pout. Fashion models – especially those advertising high-class goods – hardly ever pout, thereby drawing attention to their lips. However, in men's magazines like *Weekly Playboy* and in less glamorous magazines for younger women, the pout is not so rare (Figure 5.3). Disheveled hair, a crouching or sprawling posture, and a natural setting – particularly one involving sand or water (the latter having its own sexual symbolism) – are other common characteristics of men's magazines. Most of the models are fresh-faced, smiling, and very much affect a 'natural' look. The name, age, statistics and other personal data often accompany the photographs. Photo spreads (in *Urecco*, for example) are often accom- panied by captions such as 'Fresh shot', and by descriptions of the model as a 'flower girl', 'flower child', 'sweet angel', or 'sports girl'. Many of the models are half clothed or in bathing suits and there is a heightened attention to breasts.[1]

Mass circulation news and gossip magazines also make their

Figure 5.3 Striking similarities in the representation of women in men's and women's magazines (advertisement for zit cream from women's magazine and front cover of *Weekly Playboy*, May 1990)

contribution, not only by including material on health (*Focus*, for example, has a weekly health page), but also by playing up to their reputation amongst the Japanese media for being provocative and a little more daring (and no doubt, given their need to compete against one another, to gradually stretch the limits). All of the three magazines surveyed, in the style of a lot of the popular media, have a few pages of nudes: in its September 24 number of 1993, *Focus* broke through one limit by having a black model. In the same month *Flash* broke through another barrier by not only quite openly depicting pubic hair (formerly a privilege confined, if allowed at all, to 'art' magazines), but by depicting it on a model in her mid-thirties. Other excuses for depicting the female body in these publications are either in the form of 'news', or in reporting the latest actresses in the vast adult video industry – as well, of course, as in straight advertising. This category of magazine, while evidently bought mostly by men, especially salaried workers, is widely read by both sexes.

A number of points of interest can be drawn collectively from these depictions. The first thing that might strike the observer familiar with western counterparts is that, in general, the images convey a picture of 'wholesomeness', and even of innocence. In fashion magazines, the images certainly convey impressions of happiness, femininity and marriageability, or if the reader is already married, of calm assurance, of being sensible. As we have noted, in men's magazines the models are usually young and convey an image of a budding sexuality, attractive but nonthreatening. Where a 'stronger' sexuality is implied, the models will be older, have longer and more unkempt hair, and will pout and gaze with even more directness. Alternatively, they will be foreign women. Even in these cases, the range of facial expressions and postures is very limited and stereotyped.

Reading the Images

We have, then, a repertoire of images, surprisingly consistent in its iconography, although clearly located along a continuum. The women's magazines are concerned with the body as wholesome, and through its wholesomeness with promoting 'good taste' (i.e. status-based, and even ethnically-based, consumption). The men's magazines represent the body as the object of desire, to be consumed visually (and perhaps in the imagination), although the desired object is not that different from the images portrayed in women's magazines, except that they have generally fewer clothes on. The news magazines present the body as spectacle, of interest not as cultural role models or as physical models, but as exemplars of the human condition, interesting because of their existential predicaments. The emphasis is very much on *depiction* – which takes us back to the question of self. Where is the self in the image? It could be argued that the preoccupation with representation of the body suppresses selfhood. But our data by now should have brought us to a rather more differentiated conclusion. The pure image may exist: here is representation but no self; here is a body but not a woman. But this is only achievable in certain contexts, and here we run into a paradox: which is that it is the *women's* magazines that manage the most thorough suppression of selfhood, replaced instead by what are really categories – the perfect housewife, the young mother, the elegant professional woman – and this is especially true in the way in which women are depicted in advertising. *Fujin Gahō* reaches the apogee here: beautiful women, elegantly posed in fine clothes, a spacious interior or natural settings, representing not themselves but an (ideal) type. If one were to seek anywhere for the alleged lack of individuality in Japanese culture, it might well be here where self is submerged into the model (in both senses of the word!). But in men's magazines, where it might be supposed that there is much more complete objectification of the female body as purely the object of the (male) gaze, this is not so. Rather, two things happen. Firstly, the model gazes back, often with disconcerting frankness. There is eye contact which asserts the personhood of the model, even a gaze that makes it clear that here there is power which is the woman's, not the man's. Secondly, rather disarmingly, photo spreads are accompanied by personal information – the model's name, her age, statistics, what she likes doing, where she comes from (all of which, of course, may be made up) (Figure 5.4). She is personalized in a way in which the fashion model in *Fujin Gahō* or *CanCam* is not, and which has to do with the fact that these men's magazines are selling their readers the fiction of meeting the other. In the fashion magazines, the selfhood of the women depicted is not in the images; if it is there at all, it is in the text – this is so-and-so, she is traveling in Italy, eating organic foods that enhance her personhood by improving her body, and so on. Underlying this is a deeper ontology. Whereas in western philosophy and religion, especially in traditional Christianity, body and self (soul, personhood) are separated and unequally weighted, in Japan they are not. Not only is the body natural, pleasant to see and worthy of care, but the 'true self' even beyond society is seen to be linked to nature. Body, self and nature are thus fused (Picone 1989; Yuasa 1987).

Figure 5.4 Double-page spread in *Playboy* (October 1993)

Japanese Bodies/Cultural Theory

At this juncture, several main points should be clarified. Firstly, while it is obviously impossible to generalize about the Japanese media as a whole, within the group of magazines examined here there are certain continuities. These are expressed in the visual images via concern with fashion in *Fujin Gahō*, *CanCam* and to a lesser extent *Caz*, and with the body itself as the object of desire in *Urecco* and *Weekly Playboy*, as well as in the photo spreads of the weekly news trio. They are also expressed in the text of *Fujin Gahō* and *Caz* and especially in *Hanako*, the least visual of all the women's magazines, where the female body is not desired but itself desires, and where selfhood of the female reader is constructed through consumption. And the body is central here – it is to be clothed, fed, decorated, manicured, exercised and protected – which is, of course, a very realistic view, where the body is the vehicle for the multi-faceted interaction with the environment that constitutes actual human experience.

An important aspect of this is the construction of gender, both through the assigning and reproduction of certain attributes to each sex through fashion, body decoration, ideas of appropriate sports and diet (especially drinks, where beer and whisky, for example, are decidedly 'masculine' beverages), and through the clear separation of the sexes. This is done again by symbolic means (hair styles and clothing colours, for instance), and by the extreme segmentation of the magazine market. Interestingly, men's magazines such as *Fine Boys* are the almost exact masculine counterpart of female fashion magazines, full of images of the young male body, advice on hair, clothes, skin, diet and accessories. And all this, almost absent in the western media, is aimed at decidedly hetero-sexual men. The parallels in the print media for women and for men are remarkable.

The favoured female body is young, firm, fair, middleclass, average and cute. *Kawaii* culture discussed by Kinsella operates here with a vengeance. True sensuality is an attribute of the older woman; glamorous cuteness of the younger one. The text that often accompanies the photos in *Urecco* is revealing in this respect: sometimes it is a kind of vague poetry; at other times it tells you the model's name, age, tastes, hobbies and blood group – itself an interesting minor phenomenon in the sociology of the Japanese body (Figure 5.5). In fact, the impression that comes across very clearly is essentially a juvenile one. In the mass press, women are not so much humiliated as in control in an ambiguous way; these are not demon women, but mothers and (usually) sisters. While not

Figure 5.5 Example of feature on fortune telling by blood type and an advertisement for constipation pills (*non-no*, Jan. 20–Feb. 5, 1984)

exactly doll-like, many are immature. Speaking of a similar phenomenon, Rosalind Coward comments:

> The sexually immature body of the current ideal fits very closely
> into these ideologies (of women having a sexuality somehow in
> spite of themselves). For it presents a body which is sexual – it
> 'exudes' sexuality in its vigorous and vibrant and firm good health
> – but it is not the body of a woman who has an adult and powerful
> control over that sexuality. The image is of a highly sexualized
> female whose sexuality is still one of response to the active
> sexuality of a man. The ideology about adolescent sexuality is
> exactly the same: young girls are often seen as expressing a sexual
> need even if the girl herself does not know it. It is an image that
> feeds off the idea of a fresh, spontaneous, but essentially *re-
> sponsive* sexuality.
>
> (Coward 1987:42–43)

Well said.

I have already suggested that there is a real, if largely invisible,
discourse of race apparent in the depiction of the body in the Japanese
media, even as there is at work a not-so-subtle process of class distinction of a positively Bourdieuian kind, but which becomes evident when
one compares the imagery of, say, *Fujin Gahō* with that of *CanCam*.
This discourse of race largely takes the form of establishing, principally
through visuals and to a lesser extent through text, a notion of what it is
to be a Japanese. In *Fujin Gahō* – as in *Katei Gahō*, as discussed by
Moeran – this takes the form of an unabashed traditionalism – features
on the kimono, profiles of traditional inns, craftspeople and hot spring
resorts, a concentration on Japanese food in the cuisine articles and the
use of models of a classically 'Japanese appearance'. 'Japan' here means
the very elegant, the traditional, the aesthetically pleasing, restrained,
dignified, natural. A certain type of face and body fits this image very
well, and wrapped in the right clothing to give the appearance of sophistication, with just a hint of internationalism, the picture is almost
complete. But it still needs the reinforcement of the right kind of diet to
maintain not only that slim body and clear complexion, but also a sense
of almost spiritual Japaneseness. The management of the body is not just
to keep fat or age at bay: it is also to enhance the qualities of race. This
is equally apparent in the magazines for men, where not only are the
models always Japanese, but are written up as such – as representing the
essence of Japanese womanhood – and are also often depicted in 'traditional' settings (the hot springs being a favourite).[2]

Actually, we see in these magazines several tendencies standing in a complex and subtle relationship to one another. The primary differentiation by sex we have already noted. Secondarily, we see differentiation by race and the establishment of distinct images of 'Japaneseness'. The position of the foreign (almost always Caucasian) models who do occasionally appear in the pages of the women's magazines now becomes clearer: they either promote the consumption of that which is hidden (underwear); or that which is distinctly exotic (such as French perfumes) and, as such, that which is by definition not Japanese, but enjoyable by the Japanese woman as an indicator of her internationalization and sophistication. It is no accident that the foreign goods promoted in *Fujin Gahō* are of the same kind as, and often identical to, those in *Katei Gahō*: expensive, European, and clear markers not only of high income, but also of an elegant self-image not very different from that portrayed in distinctly upperclass British magazines – such as *Home and Garden* or *Country Life*, as opposed to – say – *Women's Own*. In other words, the concern with Japaneseness (race) also conceals a preoccupation with social distinctions (class). While the two are not precisely conflated, they certainly converge.

For many Japanese women the choice of magazine is an indicator of class in its simplest definition as 'socio-economic status'. For the small shopkeeper, wife of a lower grade manager, school teacher or salaryman, or for an unmarried woman living off part-time work, her class status is not going to improve. But for others, their choice of magazine is more a function of age. The daughter of the factory owner may now read *Hanako*, but she might possibly also read *Fujin Gahō* in the not-so-distant future. She is also likely to consume travel magazines because she travels, and to be preoccupied with lifestyle decisions involving her – at least partial – assimilation into Japanese tradition, as signalled especially by fashion which is critical to the presentation of the classed as well as racialized body. In time she will probably marry, and her concerns will shift from travel and personal consumption to children's fashion and consumption, as well as to interior decoration. But, while she is still what Rosenberger calls an elite cosmopolitan, her reading will reflect this, just as – when a teenage or pre-teen girl – she bought comics and consumer items associated with other media tie-ins (plastic jewelry, toys, lunch boxes and other items bearing the images of the fictional characters populating the pages of such magazines and filling the children's cartoon slots on television). If race and class intersect in the Japanese media, so do age and class.

Japan, Consumption and Theories of Body

We started from the assumption that an exploration of even a limited segment of the Japanese media, while interesting ethnographically in itself, also provides a very fruitful way into a dialogue with the burgeoning literature on the sociology of the body that has emerged in the west.

Frank (1990), for instance, suggests that essentially the media present the body as medicalized, sexual, disciplined and talking. Our review of a range of Japanese material suggests that the contents of these categories need to be extended and/or redefined. The idea of disciplined, for example, needs to contain the area of 'sportiness'; that of sexual requires the addition of the gaze, as well as attention to posture and to the detailing of particular body parts. The medicalized dimension seems to be repressed, but is substituted for by the preoccupation with diet found especially in women's magazines, including the primarily informational ones like *Hanako*. So while concern with bodily presentation has always been a part of Japanese culture, its centrality in the self-conscious presentation of self appears to be a relatively new phenomenon promoted by the reflexivity of late modernity – to use Giddens' terminology (1991) – where 'the body has become a fundamental feature of taste and distinction in which the management of the human form becomes part of the major aspect of cultural or physical capital' (Turner 1992:47). Turner, however, sees body management as being mainly conditioned by medical practices. What he does not analyze is the structuring of taste as a function of the media.

Here we enter rather uncharted waters – the influence of literacy and of 'visualcy' on behavior. The consumption of the sign rather than of the thing itself (although Baudrillard would presumably deny that there is a distinction) has behavioral and psychological ramifications. It may be that the 'concrete' nature of Japanese culture (Hasegawa 1982) has protected itself from too much damage here yet; or, rather, that the visual qualities of the culture (to which some trace the origins of *manga*) permit consumption of the sign to have mostly positive or even cathartic effects – and, again, some have traced the lack of overt violence in Japan to its open depiction, often in a highly sexualized way in comics, movies and 'adult videos' (Buruma 1984). The work ethic and the aesthetic are consequently not opposed, as in a Weberian understanding of the origins of capitalism. Appearance and reality are thus assimilated to each other in culturally new ways (cf. Maffesoli 1990).

Some aspects of Turner's work have already been mentioned. Another emerging theorist is Chris Shilling who, on the opening page of his recent book on *The Body and Social Theory* (1993:1) suggests that 'the position of the body within contemporary popular culture reflects an unprecedented individualization of the body'. This he relates particularly to the emergence of the 'new' middle class (who presumably have the time, money and education, plus the desire for symbolic competition). In Japan, too, it is the recently urbanized salaried workers, and especially their spouses, who consume the huge amounts of printed material, some examples of which we have here examined. But at the same time, individualization is limited by the standards of some urban western social groups. And even when extravagant displays of dress and/or body do occur, they often not only have a ritual quality, but also partake of the common Japanese custom of, in effect, wearing a uniform. A strong sense of what is appropriate pervades the Japanese fashion scene and also the presentation of the body. The overall result is an expanding display of the body in the media, together with a slow testing of the limits of how much of the female body can be exposed, but with very little individuality in its actual expression. A tendency towards normalization prevails, despite the growing opportunities for display.

The end result of all this, to return to Frank's ideal types, is the appearance of the *disciplined* body – based on what appears to the outsider, and to some insiders, to be a clear example of regimentation, but of a very different kind from the rationalized monasticism which is his model example. Disciplined bodies in Japan coexist with emotionalism, with sensuality, and with forms of efficiency which do not exactly correspond to any form of Weberian rationalization. The *mirroring* body, whose medium of expression is *consumption* (the model example being the department store), is easily recognized in Japan, although, of course, with its culturally specific qualities, some of which we have noted. The *dominating* body (medium: force; model: war), while present in *manga*, is largely absent as a type from the rest of the media – no doubt because of a combination of sensitivity to war-time atrocities and to the ornate rules governing activities such as sport in which overt competition or joy-in-winning is at least externally subdued. This is not to argue for the absence of conflict, but to draw attention to the social management of conflict and to ideologies of pacifism and harmony, which cannot simply be dismissed as false consciousness. Frank's talking or *communicative* body (medium: recognition; model: communal rituals, caring relationships) is also easily recognized in the images portrayed in the Japanese media.

We see here also an issue that we raised earlier: the constructing of *gendered* bodies through images of appropriate fashion, activities, posture, diet, decoration and appurtenances (e.g. cigarettes, cars, golf clubs). Newly created social categories (e.g. the 'sporty' woman) impose new meanings on the biological foundation, which in turn influence behaviour, dress and self-images. The huge-eyed, non-Japanese looking characters of girls' comics and the androgynous men (*bishōnen*) who inhabit the same pages may not only be figures of fantasy. A parallel phenomenon is reproduced in the very real and hugely popular activities of the Takarazuka opera company. In other words, such images are manifested in social practices which shape and form particular images of femininity and masculinity.

A characteristic of bodily presentation is the *regulated* display of class, age, or sexuality. Western writers on the body in consumer society have tended to argue that values about the desirable attributes of the body change rapidly, leading to uneasiness and uncertainty about being embodied. The evidence would seem to suggest that this process, while not absent, is very much slowed down in Japan, and we could speculate on the reasons for this. For while the Japanese media present docile and disciplined bodies, to use Turner's terminology, they also present liberated ones: it is no longer necessary to wear a kimono, for shorts are fine. While some of the attributes of all consumer societies are present – including emphasis on body management through jogging, fashion, cosmetics, and diet, and with increased emphasis on the performing self, rather than the self which just occupies a status or office (although that is still a very real factor in Japan) – it needs to be remembered that while the media present stylized images, they do so in Japan in the context of a very stylized culture. The emphasis on the image, which some commentators (e.g. Featherstone 1991b) see as being new, is not new at all in Japan.

The Body, Media and Consumption

In essence, the social construction of the body that takes place in Japanese print media can be seen as the commodification of the body: its presentation in such a way as to induce desire; to engineer the shape, size, colour, and posture of the body through fashion, decoration, diet, 'fitness' and even surgical alteration; to fit largely media-induced images of what the body 'should' look like (for a good account, see Lee 1993). But here several points can be made, beyond simply asserting the generalized commodification of areas of life which have hitherto been outside the consumption nexus. Firstly, amongst all manifestations of the media, advertising is heavily implicated in this whole process. In the context of the presentation of the body, a much wider range of material – including comics, 'glamour' magazines, the tabloid press and TV – is involved. Secondly, there are cultural variations in the way in which commodification proceeds, as this essay has attempted to demonstrate. So while commodification has certain qualities that define it as commodification, there are also important local variations (Tobin 1992b).

Thirdly, both advertising and the other manifestations of the media do not just sell things. They also create, to use Judith Williamson's phrase, 'structures of meaning' (1978:11). Commodities function at several levels – as signs and symbols, as regulating agents, as meaning conferring things, as markers of the categories of a culture. As such, they connect with many corresponding levels of behaviour and identity, including conceptions of the self, which are deeply embodied. And fourthly, commodification cannot be seen only in the dimension of the imposition by capital of compulsory patterns of behaviour: it also involves freedom, competition and choice. Since Bourdieu (1984), it is necessary to see consumption, even amongst people of objectively similar incomes, as the principal mechanism of differentiation which allows both symbolic competition for status and relative freedom to define and pursue choice about lifestyle. The question of lifestyle, which can itself be seen as part of the reflexivity of late modern society, is not a trivial issue. It is precisely the means by which a large number of people, including people in Japan, define their relationship to things. As such, they constantly make decisions about consumption in general, and in this context their bodies in particular, as the means of symbolizing and manifesting the chosen lifestyle.

All these are connected to shifts in the nature of contemporary capitalism. As Shilling suggests (1993:35), there has generally been in advanced capitalist societies a shift from production, frugality and denial towards a shortened working week, increased leisure, disposable income and expanding social incentives to consume. While we can forget the accompanying suggestion that within consumer society the body ceases to be a vessel of sin and becomes an object of display, since in Japan it never was generally regarded as sinful in any sense, that consumer culture has sanctioned the presentation of the body in fresh ways. The fact that Japan is, sociologically if not physically or geographically, seen as a low-risk rather than a 'risk society' (to use Ulrich Beck's [1992] now rather fashionable term), modifies the emergence of extreme versions of western style body-based individualism. A point made by Goffman (1963) of greater relevance to Japan, mentioned but not developed by Shilling, is the pregnant suggestion that:

217

as well as allowing us to classify information given off by bodies, shared vocabularies of bodily idiom provide categories which label and *grade hierarchically* people according to this information. Consequently, these classifications exert a profound influence over the ways in which individuals seek to manage and present their bodies.

(Shilling 1993: 82)

This is in fact correct and provides a check on the tendencies in Bryan Turner's work to equate commodification with social fragmentation. Yet, as we have suggested, the analysis of Japanese magazines does suggest that, as in Bourdieu's France, there is also a constant struggle for symbolic dominance in Japan. This occurs especially through struggles over taste – important where class differences became centered on consumption devices, rather than on objective socio-economic differences (Bourdieu 1984).

Japanese media represent a large, diverse and varied field containing the pursuit of many agendas, conflicting ideologies, technical procedures and distinct styles. Here we have only explored a tiny corner of this enormous field: a selection of magazines which nevertheless provides some fruitful ways into the problems of adequately theorizing contemporary Japanese society. This does suggest certain continuities, but also illustrates the differences, even oppositions, within the field which arise from a number of sources; but especially from the fact that the images within the magazines are targeting specific audiences, and are thus the outcome of marketing categories.[3]

What has hopefully been suggested is something of the complexity of the relationship between images and practices, including the reflection in the images of questions of class and race. There is no one Japanese female body and no one homogeneous representation of it. In fact, the magazine world seems to reflect, or itself partly creates, a breaking up of homogeneity. Certain codes are still in place – a coding of race, class and sexuality, for example – but not in a hegemonic way: the range of body types deemed attractive continues to expand. This is part of a dynamic process – shifting norms within Japanese culture, the influence of foreign experiments, the market-driven nature of much media innovation, and the effect that images have on women's perception of themselves and on men's perception of women. The illustrated magazine – highly visible artefact of contemporary Japanese culture – proves to be a rich field indeed for the exploration of Japanese society.

NOTES

1 Whether this reflects the alleged mother complex of the *amae* dependence factor, I leave to those more psychoanalytically inclined.

2 Indeed, the diet columns of women's, and the photo spreads of men's, magazines both provide a rather fresh angle on the old issue of *nihonjinron* (theories of Japanese uniqueness or of what it is to be a Japanese), a subject which has generated a huge literature and interest among those concerned with Japanese Studies.

3 We have also implied questions which are beyond the scope of a single paper, such as the social organization of magazine production – including the gender, educational background, international experience and ideology of magazine editors and publishers.

6

CUTIES IN JAPAN

Sharon Kinsella

mina totemo kawaii kedo
everyone's very cute
dakara totemo kawaisō nanda keredo!
and therefore everyone is pitiful!

(*La Pissch*)[1]

Kawaii style dominated Japanese popular culture in the 1980s. Kawaii or 'cute' essentially means childlike; it celebrates sweet, adorable, innocent, pure, simple, genuine, gentle, vulnerable, weak, and inexperienced[2] social behaviour and physical appearances. It has been well described as a style which is 'infantile and delicate at the same time as being pretty' (Yamane 1990) (Figure 6.1). Cute style saturated the multi-media and consumer goods and services whilst they were expanding rapidly between 1970 and 1990 and reached a peak of saccharine intensity in the early 1980s.

Cute people and cute accessories were extremely popular. So much so that original cute fashion became a basic style or aesthetic into which many other more specific and transient fashions such as preppy, punk, skater, folk, black and French were mixed. Cute fashion gradually evolved from the serious, infantile, pink, romanticism of the early 1980s to a more humorous, kitsch, androgynous style which lingered on into the early 1990s. The results of a survey I conducted as late as 1992 showed that 71 per cent of young people between eighteen and 30 years of age either liked or loved kawaii-looking people, and 55.8 per cent either liked or loved kawaii attitudes and behaviour.[3] Although many respondents encountered difficulties deciding what social class they were in and what politics they supported, few had any problems explaining their relative fondness for the cute.

The word kawaii itself was by 1992 estimated to be 'the most widely

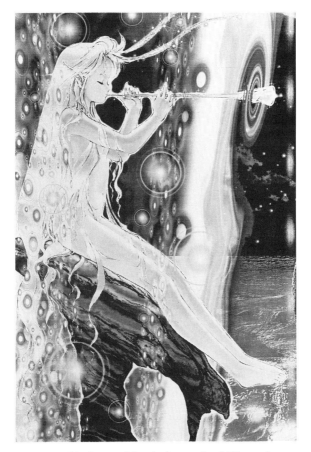

Figure 6.1 Cute and free in fantasy land. Illustration
courtesy of Tsuzuki Katō at Kadokawa Shoten

used, widely loved, habitual word in modern living Japanese' (*CREA*,
November 1992: p.58). Iwashita, president of the *Kikan Fanshii* (Fancy
Goods Periodical) trade journal, recalls that, 'Rather than being another
postwar value, the present meaning of kawaii has not been in existence
for any longer than fifteen years' (Shimamura 1990:225). The term
kawaii appears in dictionaries printed in the Taishō to 1945 period as
kawayushi. In dictionaries printed after the war until around 1970
kawayushi changed into *kawayui*, but the meaning of the word remained
the same. Kawaii is a derivation of a term whose principle meaning was

'shy' or 'embarrassed' and secondary meanings were 'pathetic', 'vulnerable', 'darling', 'loveable' and 'small'. In fact, the modern sense of the word kawaii still has some nuances of pitiful, while the term *kawaisō*, derived directly from kawaii, means pathetic, poor, and pitiable in a generally negative, if not pleasing, sense.

Cute Handwriting and Slang

The emergence of the modern term kawaii in the early 1970s coincides with the beginning of the cute handwriting craze and childish fashion. In 1974, large numbers of teenagers, especially women, began to write using a new style of childish characters. By 1978 the phenomenon had become nation-wide, and in 1985 it was estimated that upwards of five million young people were using the new script.

Previously, Japanese script had been written vertically, using strokes that varied in thickness along their length. The new style was written laterally, preferably using a mechanical pencil to produce very fine even lines (Figure 6.2).[4] Using extremely stylised, rounded characters with English, *katakana*,[5] and little cartoon pictures such as hearts, stars and faces inserted randomly into the text, the new style of handwriting was distinct and the characters difficult to read. In middle and high schools across the country, the craze for writing in the new style caused discipline problems. In some schools, the writing was banned entirely, or tests which were completed in the new cute style would not be marked. The new style of handwriting was described by a variety of names such as *marui ji* (round writing), *koneko ji* (kitten writing), *manga ji* (comic writing) and *burikko ji* (fake-child writing). Through the 1980s magazines, comics, advertising, packaging, and wordprocessor software design (Macintosh) adapted the new style. Yamane Kazuma carried out two years of research into cute handwriting (between 1984 and 1986) which he officially labelled, 'Anomalous Female Teenage Handwriting'.[6] Arguing against the common view that cute handwriting was something young people had mimicked from the lettering in comics, Yamane furnishes evidence that in fact the craze for rounded lettering pre-dates its use in comics, which relied on the later invention of photo composition methods in order to be able to use the round characters. Instead, he concludes that teenagers 'spontaneously' invented the new style. Results of Yamane's survey carried out in 1984–85 amongst middle and high school students showed that the older students were, the more likely it was that they would use the childish hand writing. 22.5 per cent of eleven to twelve-year-old female pupils, 55.3 per cent of twelve

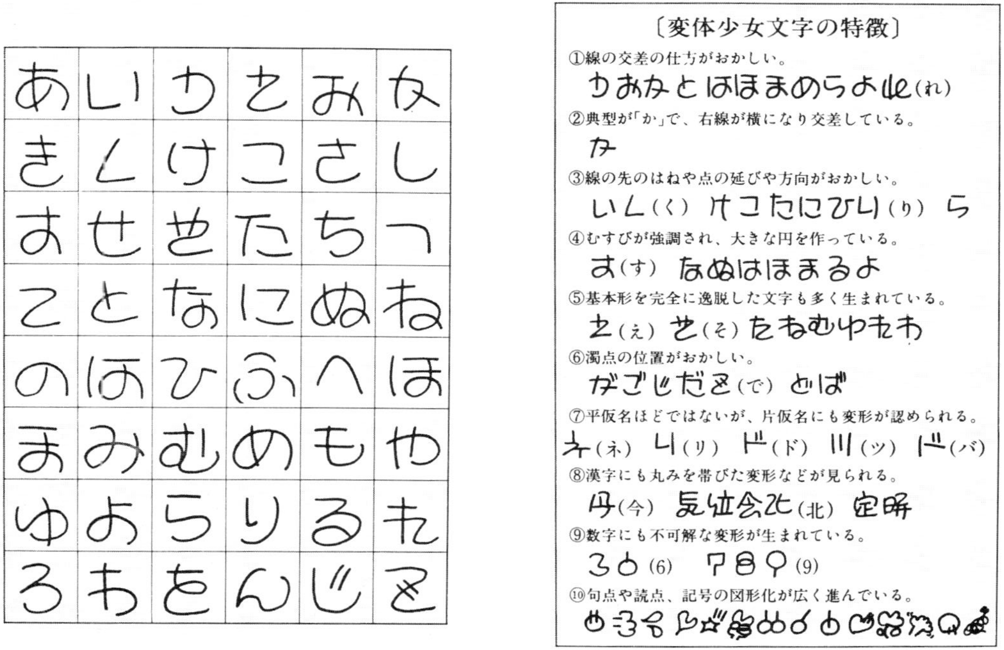

［変体少女文字の特徴］

① 線の交差の仕方がおかしい。
うあから ほほまめらみ れ(れ)

② 典型がわかって、右線が横になり交差している。
カ

③ 線の先のはねや点の延びや方向がおかしい。
いし(く) ナコにに てい(り) ら

④ むすびが強調され、大きな円を作っている。
す(す) ほめほまるみ

⑤ 基本形を完全に逸脱した文字も多く生まれている。
そ(え) とをむゆそや

⑥ 濁点の位置がおかしい。
がづじぜ(ぜ) をは

⑦ 平仮名はどてはないが、片仮名にも変形が認められる。
ネ(ネ) ニ(リ) 凸(ド) 川(ツ) 凸(ハ)

⑧ 漢字にも丸みを帯びた変形などが見られる。
丹(今) 気地会比(北) 定呼

⑨ 数字にも不可解な変形が生まれている。
3 6 (6) マ 8 9 (9)

⑩ 句点や読点、記号の図形化が広く進んでいる。
ゆう。も☆等 ♡♡回☺♡♡Q♋

Figure 6.2 A sample of cute handwriting from 1985, courtesy of Yamane Kazuma

to fifteen-year-old female middle school pupils, and 55.7 per cent of fifteen to eighteen-year-old female high school pupils used the cute writing style. Amongst young men, ten per cent of twelve to fifteen-year-old middle school, and 17.5 per cent of fifteen to eighteen-year-old high school pupils used the cute style. Its increasing incidence amongst older students illustrates that cute handwriting was a style acquired with maturity and exposure to youth culture rather than the result of any adolescent writing disability. Yamane asked some of these young people why they used the round hand writing style and was unequivocally informed:

'It's got a kind of cute feel.'
'I think it's cute and it's my style.'
'I think these letters are the cutest.'
'Cute! They are hard to read but they are so cute I use them.'

(Yamane 1986:132)

It is interesting that cute style did not start in the multi-media which are frequently criticised for originating all the trends of youth culture, if not exercising a virtual mind control over young people. Rather, it began as an underground literary trend amongst young people who developed the habit of writing stylised childish letters to one another and to themselves.

Cute handwriting was arrived at partly through the romanization of Japanese text. The horizontal left to right format of cute handwriting and the liberal use of exclamation marks, as well as English words such as 'love' and 'friend', suggest that these young people were rebelling against traditional Japanese culture and identifying with European culture which they obviously imagined to be more fun. By writing in the new cute style, it was almost as though young people had invented a new language in which they were suddenly able to speak freely on their own terms for the first time. They were thus able to have an intimate relation with the text and express their feelings to their friends more easily. Through cute handwriting, young people made the written Japanese language – considered to be the lynch pin of Japanese culture – their own.

The spread of cute-style handwriting was one element of a broader shift in Japanese culture that took place between the mid-1960s and the mid-1970s in which vital popular culture, sponsored and processed by the new fashion, retail, mass-media and advertising industries, began to push traditional arts and crafts and strictly regulated literary and artistic culture to the margins of society.

At the same time as Japanese youth began to debase written Japanese, infantile slang words began to spread across the nation – typically coming into high-school vogue for only a few months before becoming obsolete again. In 1970 the *Mainichi Shinbun* carried an article describing how the common word *kakkoii*, meaning cool or good, had sprouted a deformed infantile version of itself. The term kakkoii was deliberately mispronounced as *katchoii*, thus mimicking the speech of a toddler incapable of adult pronunciation. There are even a few examples of deliberately contrived childish speech such as *norippigo* officially invented by pop-idol Sakai Noriko, alias Nori P, in 1985. *Norippigo*, now obsolete, consisted of changing the last syllable of common adjectives into a *pi* sound. Therefore *kanashii* (sad) could be changed into *kanappi*, and *ureshii* (happy) could be changed into *ureppi*. Meanwhile, Nori P invented a few words of her own, such as *mamosureppi* (very happy). However, infantile slang was not limited to the contrived overuse of puritanical kindergarten adjectives. 'Sex' became popularly referred to by the morbid term *nyan nyan suru* (to meow meow).

Cute handwriting is strongly associated with the fashion for using baby-talk, acting childish and wearing virginal childish clothes. Young people dressing themselves up as innocent babes in the woods in cute styles were known as *burikko* (fake-children), a term coined by teen starlet Yamada Kuniko in 1980. The noun spawned a verb, *burikko suru* (to fake-child-it), or more simply *buri buri suru* (to fake-it). Another 80s term invented to describe cute pop-idols and their fans is *kawaiikochan* which can be roughly translated as 'cutie-pie-kid'.

The Fancy Goods Industry

Cute culture started as youth culture amongst teenagers, especially young women. Cute culture was not founded by business. But in the disillusioned calm known as the *shirake* after the last of the student riots in 1971, the consumer boom was just beginning, and it did not take companies and market research agencies very long to discover and capitalise on cute style, which had manifested itself in manga and young people's handwriting.

In 1971 Sanrio, the Japanese equivalent of Hallmark Cards, experimented by printing cute designs on previously plain writing paper and stationary. Sanrio began to produce cute-decorated stationary and fancy diaries for the dreamy school students hooked on the cute handwriting craze. The success of this early prototype of *fanshi guzzu* (fancy goods), inspired by cute style in manga animation and young people's handwriting,

225

encouraged Sanrio to expand production, and its range of fancy goods proliferated. The company established a firm monopoly in the fancy goods market and during 1990 sold ¥200 billion worth of goods (Shimamura 1990:60–62), whilst the fancy goods business as a whole reached an estimated turnover of ¥10 trillion in 1990 (*Japan Times* January 5, 1991). Typical fancy goods sold in cute little shops were stationary, cuddly toys and gimmicks, toiletries, lunch boxes and cutlery, bags, towels and other personal paraphernalia.

The crucial ingredients of a fancy good are that it is small, pastel, round, soft, loveable, *not* traditional Japanese style but a foreign – in particular European or American – style, dreamy, frilly and fluffy. Most fancy goods are also decorated with cartoon characters. The essential anatomy of a cute cartoon character consists in its being small, soft, infantile, mammalian, round, without bodily appendages (e.g. arms), without bodily orifices (e.g. mouths), non-sexual, mute, insecure, helpless or bewildered. Sanrio invented a large cast of cute proprietary characters to endorse and give life to its fancy goods: *Button Nose, Tiny Poem, Duckydoo, Little Twin Stars, Cheery Chums, Vanilla Bean* and, most famous of all, *Hello Kitty* and *Tuxedo Sam*. Not only do these cute characters inhabit cute-shops; they have also worked hard selling under license the goods and services of over 90 Japanese companies. A large number of these are financial institutions such as 23 banks, including Mitsui, Sumitomo, Sanwa, and Mitsubishi; fourteen stock companies, including Yamaichi, Daiwa and Nomura; and seven insurance companies, including Nihon Seimei, Sumitomo Seimei and Yasuda Kasai (Figure 6.3).

Cute design was not limited to banking cards and stationary, however. For the privileged, whose passion for cute was stronger than their sense of traditional good taste, there was the option of purchasing a 'short cake' house resembling a little cottage or fairyland abode in Hiroo or Seijō, or a cute rounded apartment in Roppongi or Akasaka-Mitsuke. The 1980s was the decade which left behind police boxes designed as gingerbread houses (*okashi-no-ie*).

Meanwhile Sanrio organised Sanrio festivals and athletics meetings, *Hello Kitty* Santa tours, a *Strawberry Mate* travelling caravan, Halloween and Valentine extravaganzas, and printed *Ichigo Shinbun* (The Strawberry News). Sanrio built cute shopping arcades such as the Sanrio Ginza Gallery, and Sanrio Fantagen – a cluster of eighteen cute goods shops in Funabashi – Ichigo Hall in Den'en Chōfu, Sanrio Theatre in Matsudo, Harmony Land in Kyūshū, and Puroland in Tama City, Tōkyō.

Cartoon characters printed onto goods literally add character to their

226

Figure 6.3 Mitsubishi Bank credit
card advertisement

lifelessness and slogans etched onto the actual good or printed on the
packaging put across more forcibly the same notion of light fun. Cute
slogans were more often written in fractured English or pseudo-French
than in Japanese. A toilet bowl called *petit etoile*; a pink toaster in the
shape of a cottage called *My Sweet Bread Toaster*; a can opener which
says: *This can-opener is not just a kitchen tool. Treat it kindly and it will
be our loyal friend*; school note paper inscribed with the message: *OK!
You're in my team. Let's have fun together!*; and a set of plates saying:
Life is sweet like a poem when you are with kind friends.

227

The industrial, impure or masculine nature of some of the objects decorated in fancy style can produce incongruous images, such as the almost transvestite-like character of baby pink road diggers or adult gambling machines called *My Poochy* and *Fairies*. But there is no mischievous conspiracy of camp designers behind these articles. Despite appearances to the contrary, there is no sense of camp in Japanese culture. In some cases this mismatch between the good's function and its design has simply gone unnoticed; at other times an attempt has been made to camouflage and mask the dirty image of the good or service in question. The typical household toilet, maybe unconnected to a sewage system and sometimes foul smelling, was often made to resemble a tiny grotto, festooned with puffy gingham curtains, quilted toilet brush covers and toilet roll dispensers, fluffy toilet seat covers, fancy cartoon slippers. Love hotels, which sell room space for sex, are named after good, sweet girls like *Anne of Green Gables* and Laura of the *Little House on the Prairie*. Yakuza-run *pachinko* gambling parlours are recognisable as the light buildings full of pink and blue neon with baskets of plastic flowers arranged on the pavement outside.

Cute style gives goods a warm, cheer-me-up atmosphere. What capitalist production processes de-personalise, the good cute design re-personalises. Consumption of lots of cute style goods with powerful emotion-inducing properties could ironically disguise and compensate for the very alienation of individuals from other people in contemporary society. Cuteness loaned personality and a subjective presence to otherwise meaningless – and often literally useless – consumer goods and in this way made them much more attractive to potential buyers. The good could appear to have a character of its own because of its winsome UFO or mammalian shape, such as little round, weeping digitalized vacuum cleaners and rice cookers, or the 1980s' *mini kāsu* (little cars) designed to feel playful and cuddly.[7] Modern consumers might not be able to meet and develop relationships enough with people, but the implication of cute goods design was that they could always attempt to develop them through cute objects.

Cute Clothes

Adverts and articles printed in *an-an* and *non-no*,[8] two of the leading women's fashion magazines, suggest that the desire for a more than just youthful, but distinctly child-like, cutie-pie look began in the mid-1970s. In May 1975, *an-an* ran a special article introducing its readers to the novel new concept of cuteness:

228

'**PLAY! Cuteness! Go for the young theme!** On dates we only want feeling, but our clothes are like old ladies! It is the time you have to express who you really are. Whatever you say, co-ordinating a very young theme is cute. Wear something like a French slip . . . for accessories try a cute little bracelet. BUT! It will look much cuter if you don't use high quality exclusive materials. Cute-looking plastic and veneer look younger. For your feet try wearing colourful socks with summer sandals, it will exude a sporty cuteness! Hair is cutest styled straight with children's plastic hair pins fixed in the sides.'

Cute clothes were – and are – deliberately designed to make the wearer appear childlike and demure. Original cute clothes were simple white, pink and pastel shades for women and more sort of bright and rainbow-coloured for men (Figure 6.4). The clothes were often fluffy and frilly with puffed sleeves and lots of ribbons – a style known as 'fancy' – or alternatively were cut slightly small or tight and came decorated with cartoon characters and slogans. In the first half of the 1980s the most fashionable design house in Tōkyō was 'Pink House Ltd.' which produced adorable outfits for budding cuties. Pink House was so sought after that the Hakuhodo Institute of Life and Living (HILL) began to refer to young people aspiring to the Pink House image as the 'Pink House movement' (HILL 1984: 227). Women's underwear was also cute, the dominant taste being for puritanical white pants and vests, in addition to the infamous white tights, frilly ankle socks or knee length 'school-girl' socks. Then there was the understanding habit of manufacturers in placing great lengths of elastic in underwear so that women's pants often looked like a little girl's when not worn, but fortunately stretched to three or four times the size when in service.

By the late 80s, cute fashion had matured into a cheeky, androgynous, tomboy sweetness. Apart from the perennially popular tight, white, baby vest-like T-shirts, nursery colours, cartoon characters and baby doll frills mellowed out into woolly Noddy hats, dungarees and tight little sweaters. This change is well illustrated by the fashion magazine *Cutie For Independent Girls*,[9] first published in spring 1986 and attracting a readership of 100,000 by October 1989. Obviously, *Cutie* takes cuteness as its starting point, but on top of the basic ingredient of childlikeness, *Cutie* style is also chic, eccentric, androgynous and humorous (Figure 6.5). *Cutie* is published monthly by the odd-ball media corporation Takarajimasha, which was founded by a group of ex-revolutionary Waseda University students, and is better known for publishing the

229

Figure 6.4 Pop-idol Kawai Sonoko in a little doggy outfit

sub-culture oriented magazine *Takarajima* through the 1980s; in *Cutie* the rebellious, individualistic, freedom-seeking attitude embodied in acting childlike and pursuing cute fashion is very clear. The magazine prints pages of photographs of readers, whom it calls 'kids', posing in clubs and streets trying to look bad and cute at the same time.

Figure 6.5 Funky-sweet – the front cover of a 1993 issue
of *Cutie For Independent Girls*

Cute Food

Young people took to purging themselves on cakes and sweets. Eating confectionery is not only a habit with child-like connotations, but also symbolically stresses personal sweetness which in Japanese (*amai*), as in the English, refers interchangeably to both edibles and charming people. The association between sugary foods, especially cake, and children's culture is strong in Japan, as Edwards elaborates:

Alcohol in general is considered one of the spicy foods which as a class are the province of adults, and which children are taught to avoid in favour of sweet ones. Cakes, as sweet foods, have a close association with children in Japan. Special cakes were made in pre-war times at the naming ceremony of a new born child.

(Edwards 1987:66)

The most popular and fashionable foods of the 1980s were soft, sweet and milky, including icecream, cakes, milk drinks and soft deserts. The yearly growth rate of the icecream market in the 1980s was five per cent and, by 1989, the sale of high-class icecream in Japan accounted for US$100 million per annum. Most of this icecream was sold in the fancy icecream parlours which arrived on the streets of Tōkyō and Ōsaka in the early 80s at the beginning of the 'icecream boom' caused by the sudden increase in adult consumers:

Until now icecream was always considered as 'something for the kids', however it has recently become fashionable and achieved a certain adult respectability . . .

(*Focus Japan* August 1986:4)

Icecream, puddings and cakes purchased at 'fancy patisseries' and cafés, and cleverly invented baby food like *cheezu mushi pan* (squashy, cheese-flavoured cake) were popular throughout the 1980s, whilst other sweet foods such as creme caramel, tiramisu, nata de coco, tapioca pudding and panacotta attained briefer fad followings (Figure 6.6).

The ideal 'cute' food carried with it a marketing image, frequently something petite, frilly and Victorianesque; rustic and olde worlde; or derived from fairy-tale images scavenged from the nursery. A good example is Rolly Doll, founded in 1985, which operates and franchises over sixty fresh-baked cookie shops across Japan and owes most of its ¥5 billion annual sales to nostalgia. Its founder explains:

Drifting through sweet memories of childhood I recalled the special aroma of fresh baked cookies, emanating from Aunt Stella's farm kitchen in Pennsylvania's rustic Amish country. The concept was complete in a flash: the image, the taste, the aroma, the wholesome goodness of an earlier America where 'kinder and gentler' were the norm.

(*Focus Japan* 1990:8)

Figure 6.6 Very fancy. Fujiya chocolates

Figure 6.7 Typical Matsuda Seiko, waking up in her nightie, and cuddling dolls and foreign children

Cute Idols

Matsuda Seiko was to cute what Sid Vicious was to punk. Between April 1980 and 1988 she became the reigning queen and prototype for a whole new industry of 'idol singers' that flourished in the 1980s.[10] Matsuda was flat-chested and bow-legged and on TV she wore children's clothes, took faltering steps and blushed, cried, and giggled for the camera (Figure 6.7). Every one of her 23 singles, released between 1980 and 1988, became number one smash hits (Imidas 1991:746). Matsuda gained her popularity by being childish. She published several books for her fans, filled with large wobbly handwriting, small words and 'heart-warming' poems like the one below:

> Seiko always . . . . .
> Wants to see a dream.
> What I'm thinking,
> I want to try and put in a poem.
> So my little heart,
> Can reach out to you a little.

(Matsuda 1982: 147)

Following in Matsuda's footsteps, most of the 1980s idols were released in time to become famous between the ages of fourteen and sixteen. The debut age of packaged pop-stars has in fact been getting progressively younger since 1974. This includes male sweety bands like Tanokin Trio aged fourteen to nineteen (debut 1980), SMAP aged fourteen to fifteen (debut 1988), and Hikaru Genji aged fourteen to sixteen (debut 1988), as well as female idols such as Kyon Kyon aged fourteen (debut 1982), Nakayama Miho aged fifteen (debut 1984), and WINK aged fourteen (debut 1988).

Cute stars dominated television and magazines as well as pop-music. Known by the collective term 'talents', their appearance as hosts, contributors or ornamentation in a great many television programmes was an innovation that partly originated with Fuji Television's *Yūyake Nyan Nyan* (Sunset Kittens) programme in 1985. Katō Kōichi describes the original reasons for the programme's popularity:

> They responded to the host's questions, and played silly games, like a competition to see who could stay in an extremely hot bath the longest. Childish and frivolous as the show was, it neverthe-less attracted far more viewers than programmes featuring the performances of professionals and celebrities.

(Katō 1987:89)

235

Sunset Kittens, on air daily at five o'clock, became such a popular programme that it has since achieved the status of a TV classic. The programme was hosted entirely by school girls and consisted of games, songs, sketches ridiculing adults, and an ongoing competition amongst school girls who wanted to join the team of amateur hosts, otherwise known as the *Onyanko Club* (Kitten Club). Eventually the number of kittens expanded to 52, and over the following years some of the most popular girls, such as Kawai Sonoko and Kokusho Sayuri, began to branch out into separate careers, releasing hit singles and diffusing into other television programmes. However, the practice of using cute childish stars with no specific talent, such as singing or acting, to increase the interest value of programmes began to fade out by the 1990s.

Instead, in 1991 there was a national craze for the 100 year old twin sisters, Kin and Gin, who made frequent appearances in talk shows on television, had their faces printed on all kinds of fancy merchandise – such as Kin-san and Gin-san hard boiled orange sweets – and even recorded a song on CD together. They were described by young and older people alike as both kawaii (cute) and kawaisō (pitiful). Kin and Gin were sweet, frail old ladies with girlish old-fashioned ways of expressing themselves and, like many very old people, they were slightly out of touch. The case of Kin-san and Gin-san illustrates that, although cute was principally about childishness, a sense of weakness and disability – which is a part of childishness – was a very important constituent of the cute aesthetic. In fact cute and pitiful were often the same thing (Figure 6.8).

Toddlers, baby animals, and frail old ladies are the natural models for cute, and cute characters produced by the fancy goods industry were deliberately designed to be physically frail, emulating weak members of society. Cute characters like *Hello Kitty* and *Totoro* have stubbly arms, no fingers, no mouths, huge heads, massive eyes – which can hide no private thoughts from the viewer – nothing between their legs, pot bellies, swollen legs or pigeon feet – if they have feet at all. Cute things can't walk, can't talk, can't in fact do anything at all for themselves because they are physically handicapped. Discussing cuteness in America, Harris makes this point very clearly:

> Although the gaze we turn on the cute thing seems maternal and solicitous, it is in actuality a transformative gaze that will stop at nothing to appease its hunger for expressing pity and big heartedness, even at the expense of mutilating the object of its affections.
>
> (Harris 1993:134)

Figure 6.8 Pop-idol Hiroko spills her adorable tears for
the fans

However, cute fashion in Japan was more than merely cuddling cute things; it was all about 'becoming' the cute object itself by acting infantile. Young Japanese, especially women, purchased cute accessories and filled their rooms, cars, desks at work, and handbags with sweet paraphernalia as a way of surrounding themselves by cuteness, to the point where they felt transformed and could enter this cute-only world themselves. Being cute meant behaving childlike – which involved an act of self-mutilation, posing with pigeon toes, pulling wide-eyed in-nocent expressions, dieting, acting stupid, and essentially denying the existence of the wealth of insights, feelings, and humour that maturity brings with it. In cute culture, young people became popular according to their apparent weakness, dependence and inability, rather than be-cause of their strengths and capabilities.

Cute Ideas

During a survey amongst 18 to 30-year-old men and women carried out in Tōkyō in 1992, I asked respondents to write down freely what cute meant to them. The question asked was: 'In what kinds of situations might you use the word kawaii?', and the replies were dominated by themes related to childhood. Respondents said they used kawaii when they felt people were *childlike*:

'Children and adults are innocently frolicking about.'
'When you have treated your companions a little contemptuously as though you thought they were little fools.'
'I use it as a complimentary word when people are childlike.'
'When people's faces are perpetually childlike.'
'People who experience things in a childish way.'
'When my friends seem precocious and their clothes and gestures childish.'
'People that in places are as pure as children.'

These childlike people were often childlike because of their apparent *innocence*:

'Loveable idiots.'
'Cute is people so lacking in experience that they can't communicate.'
'When I see a clear girlish innocence in someone.'
'Tiny innocent things.'
'Babies, children and people younger than me with an expression of innocent obedience.'

Beyond mere innocence, some respondents felt that kawaii referred to people in a state of *naive* unity with their world:

'When children and friends are happy and quite indifferent to their lack of common sense.'
'People who fit into their surroundings and lose sight of themselves.'

Cuteness was also a very *unconscious* thing, as is reflected both in the degree of unawareness respondents displayed in their answers and in a few outright admissions that kawaii was about not thinking at all:

'The word just pops out unconsciously.'
'When people are acting without thinking at all.'

Kawaii was also considered to be a *natural* thing:

'When I feel natural.'
'When a friend is genuinely and naturally lovely.'

Secondly, respondents used kawaii when they felt that warm *emotional contact* between individuals had been expressed:

'The effort people expend for other people is cute.'
'When I see something that is dear to me.'
'When people make contact with someone else.'
'When my feelings are softened and made culpable.'
'When I see an incredibly sympathetic face.'
'When without any connection to profit the mood of your heart is expressed.'

These sociable, sincere emotions tended to come from *inside individuals* where it was normally hidden:

'It is about the internal part of you seen when you make a chance gesture or move that is disarming.'
'The greatness inside someone oozes out.'
'When things warm the spirit.'
'When from the bottom of my heart I am able to think that something is sincerely cute.'
'When it is hard to say "I love you".'
'When people show their real selves without any affectation.'

The *fashionability* of cute was apparent in the answers of respondents who associated cute predominantly with fashion items and attractive people, or who mentioned the peer pressure they felt to use the word cute:

'Attractive faces.'
'Things to my taste. When I see and touch things.'
'When I see the kind of little things and clothes I like.'
'When I realise my friends want me to say "cute".'

Cute was also strongly associated with animals, or more precisely pets, which – needless to say – were very popular during the 1980s.

'When animals and children play for my attention (*amaeru*).'
'When I see the gestures of the animals I look after.'

Some respondents directly described as cute an individual's *weakness* and inability to deal with everyday life:

'When I look and I feel that someone is trying as hard as they can and grappling with something.'
'When someone's situation overwhelms them more than my situation overwhelms me.'
'When someone is happy and then suddenly their smile drops, or when someone is relieved.'

It is quite apparent from these statements that, for cute fans, cute sentiments were all about the recovery of a childlike emotional and mental state. This childlike state was considered to be innocent, natural and unconscious. And it was one in which people expressed genuine warm feelings and love for one another. But most of the time this expressive emotional state was hidden, trapped inside each individual and something not often visible to other people. For the fans, cute people and things seemed to be in a state of happy, naive, and natural unconscious unity with life and other people.

The idea underlying cute was that young people who had passed through childhood and entered adult life had been forced to cover up their real selves and hide their emotions under a layer of artifice. But the original childlike innocence of each individual, rather than disappearing forever, was still present in some naive individuals and could be glimpsed occasionally in the gestures, expressions and attitudes of almost any kind of person. Cute childlike behaviour was considered genuine and pure – implying that the experiences and social relations acquired after maturation were considered to form a false, shallow, external layer.[11] The logic of this assumption is quite coherent, although ironically cute is in fact extremely artificial and stylised. Cute is the particular style derived from adults (and children[12]) pretending to be childlike. Furthermore, the 'childlikeness' aspired to is not so much real childish behaviour – which must include subservience, temper tantrums, bed-wetting and frustration – as the idolised childlikeness described in the neo-romantic tradition.

Respondents tended to think of cuteness manifested in the minutiae of friends, gestures and behaviour as profoundly natural. At the same time as they imagined cute to be natural, they did not tend to view it as a historically defined style. Young people fond of cute things and acting like *burikko* (fake children) did not consider themselves to be engaging in a current fashion at all. This apparently unconscious involvement was very distinctive of cute fashion. I say 'apparently' because one of the ideals of the cute fashion, as we know, is precisely to be uncontrived and genuine, so that any real cutie was obliged to cover up the traces of her conscious effort to look sweet.

Childhood Romance, Adulthood and Individualism

We have established that cute style was all about acting childish in an effort to partake of some of childhood's legendary simplicity, happiness, and emotional warmth. Underpinning cute style are the neo-romantic notions of childhood as an entirely separate, and hence unmaligned, pure sphere of human life. In fact, the general belief that childhood is 'another world', in some ways an ideal world, has been the dominant perception of childhood throughout the developed world for most of the twentieth century. Early European criticism of the spiritual poverty of modern society, which developed in response to industrialisation and urbanisation, led to a romantic re-evaluation of pre-industrial society. For the first time, past and more primitive lives in rural communities and in childhood were described as a period of innocence, simplicity and spiritual unity which had been ruptured and destroyed by the corrupting and alienating forces of modern social relations and cities.

Urban nostalgia for this wholesome country life did not result in a cute aesthetic until this sentiment was captured by Disney animation and delivered to a mass audience. Disney made his first animations in the interwar years, producing *Steam Boat Willy* in 1928 and *The Opry House* in 1929. As with Charlie Chaplin, Disney animations were adored in Japan, as much as, if not more than, in America, until they were banned for the period of the war. But from 1950, Disney comics and animation, this time full-length productions such as *Snow White and the Seven Dwarfs*, flooded into the country again. Going to visit the cinema to see Disney films on specially designated days became a part of primary school education (see Ono 1983). Disney had a big influence both on Japanese animation and comics and on the introduction of the modern cute aesthetic into Japan.

However, whereas Disney cute was based more on a sentimental journey back into an idealised rural society populated with happy little animals and rural characters taken from folk stories, Japanese cute fashion became more concerned with a sentimental journey back into an idealised childhood. As Disney romanticised nature in relation to industrial society, so Japanese cuteness romanticised childhood in relation to adulthood. By idolising their childhoods and remnant childishness, young Japanese people implicitly damned their individual futures as adults in society. Condemning adulthood was an individualised and limited way of condemning society generally.

In the survey I conducted in 1992, I also asked respondents to describe the way they felt about adulthood and childhood. In relation to adulthood the question I asked was: 'When you think of adulthood what images come to mind?' Although some respondents gave positive appraisals of adulthood, describing it as a period of 'freedom' and 'potential', the great majority of respondents – who, we must remember, are not teenagers but young people already well embarked in their adult lives – described adulthood as a bleak period of life:

> 'The harshness of having to make do everyday and make a living, the harshness of supporting a family.'
> 'Controlled society, hard work to help society, responsibility and effort.'
> 'It is a hard society where you take responsibility for all your actions, working hours are long and free time is lacking, fun, gentleness and naturalness are hard to give and let out.'
> 'A dirty world of power.'
> 'The degree of freedom on the spiritual side is lower than that of a child, responsibility to big organisations becomes very large, dreams disappear as the necessity to conform comes nearer.'
> 'Strictness day in and day out, you can't stop working.'
> 'Life is lonely'

The negativity of the answers given is startling. Their assessments of Japanese society were very dark, and their impressions of an adult life in that society equally depressing. Adulthood was directly understood to mean society, and vice versa; it was not viewed as a source of freedom or independence, it was viewed as quite the opposite, as a period of restrictions and hard work. The most common impression of adulthood was that it involved responsibility (*sekinin*), typically a huge responsibility, which was not an abstract individual, but specific, responsibility to society, to one's family, and to large organisations, in which one had to work hard and conform to expectations. After social responsibility, respondents cited a general lack of free time and tight social regulations as the unhappy characteristics of adulthood. The mid-1970s to mid-1980s was a period notable for its lack of political and social imagination in Japan and, in relation to this widespread understanding that adulthood was a period of restriction and overwhelming obligations, childhood – one of the oldest and most immediate sites of imagined freedom – became extremely popular. Cute fashion idolises childhood because it is seen as a place of individual freedom unattainable in society.

There is in Japan no strong pattern of thought which links adulthood with individual emancipation. Maturity, which in the west has been linked to the authority and rights of the individual, still tends to be thought of according to the Confucian model in modern Japan. That is, maturity is commonly considered as the ability to cooperate well in a group, to accept compromises, to fulfil obligations to parents, employers, and so on, and carry to out social responsibilities. This underlying ideology is another reason why rebellion against society in Japanese youth culture has developed into a rebellion against adulthood as well. For the same reason intellectuals, ascetics and artistic outsiders from Japanese society have long carried the stigma of infantilism, and some have possibly even played up to the image of being childlike eccentrics.

Cute fashion was, therefore, a kind of rebellion or refusal to co-operate with established social values and realities. It was a demure, indolent little rebellion rather than a conscious, aggressive and sexually provocative rebellion of the sort that has been typical of western youth cultures. Rather than acting sexually provocative to emphasise their maturity and independence, Japanese youth acted pre-sexual and vulnerable in order to emphasise their immaturity and inability to carry out social responsibilities. Either way the result was the same; teachers in the west were as infuriated by cocky pupils acting tough, as Japanese teachers were with uncooperative pupils writing cute and acting infantile.

Cute Ladies

Young women were the main generators of, and actors in, cute culture. From the consumption of cute goods and services and the wearing of cute clothes, to the faking of childish behaviour and innocent looks, young women were initially far more actively involved in cute culture than were men. This is not to say that cuteness was not popular amongst young men – on the contrary it was very popular – but young men were largely relegated to the passive, wistful audiences of the performance of cute culture put on by women. Towards the late 1980s, more and more young men did in fact join the ranks of cute young women themselves, and cute style became more androgynous and more asexually infantile. The gender-related nature of youth culture in itself is not new. Nearly all originally western youth cultures in the postwar period – such as mods, rockers, new romantics, techno, punk and hip hop – have been dominated by young men with young women playing a more passive, side-kick role. To date, the much greater original involvement of men than women in other youth cultures has attracted little specific notice – perhaps for the simple and valid reason that the greater active involvement of young men had seemed to be normal or natural, given the general structure of modern societies. Consequently, the creation of cute youth culture around young women has attracted a lot of notice. While old-fashioned mums in England grumble that they can no longer distinguish between girls and lads because the girls all dress like boys these days, Japanese social commentators have bemoaned the domination of modern culture by young women and the increasingly cute, little-girlish appearances of young men.

The position of the young unmarried woman in contemporary Japanese society represents greater freedom than that of the young man. Young women – by virtue of the strength of their oppression and exclusion from most of the labour market and thus from active social roles – have come to represent in the media the freest, most un-hampered elements of society. Young women pushed outside mainstream Japanese society are associated with an exotic and longed-for world of individual fulfilment, decadence, consumption and play. Young men do not represent freedom in the same way. Nor, in their role as subservient company employees, do they embody any of the characteristics of the powerful, antagonistic, macho individualism of the male in western societies and their youth cultures. For many young men, cute fashion represents freedom and an escape from the pressure of social expect-ations and regulations. Typically these young men both wear cute fashions, emulate cute behaviour themselves, and fetishize young women – either real girl friends or syrupy sweet little girl heroines depicted in lolita complex comic books for adolescent boys. Adolescent women (*shōjo*) provide the elusive model for cute culture. As John Treat discusses in some detail in a later chapter of this book (see also Treat 1993), *shōjo*, the leaders of cute, have been transformed into an abstract concept and a sign for consumption in the Japanese mass-media and modern intel-lectual discourse.

For their part, young women – even more than young men – desire to remain free, unmarried and young. Whilst a woman was still a *shōjo* outside the labour market, outside of the family she could enjoy the vacuous freedom of an outsider in society with no distinct obligations or role to play. But when she grew up and got married, the social role of a young woman was possibly more oppressive than that of a young company man. In her role as an unmarried woman, she was pushed to the margins of society, but was still able to work as an OL on a temporary contract in company offices, spend her money on herself and her friends, and socialise in urban centres. Maturity and marriage threat-ened to separate her from these privileges, and very likely to shunt her off to a small apartment in a remote and unattractive suburb, with only her devotion to her children and their school books to occupy her. While the 'moratorium mentality' and lack of desire to grow up and take on adult social roles and responsibilities was a feeling spread right through Japanese society in the 1980s, for women the urge to prolong youth and its appearances took on the form of a profound struggle. These young women thus savoured their brief years of freedom as unattached urban socialites through decadent consumption, and also expressed their fear of losing that freedom and youth through the cute aesthetic. Shimamura (1990) notes that, as young women get older and particularly in the period immediately prior to marriage, their fascination with and immersion in cute culture becomes still more acute.

Cute Consumption

Young people entered cute culture through consumption of cute goods with cute appearances and emotional qualities. The increasingly large disposable incomes of youth and young women in particular throughout the 1980s, and the inventiveness of Japanese businesses in providing goods to make them part with their money, had the greatest determining influence on the highly commercial nature of cute culture. Cute did, however, seem to be accessible *exclusively* through consumption. This was both because it encouraged hedonism and sensual pleasure necessitating consumption, and because, even during their youth and bachelor days, it was very difficult for Japanese to be cute full-time. Cute culture along with other youth cultures could only be enjoyed during brief moments of private time, such as at home between working and sleeping, or in the car, and in tiny private places such as inside handbags, presents and pencil cases. There was not only no space for cute to ever become part of a 'lifestyle'; the fantastical nature of cute culture itself contained so few references to real life and society that there was in any case little way of understanding it in terms of everyday life. Cute culture had to be entered and left in a matter of minutes or moments, which lent it to construction by ephemeral products and places of consumption of goods and leisure services.

And childlikeness was an expensive youth culture. There is no upper limit to the cost of childish clothes and accessories because perfect childlikeness is a particularly unattainable ideal that becomes less and less attainable with time. The demanding ideal of cute fashion generated a built-in orientation towards the consumption of goods which could transform a young person to look and feel something like a child.

Unlike even those ironically well-marketed western origin youth cultures such as punk and grunge, cute culture did not condemn materialism or the display of wealth. Many contemporary western youth cultures have been distinctly opposed to, amongst other things, modern consumer culture, encouraging a tendency among hip youth to condemn materialism, to appear to or actually buy little, to dress down, and to find cheap, second-hand goods with which to adorn themselves. In contrast, personal consumption is portrayed as something rather anti-social and immoral in mainstream Japanese society, and cute youth culture went against the grain of older social values by sanctioning consumption.

Anti-cute Ideas

There were anti-cute elements. Anti-cute people can be divided into two social categories: young people who considered cute to be too weak and stupid; and conservative intellectuals in academia and the civil service who were appalled by the spread of a new female-led youth culture which did not accord to traditional canons of good taste, let alone good morals.

Punks, rockers and young people attracted to the 'indies' scene felt that their own fashion was more politically progressive, intelligent and sophisticated. These types of independent young people would have been likely to read magazines like *Takarajima*, Japan's main sub-culture magazine which frequently criticised the commercial pop-idol industry whilst promoting *YMO*, Japanese indie bands, 'New Age Fashion', encouraging the import of UK punk music and fashion, and challenging pop-stars like *David Bowie*, *The Jam*, and *Siouxie and the Banshees*. Many of these young people, who in the 1990s are in their late twenties and early thirties, entered *katakana* and multi-media professions as producers, editors, freelance writers, and designers, and brought their disdain for cute and other common cultures with them.

Amongst intellectuals, criticism of cute style blended with the general moral attack on youth – and especially young women's behaviour and social values – which was sustained through the 1970s and 1980s. Ironically, this is also the period in postwar history when Japanese youth were most politically passive and untroublesome for the establishment. But in fact it is this extremely passive behaviour at which intellectuals began to take offence. Rather than reflecting on 1968 and being grateful for the enormous inactivity of Japanese youth, moral academics complained that this passivity was part of an attempt on the part of youth to shrink away from their active duties and obligations in society, at work, in the public space, in the home. Intellectuals demanded that youth show their commitment to the social order by an eager, positively motivated, moral engagement with their traditional social roles as company man and housewife, rather than merely refrain from active criticism of society. Cute fashion was perceived correctly as one more example of social disaffection and malaise amongst youth. Rather than attempting to grow up and take on social obligations that adulthood brings with it, youth were quite obviously attempting to avoid all these oppressive demands made on them by aspiring not to grow up at all and immersing themselves in cute culture.

Cute 'boys' and 'girls' were portrayed as spending horrendous amounts of money on music, clothes and cute 'things' in Harajuku and Aoyama, or meeting their friends at trendy restaurants and bars, and going on frequent holidays skiing or abroad. And this they surely did where possible – but it wasn't cute youth in particular that consumed, but the goods consumed that were particularly cute. Retailers, advertisers and manufacturers scrambled over one another to invent new goods, services and gimmicks to sell on the expanding domestic consumer market, as they sought to appropriate the cute style.

Conservative critics felt that allowing this consumption to continue out of control could only encourage the idea that life was about the pleasure of the individual and not about gaining moral satisfaction through fulfilling social obligations and responsibilities. Individualistic consumption and the cute values of sensual abandon and play, which provided an apology for consumption, were accused of undermining Japanese tradition:

> Play can only be truly satisfying when a sense of balance reveals the substance of tradition. True play by drastically diminishing one's own stature in relation to tradition, expands one's world. Puerile play by exaggerating one's position in relation to tradition, constricts one's world. I bear no ill will towards commercial civilisation. Like it or not, I am very much its beneficiary. This does not mean, however, that I feel the least inclination to glorify it in any way. The maturity of culture requires a certain degree of serenity and moderation, but commercial civilisation spreads noise and excess in the name of vigorous differentiation. As little as I know about foreign lands I am well aware that the 'Japan problem' brought on by our commercial civilisation has grown to serious proportions. As Ishikawa Yoshimi has pointed out, the basic Japan problem is not the trade surplus but implicit and explicit disdain for the Japanese way of life itself.
>
> (Nishibe 1986:41–42)

Nishibe directly equates play with consumption and makes it quite clear that the concept of play (*asobi*) in the contemporary Japanese context was no more than a cute way of saying 'do what you want'.

But the play motif ran right through the core of advertising, retailing, and the multi-media in the 1980s. For these industries, which had to appeal to the private, often solo, consumer to purchase their goods, the idea of play became a useful aphorism for individual fulfilment through consumption. Incidentally, the patronising implication of the equation of individual free time and consumption with play, made both amongst the Japanese intelligentsia and in the mass media, was that Japanese youth were insignificant people even to themselves whose private activities amounted to little more than child's play.

Cuties were also denigrated for being infantile. For a style which labels its self as infantile it is hardly a critique to say that it is infantile. However Fujioka, PR director for Dentsū, certainly came up with an original reason for why cute might be literally 'stupid' when he described cuteness as the epitome of thought without reason:

> Cuteness can not be developed by reason and cannot be evaluated without being seen. Thus it is really not in the least surprising that for grasshoppers *[modern youth, spendthrifts]*, making what one would want oneself means responding not to any practical demand but to the subjective, intuitive demand for cuteness.
>
> (Fujioka 1986:35–6)

Fujioka was using post-modernist theory to make his point, but most critics were not so generous. The general opinion of cute was that it was 'juvenile, effeminate and tasteless' (Shimamura 1991). In this equation the feminine, the tasteless, the infantile, and the popular were used as virtually interchangeable concepts, giving a good idea of the kind of narrow prejudices of the critics. Yamane, in particular, took it for granted that infantile meant feminine:

> What can we conclude about this complete infantilisation of Japan? The answer is straightforward. The girl has jumped up. The girl is boisterous.
>
> (Yamane 1990:11)

Nakano Osamu, a leading intellectual and expert on youth echoes Yamane's sentiments:

> With the action of one selfish nod of their head in response to a question, a response originally typical of children, young people display their infantilism. At times female university students babble

to themselves and from their attitude and demeanour to their facial expression they act just exactly as though they were children.

(Nakano 1985:62)

One gets the strong impression that Nakano feels that the problem of ingratiating 'selfish' cute fashion could be solved if only women were banned from universities altogether. Women were blamed for feminizing society. But the so-called feminine behaviour described by critics is not actually traditional feminine behaviour at all, but a new kind of petulant refusal to be traditional subservient females which can be observed in modern young women following cute fashion. Cute behaviour was perceived as 'selfish' not just because of its seeming refusal to co-operate with social expectations – in this case respectful and polite behaviour in the presence of superiors like Mr Nakano – but because it was strongly correlated with indulgence and individualistic consumption.

Young women, in particular, have born the brunt of the criticism of consumer culture throughout the 1980s and 90s. Cuties have been scapegoated. Their recent and highly conspicuous participation in decadent consumption activities, together with the older association of personal consumption involving interest in fashion and emotional abandon with femininity, has helped critics of modern culture to point the finger at women. Overworked salary men have been encouraged to see the source of their misery as the new generation of stroppy decadent young women, who selfishly do whatever they wish and make unreasonable demands on men. There is a general consensus that, today, men are hard done by and humiliated by manipulative, choosy, cute young women. In fact, in the first half of the 1980s, young women worked more than at any time previously in the postwar period. However, the greater involvement of young unmarried women in the labour force has also been interpreted as another act of willful selfishness on the part of women, who were accused of deliberately vying with men for good jobs and simultaneously denying them marriage partners.

There is an interesting, though incidental, similarity both between the particular forms of black culture and the ways in which black Americans have been discussed in academic and media discourses in the USA, and the particular form of feminine cute culture and the ways in which women have been discussed in academic and media discourse in Japan. In the 1980s, a strand of black American culture responded to the mainstream stereotyping of blacks as vain, emotionally unstable, immature, violent, criminal, and so on, by adopting the stereotype of the 'nigger' and raising it into a positive stereotype. They proudly described themselves as 'niggers' (for example *Ice T* and *NWA*), and flaunted their potential for criminality, violence, and sexual prowess in their fashion, in hip hop, and in rap music. In Japan, a barrage of sexist stereotyping and insults – frequently propagated under the guise of media or academic social analysis about the new position of women in Japanese society – began flowing in the mid-1970s and continued throughout the 1980s, producing, by now, a mountain of books on 'women'. Aspects of cute culture engaged in by young women appear to respond to this criticism by defensively strengthening a 'girls only' culture and identity.

Women debased as infantile and irresponsible began to fetishize and flaunt their *shōjō* personality still more, almost as a means of taunting and ridiculing male condemnation and making clear their stubborn refusal to stop playing, go home, and accept less from life. Popular examples, true or false, of young women's triumphal manipulation of men using their cute appearances as a bait, abounded in late 80s Japan. Apparently the cutest and most innocent-looking of young women were keeping several dates on the boil at once in order to service their materialistic needs. Each date would have a separate function and name – *ashi-kun* (Mr Legs) being awarded to the man who could provide a free late-night taxi service, and *meshi-kun* (Mr Food) to the man who provided free meals out on the town.

Cute Against Society

Cute fashion, as we have seen, idolises childhood. The aims of playfulness, individual emotional expression, and naiveté incorporated in childlikeness are not consistent with traditional social values. The people who persist in play and 'refuse to grow up' are what Okonogi Keigo would call moratorium people:

> Present day society embraces an increasing number of people who have no sense of belonging to any party or organisation but instead are oriented towards non-affiliation, escape from controlled society, and youth culture. I have called them the moratorium people.
> (Okonogi 1978:17)

The concept of 'moratorium people' invented by Okonogi in 1978 became very widespread and influential, to the point that students and individuals on the periphery of Japanese society happily identified themselves as *moratoriamu*. But, in fact, the contemporary association of social disaffection or social rebellion with childishness began during the students' movement at the end of the 1960s. One of the reasons for this was the adoption of children's culture as an alternative to mainstream 'adult' culture by *students* who refused to accept any longer the values taught by the universities. Rather than reading the classics and doing as they were told, students started to read instead children's and adolescent comics, more or less adopting the comic medium as their own. The common motto of the day was 'never trust anyone over thirty', and students showed their loathing by spending hours with their noses in comics which came to be considered somewhat risqué and underground. 'Adult' came to have the additional meaning of conservative, while 'childlike' and play came to have the additional meanings of progressive and open-minded. This explains the logic behind Doi Takeo's thinking when, in 1973, he neatly described internationalism and social equality as infantilism:

> In practise, the present tendency to shelve all distinctions – of adult and child, male and female, cultured and uncultured, east and west – in favour of a universal form of childish *amae* can only be called a regression for mankind.
>
> (Doi 1973:65)

Okonogi Keigo's vision of moratorium people who evaded responsibilities, social duties and adulthood is an extension of Doi Takeo's theory of childishness. Nakano goes on to recall bitterly that cute behaviour is a direct expression of the moratorium mentality:

> They deliberately affect a pitiful cuteness. Growth, maturity and becoming an adult are not positive values: they want to remain children forever. This subjective childishness is related to the prolongation of the *moratorium period*, which is made evident by the striking infantilism of young people after they have entered university.
>
> (Nakano 1985:63)

Cute style is anti-social; it idolises the pre-social. By immersion in the pre-social world, otherwise known as childhood, cute fashion blithely ignores or outrightly contradicts values central to the organisation of Japanese society and the maintenance of the work ethic. By acting childish, Japanese youth try to avoid the conservatives' moral demand that they exercise self-discipline (*enryō*) and responsibility (*sekinin*) and tolerate (*gaman*) severe conditions (*kurō, kudō*) whilst working hard (*doryoku*) in order to repay their obligation (*giri, on*) to society. Rather than working hard, cuties seem to just want to play and ignore the rest of society completely.

251

Cute is one element of the vast popular culture which has flourished in Japan during the last quarter of a century, overwhelming and threatening traditional culture. This popular culture is almost entirely devoted to an escape from reality, and its dominant themes have been cuteness, nostalgia, foreignness, romance, fantasy and science fiction. Cute culture has provided an escape exit into childhood memories; nostalgia has been a door to people's collective past; foreign travel and fixation with foreign culture have provided another escape hatch; whilst syrupy monogamous romance has beckoned people into their narrow, inner lives. Fantasy and science fiction – most visible in comics, animation and computer games – have opened an escape route into alternative universes. The rule for Japanese popular culture has been any space or any time, but here and now in Japan.

In any modern society, culture is the sphere to which people turn to fulfil spiritual, emotional, intellectual and sexual needs and desires which are not met within the fabric of their lives at work, at school, at home. The overwhelming desires of young Japanese people in the 1980s, reflected in cute culture, were to escape from real life as completely as possible. For Japanese youth, as for Sid Vicious, there was NO FUTURE; in fact, there was not even a present.

NOTES

This chapter is based on the following materials:

> Magazines: *Takarajima, an-an, JJ, non-no, Cutie for Independent Girls, Popeye, Heibon, CREA, SPA!*
> Journals: *Japan Echo, Look Japan, Focus Japan, Takarajima 30*
> Interviews with: Shimamura Mari, Yamane Kazuma, Okonogi Keigo, chief editors of *Cutie For Independent Girls* and of *Takarajima*.
> Survey: Analysis of the free answers in the self-completion written questionnaire I distrubuted to 110 men and women between the ages of 18 and 30 in the summer of 1992.

1 *La Pissch* are a main stream ska/rock band from Tōkyō. These lyrics are taken from the song *Sanbon Tsuji ni Shōjo Murete*, on the album *MAKE* released in 1988. The two words *kawaii* and *kawaisō* in the first and second lines work together as a play on words. Kawaii means cute and kawaisō, which is a slight variation of the word kawaii, usually using the same Chinese characters, means pitiable, pathetic or vulnerable.
2 In Japanese, *amai, airashii, mujaki, junsui, kantan, shōjiki, yasashii, kizutsukeyasui, kawaisō,* and *mijuku.*
3 The questions asked were: 'To what extent do you like or dislike cute-looking people?' and 'To what extent do you like or dislike cute behaviour

and attitudes?'. Respondents were asked to answer these questions along a boxed scale of: (1) love/like a lot; (2) like; (3) neither like nor dislike; (4) dislike; (5) dislike strongly/hate. The survey was given to a random selection of 110 people, by whom 89 answers were returned.

4 In the same years that the new handwriting cult spread, the mechanical pencil industry made record profits producing strong, thin leads and a plethora of cute mechanical pencils for young writers to choose from. Between 1969 and 1979 sales of mechanical pencils doubled, and between 1979 and 1981 trebled again.

5 There are two syllabaries in the Japanese language. *Hiragana* is the alphabet used most frequently for all normal purposes, and *katakana* is a special alphabet used originally for Buddhist texts and then for military purposes and foreign words, but now also used to give emphasis to particular words, and in advertising.

6 Yamane's research involved examining visitors' books in tourist temples and love hotels where young people left signatures and personal messages, and a questionnaire survey in which 3021 school students nation-wide participated (see Yamane 1986).

7 Nissan is a big producer of the so called mini car with models such as the snail-shaped *S-Cargo, Figaro, PAO* and the extremely popular, indefinitely sold out, bubble-shaped *BE-1*, launched in 1987, complete with extra horns and whistles. The most successful mini car of all, the *Mazda Eunos*, is also one of the most lucrative designs of car ever created. Shigenori Fukuda, chief designer of the *Eunos*, consciously set out to create a 'small, softly curved, comfortable car that would be a kind of friend like a puppy' (quoted by Ōtsuka Sachiko in Mazda's public relations magazine, *Joyful Life*, 1989).

8 *an-an* and *non-no* have been two of the most consistently popular and widely read young women's fashion magazines since 1970 and 1971 respectively when they were launched. *non-no* circulates 1,500,000 copies a week, targeted at young women between 17 and 23 years of age. *an-an* circulates 650,000 copies every fifteen days and is targeted at slightly more sophisticated 18 to 25 year old women.

9 One editor of *Cutie For Independent Girls* told me that the original plan had been to call the magazine plain *Cutie*. However, since there were five other magazines in publication at that time whose titles and copyrights were a variation on the word 'cute', the words *For Independent Girls* were added in small print. The title is not therefore intended to carry any meaning.

10 By 1988 Matsuda was married with a child and had adjusted to a more adult, sexy image, and at this point the media began to witch-hunt her, describing her as a 'bad' wife and 'cruel' mother. One or all of these events caused a decline in her popularity and all but the end of her career.

11 Sayuri Koshino, a PR representative for Sanrio, describes exactly this mentality: 'I believe we are all born with actual physical organs of cute, tiny and valentine shape, pulsing away in our cerebella. But I also believe that many of us, having developed harsh and realistic life attitudes, have repressed our cute impulses.' (Quoted in Logan 1983:12)

12 In a brilliantly perceptive book written by a photographer on the abuse and misrepresentation of children in modern society, Patricia Holland describes

how children are often forced to behave 'childlike' according to adult expectations: 'Children – especially girl children – must learn to present themselves *as* an image. They must learn a special sort of exhibitionism and reproduce in themselves the charming qualities adults long to see. They may recognise the pleasure that childhood provides for adults but they must not reveal that knowledge, observing adult behaviour only secretly. Open refusal to cooperate invites punishment and a forced return to childishness in tears and humiliation' (Holland 1992: 16).

7

THE MARKETING OF ADOLESCENCE IN JAPAN:
Buying and Dreaming
Merry White

On a visit to Japan in 1963, one year before the Tōkyō Olympics, I found the pace of change giddying: the fast-growing postwar economy and the spotlight effect of the impending Games produced a rush of development not unlike that of the Meiji and Taishō periods. There were new roads, new buildings, new subways, storefront English language academies in every neighborhood – but no teenagers, though we had come to accept them as a necessary modern evil at home.

As we know, this rapid development did not produce a wholesale adoption of western culture and social identities, and only recently has adolescence emerged as a marked stage in the cultural conception of the Japanese lifecourse, both as psycho-social experience and as a new market-driven population segment. The images and realities of teens' lives, as constructed and purveyed by the media and marketing industries in Japan, are the focus of this essay.[1]

Teenagers in any modern society are a composite construction: they are the products of biological development, of institutions (educational and occupational) preparing them for economic and social participation as 'appropriate' adults, and of their own negotiations with their environment, themselves creating new cultural models and goals. But the Japanese definition of teenagers (or *chīnēja*, the word borrowed to fill a conceptual gap) does not correlate precisely with the years called the 'teens' in the west. It does not necessarily begin with puberty, nor does it necessarily end with the termination of schooling and the beginning of 'adult' roles. It is not only a bridge between childhood and adulthood; rather it implies style, aspirations, a way of thinking and behaving. To some it may imply the older notion of 'neither here nor there', the *chūto hanpa* limbo of 'betweenness', but the consumer industries have targeted these young people in a more specific way. The 'naming' of this 'stage' has thus outlined a category permitting, and indeed demanding, diversity and slippage. Because of the speed of marketing, the case of Japan reveals the market-driven aspects of coming of age as well as the active involvement of teens themselves in creating new cultures and practises that then feed back into market definitions of adolescence.

While this relationship between media and young consumers exists elsewhere in the modern world, there are some special conditions in Japan which heighten the effect and highlight a culture-specific coming of age. These include: the relatively high affluence of young people; compression of time and space in young people's lives; information-orientation and high literacy; and a highly interactive relationship between the consumer industries, including the media, and young people.

We will investigate one aspect of this relationship in this chapter – how magazines disseminate a 'curriculum' of adolescent roles and behavior among teenagers, and the effects this has on the mass audience in terms of friendship, consumption, sexuality and other aspects of teens' lives (Figure 7.1).

The Study

From 1988 to 1992, a broad investigation of the media and marketing in Japan was carried out, through data provided by marketers, a review of magazines focussed on young people, and interviews conducted with experts and practitioners in the advertising, marketing, consumer and entertainment industries. Further interviews were held over the same period with a cohort of 50 teenagers; these were given broader context in a survey of over 100 young people from a wide range of urban and rural environments throughout Japan. The interviews were repeated annually over three years, and accompanied by special 'exchange' diaries prepared during short periods of each year for the researcher, as well as essays written by the young people on their lives and perspectives. The study produced a multilayered view of adolescence which could not have been achieved by a larger survey or a single target group.

Marilyn Ivy (1993) notes that the Japanese media have created a 'consumption definition of the middle class'. I would like to suggest that the creation of the teenager through the media does more than identify the teen as a consumer. In fact, what Ivy calls 'the culture industry' is, in the case of youth markets, a highly sensitive, reactive as well as creative force in the formation of a 'segment identity' for adolescents as consumers, but not *only* as consumers.

Of course, consumer marketing has been a factor in the creation of new categories in the lifecourse and new population segments as tagged

Figure 7.1 Japanese teen with a difference
(*Cutie*, March 1992)

markets in the west as well: for instance, the 'Pepsi Generation', Generation X, and Yuppies. Marketing to American youth has established an
interesting fiction of individualism, as in the idea that if you buy this pair
of jeans you will be completely acceptable to your friends *and* a real free
spirit. In Japan, you can all be free spirits together, without concern for
the contradiction. The consumer identity of young people also involves
peer solidarity, as Millie Creighton (1994:94) notes, saying that in Japan
'consumerism is less a way of "finding oneself" and more a way of
linking selves to others'.

257

The teen has existed as a popular concept in the United States since the 1950s, when both developmental psychologists and the market began to create a distinctive image of the teen. Most traits characterizing teens were perceived as negative: the need to separate from adults was seen as driving young people into the nets of peer pressure for delinquency and gang activity. *West Side Story* was the romanticization of this image, as was James Dean of the alternative image of the alienated loner. In Japan, however, the popular concept is still forming, and most traits popularly associated with young people of the 'teen' years are not, for the most part, seen as negative. Of course, young people in both countries are influenced by their media and material culture, but in detail there is little convergence: while American and Japanese teens share some interests – at least in the *categories* of music, clothing and television – the content and outcomes are not the same.

Consumer Society

Japan's emergence as a modern consumer society began in the 1920s, when mass production and urbanization expanded. Within the decade, city populations doubled and improved mass transportation allowed for mobility between and within cities. Tōkyō's circle rail line, the *Yamanote-sen*, was completed in 1925, allowing several suburban stops in Tōkyō, such as Shinjuku and Shibuya, to become central commercial and entertainment hubs. Commercial production became mechanized and focussed on mass markets. Further, in the 1920s, leisure activities became an industry as more people were able to afford such luxuries as baseball games, movies, and radios. Consumption itself became a leisure-time pursuit as department stores became attractive places to meet and stroll, and to learn about new products and trends. Newspapers and magazines supported the consumer boom, and especially directed readers to the attractions of foreign goods and styles.

When urban youth began to spend that leisure, as well as school, time away from home, the creation of a youth market followed. For older teens and young workers, the influence of foreign youth cultures led to Japan's version of 'flappers', the 'modern girl' and 'modern boy', or *moga* and *mobo*. Fads abounded, from ketchup to taxi dance halls (Takemura 1989). However, in the next decades, the effects of world depression, the mobilization for war, and postwar reconstruction slowed consumer-oriented production, which did not again flourish until after the economic take-off of the 1960s.

Postwar development in Japan quickly led to a proliferation of new and profitable consumer market segments. One of these was aimed at young people, and in the boom years of the late 1960s and 70s, a youth market emerged and continues to grow. It is divided into several sub-segments – chiefly 'low teens', 'high teens' (roughly, middle and high schoolers), and the new breed (*shinjinrui*) referring to those in their late teens and early twenties. Of course, these categories are not the only relevant ones, as diversity by age, taste, gender, region and other considerations complicates definitions.

The notion of the mass generation is now breaking up and, as PR director of Dentsū Fujioka Wakao (1986) says, we may now hear more of the 'micromasses', or mini-segmented populations. Fujioka persists, however, in characterizing larger-span generations, and in the following we will take a closer look at the way in which marketers like him have used historical experience to create images of generational shopping cultures.

Consumer Generations and the Teen

Consumer marketers are interested in how people experience the times they live in, and they characterize their audiences by these historical frames. There have been great changes in the experience of affluence and material culture since World War II, producing distinctions in so-called 'consumer generations'. Fujioka (1986), for example, calls those people nearing 50 years of age, the parents of the currently targeted teens, the 'ants . . . who were taught to value work and struggle towards a goal'. Their immediate followers, those about 20 to 25 years of age, he calls the 'grasshoppers', a trend-oriented 'intuition generation . . . who prefer play above all else'.

1930 ⟶ 1947 ⟶ 1955 ⟶ 1960 ⟶ 1973 ⟶ 1980

Wartime
Mobilization   Reconstruction   Recovery   Oil crisis   Prosperity

Grandparents A   Parents A (*kyūjinrui*)   Children A (*shinjinrui*)

Grandparents B   Parents B   Children B (*ichigozoku*)

Figure 7.2 Consumer Generations

259

Another more formal way of grouping consumer generations comes from Sumio Kondō of the Children's Research Institute (personal communication) (Figure 7.2). Children A, whose parents were born before the mid-1950s, have two generations of elders who knew scarcity first hand, and who have tried to instill in their children and grandchildren ideas of conservation and thrift. However, these young people, sometimes called the 'new breed' or shinjinrui (now in their college or early work years), are also the beneficiaries of at least grandparental indulgence, since people now in their sixties and over still prefer not to spend money on themselves, but rather want to provide treats for grandchildren. It is these children, and in fact the younger ones following, who are said to have 'six pockets' filled regularly by four grandparents and two parents, and thus to have relatively large amounts of money to spend on themselves. These are Fujioka's 'grasshoppers' (Fujioka 1986). There is a gap between the parents of these children, called *kyūjinrui* (the 'old breed', Fujioka's 'ants'), who did not in their own youth experience such lavish donations, and their affluent offspring.

We do not see much of a gap between the so-called 'recovery parents' (B) born in the boom years from the late 50s to the end of the 60s and *their* children B. Both generations were raised with a full kit of modern goods, including washing machines, televisions, and audio systems. They share interests in computer games and comic books, and sometimes in the same fashions, but not to the extent that parents and children do in the United States. These are merged generations, the baby boomers and what are called the *ichigozoku*, or 'strawberry gang' (a play on the one and five signifying the fifteen year olds), in terms of the experience and expectations of material comforts and luxuries. As I suggested earlier, however, generation alone is not enough to classify the new markets.

Though marketers in the west also engage in this kind of exercise, such characterizations, by age and stage, are somewhat more reliable in Japan where age cohorts tend to be more coherent in terms of behavior, particularly in terms of predictability of life-stage activities, such as school completion, marriage, childbearing, work force participation, and retirement. Japanese at sixteen tend to be in school, at nineteen in the work force, at 27 married, at 30 in mid-career and mid-parenting roles, at 55 retired and in a second job, and nearly finished with most parenting activities.

The kind of experiences Japanese children have and the degree to which they actually fit this pattern are influenced by region and social class. The media may to some extent homogenize the age cohort, but

260

there is still diversity, and children are more and more aware of these distinctions. While middle-class children can afford the ¥2,000–3,000 per month they spend on magazines, comics, and other print media, the thousands of additional yen spent on telephone party lines, *karaoke* boxes, and CD rentals (let alone on clothing and gear), are out of reach of many.

As a generational cohort, however, these Japanese teens are wealthier than previous cohorts, for although the allowances (on average ¥3,000 per month) they may receive tend to be lower than the middle class average in America (about ¥5,000 per month), they receive large amounts of gift money for major holidays and birthdays, and ask for and get money from parents as they need it. They average more than ¥100,000 in personal savings accounts.

The most popular activity among twelve to nineteen-year-olds is spending money. Middle schoolers tend to spend their money on small items such as comics, magazines, snacks and recorded music, while high schoolers spend more on expensive goods. Most middleclass low teens, however, do own things like radio cassette players, Nintendō games and other electronic items, often the contributions of grandparents.

Mass media and marketing for young people are, of course, primarily dedicated to getting them to divest themselves of their disposable income, but – both as enticement and indeed as an educative mission – they also create what I call a curriculum of identity-formation that both complements and contradicts the program for youth established in education and family. Behind this curriculum is a complex portrait of both an appropriate child (one of use to the economy and society), and a real child with whom the media and market must interact.

The communication between media and youth must address the young person's actual experience, identity and needs even as these are being constructed, even as the child is subliminally being taught to be what society and the market need. This often produces conflicting images even within the curriculum which, for efficiency and profit, favors a homogeneous cohort view of its audience. The roles on offer in the media – especially in the magazines as critical texts in the formation of identity – I have summarized as: the 'apprentice', the 'dreamer', the 'sexual being' and the 'buyer'.

On the one hand, then, the media reflect the social learning the young person experiences more directly in family, friendships and school, but instead of demanding the wholehearted acceptance of the responsibilities and behaviors that adulthood will exact, the media keep alive the notion that a young person can have – however manufactured and packaged – a variety of personae, even a 'dream'. Where these apparently ambiguous messages are mostly clearly exhibited is in the print media, most prominently in magazines.

Magazines: the Uses of Literacy

The current generation of teens in Japan receives a large dose of these messages, having been exposed more than any other postwar cohort to the blandishments of the print media. They are a natural target, for several reasons: first, they read – with nearly 100 per cent literacy, they are available to magazines; second, they are curious, engaged – as are their elders – in a habit of questing for information. Further, being pressed for time and space, they seek even the limited privacy of reading, on trains and buses or at home. Friendship and peers are their chief reference points, and magazines also provide substance which can be purveyed in relationships. Finally, most middleclass teens have enough disposable income to afford to purchase magazines, which range from ¥300 to ¥750 per issue.[2]

Girls especially disseminate fashion, pop star, and trend information to their friends, and magazines and their advertisers rely on this word-of-mouth (*kuchikomi*) amplifier effect in considering the impact of (and profit from) their messages. Word-of-mouth, of course, is not only limited to teenagers, but is an expected aspect of adult consumerism as well. These information links may actually be institutionalized by consumer industries – novelty companies like Sanrio which have specialized products such as exchange diaries with pre-established categories to fill in, like 'what I want to buy when I go shopping', or places for lists of favorite styles, colors, kits for designing one's own room, and places for itemizing one's New Year's gift money.

Advertisers also rely on *machikomi*,[3] meaning 'town-' or 'street-communication'. Through machikomi, teens do 'research' in commercial districts, in trendy shopping neighborhoods, and learn from what they see people wear, and how they behave, in public. Both kuchi- and machikomi are amplified by magazine shopping instructions which specifically direct young people to the best hangouts, where they may learn what is in.

Like the friendship groupings that define adolescent social life, magazines are gender and age-specific. Girls tend to read more general, fashion and pop star-focussed magazines, while boys read more special-interest magazines, such as publications specializing in motorbikes, fashion, sports or music. Whereas boys only occasionally cross-read girl's magazines, girls frequently borrow their brothers' fashion and music magazines. This has encouraged 'sibling magazines' such as *Hanako* and its brother magazine, *Popeye*, which purvey information on fashion, relationships, trendy goods and sex, to approximately half a million readers each per month. While age-stratification exists among these magazines, it is common for both girls and boys to 'read up', so the readership of magazines directed at 'high teens' often has a much broader range than that of 'low teen' magazines.

The Curriculum Examined

The following suggestive analysis is based on readings of magazines dedicated to young people age twelve to 25 published during the period 1985-1993. It also discusses the way in which magazine editors see their own role and responsibility in shaping a media curriculum. As outlined above, teen magazines see their readers in multiple roles, all of which they serve in some fashion: the apprentice, the dreamer, the sexual being, and the buyer. What George de Vos (1973) has called a pervasive 'role perfectionism' in Japan may help us to understand how seriously young people aim to follow this curriculum.

The Apprentice

Traditionally, a young person is an apprentice to adulthood's tasks and responsibilities, obeying, learning and doing. Even today's affluent, middleclass teenager is on track to adulthood in this sense, rather than (as in America) waiting for age-specific rights and freedoms. The apprenticeship in Japan includes social and interpersonal skills, since magazine editors feel that young people, under the pressure of examinations, have little opportunity for learning and exploring social life. The magazines take on the task of teaching the norms and values of adult society. Teens themselves, of course, are 'patrolling' each other in terms of appropriate peer culture norms for behavior,[4] and may tease or bully those who deviate even in small things.

According to readership surveys, many teens suffer from performance anxiety even in friendship, and because of the great vulnerability they feel, turn to print for help. In each area of the curriculum then, magazines provide two important components: one, the right way – whether it be dressing correctly, behaving appropriately with a lover in bed, or being a good friend; and two, the implication, at least, of choice (Figure 7.3). So, for example, in an article on how to conduct a telephone

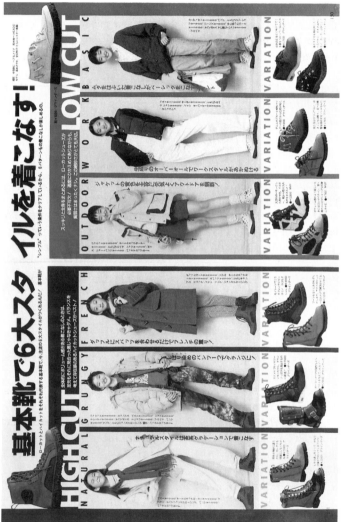

Figure 7.3 mcSister presents fashion types (January 1994)

conversation with a girl, boys are given several scenarios from which to choose, each with its own flow chart – if in response to your query B, she says Y, you have choices C and D; if she says Z, you can choose between E, F, and G; and so on.

Thus, one of the magazines' complicated functions is to set high standards for acceptability, and at the same time reassure young people that they are 'normal'. They play on the needs of young people to be appropriate, to invest deeply in friendships, and to discover – or invent – their own identities. At the same time, they exhort teens to act in a manner appropriate to adult society, and somehow still offer them support – a combination similar to that purveyed by mothers who invoke the *seken* (public opinion or the watchful community) standards as they also offer unconditional indulgence (Peak 1991).

Magazines encourage the right ways of doing things, but do so by providing minutely detailed, confidence-inspiring instructions on some easily accomplished task, such as weaving a friendship bracelet from colored string, or making muffins (for boys the task might be fixing a bicycle). At the same time they also lead the child to believe that he or she is learning these things by choice. These lessons are taught in an upbeat positive tone, a you-can-do-it exhortation, whether the topic is friendship, success in school, or thinking about one's future, but behind these messages is, of course, the more than subliminal message that keeping up to a high consumer standard is very important.

The Dreamer

Fantasy is a big portion of the media meal for children. If not in daily life, at least in fictionalized dreams, the teen can experience romantic visions and achieve her personal goals. 'Dream' is said to be the most frequently used word in Japanese advertising, especially in ads dedi-cated to women. There are television shows, newspaper columns and other media devoted to fantasy and 'dream', as in the many travel shows, or features on 'Japanese with a dream', depicting people who have pursued some life-long goal – climbing Mount Everest at 65, opening an orphanage in Vietnam, or collecting one of every known species of butterfly. In the context of teen magazines, dreaming includes both 'a dream' – in the sense of a passionately held goal of some sort – and fantasy – as in girls' magazine fiction stories which are often very romantic and often have European settings. But these are not all fairytale stories, as shown in a recent issue of *Seventeen* which inaugurated a new fiction section, rather less sentimental, called 'First Sex Story'.

Pop-star magazines retail dreams too. Most young teens read a fan magazine, such as *Duet*, which portrays practically every possible aspect of the stars' lives – including their horoscopes, blood types and personality profiles, how they celebrate a holiday and what their favorite foods are. Promotion groups, such as Johnny's Jr., work with the idol magazine researchers who collect elaborate data on their readership, and often design the next hit group on the basis of these magazine polls. Polls have shown, for example, that each girl in a typical friendship group will attach herself to one of the boys in a pop group. Learning also that the typical size of a clique is five to seven girls, promotion agencies have started to create boys' singing groups of the same size, to allow one boy for each fan in a friendship group (Figure 7.4).[5]

The magazines also feature star interviews through which the reader can vicariously enjoy her proximity to the star. This is facilitated by the fact that the reporter herself is depicted as a giggling fan, a typical girl-next-door, who can act as a stand-in for the reader. The *Duet* editors have said that their only taboo is against revealing the stars' sexual or love relationships, *not* from a puritanical motivation, but because the young girl readers would lose interest if the male stars were to be involved publicly with someone. The reader must be able to fantasize that the star is free to be with *her*. Editors' avoidance here of implications of sexual activity among pop stars is *not* an indication that they want to protect young girls from their own sexuality; in fact, they said it was to encourage the reader not to repress her own yearnings, which are dependent on the fantasy of access to the star.[6]

Another aspect of fantasy encouraged in magazines for young teens is the *omajinai*, charms or spell-casting. Junior high school girls particularly seem to love such devices. These range from a love charm – involving dropping lemon juice on a five-yen coin minted in the birth year of the boy in question, then tying it with a red ribbon to the lower right-hand corner of his framed photo, to spells for increasing one's spending money. One recent charm for middle school girls assured her that the seating order at the beginning of the next term in school would place her next to the boy she liked. Such spells are described in meticulous, step-by-step detail, for – as in other kinds of learning – success is said to depend greatly on doing it exactly the right way. Fortune-telling and horoscopes are also popular, especially among girls, and bloodtype correlations with personalities are given to guide one's choice of romantic partner.

Figure 7.4 SMAP pop group consisting of six boys (poster insert from *Myōjō*, October 1994)

Sexual Being

Similar to other aspects of the child's identity, magazines approach the issue of sexuality with both concrete instruction and a sense of the enhancement of the self – completely avoiding an admonitory, negative tone. Articles provide very concrete detail, often in pull-out sections which may be consulted, for example, when buying condoms or seductive underwear. There are also manuals on sexual intercourse and on the use of love hotels. In this way, instruction is combined with choice and pleasure. Editors further note that sex education in Japanese schools is insufficient and vague, and that the magazines have functioned to fill this gap, emphasizing pleasure over protection – for both boys and girls.

Recent examples from a boy's magazine include an enclosed dating manual with photo-assisted guidance on a date's likely reaction to the application of a boy's hand on various parts of her anatomy. The same magazine also featured interviews with girls' fathers on what their daughters would want in a man. Girls' magazines, too, encourage their readers to explore their bodies. A recent issue of a magazine for high teens and college women featured an article on orgasms, charting a variety of trajectories and experiences. Another gave detailed instructions on masturbation. These articles emphasize a kind of social-scientific approach, using case studies of individuals, interviews with doctors and psychologists, and first person accounts, as well as charts, graphs and typologies. There do not appear to be distinctions regarding sexuality and its expression by gender, but some by age, as the magazines specifically targeted at younger teens refer less to sexuality than do those for the older teens. As noted, however, young teens are known to 'read up', buying magazines for the older age groups.

The Buyer

Above all the magazines seek buyers, not just of the magazines themselves, but of the consumer goods and services offered by advertisers. And, of course, we find shopping training as a significant part of the curriculum of adolescence. During the 1980s, affluence encouraged the consumer industries to target teens as one of the most important growth segments – which in turn helped to socialize children as future big spenders and as a high volume (though usually low ticket) market in themselves. The assumption behind this development was that all teens could perform equally as consumers, or, at least, that it was only worthwhile attending to the high end of the market. However, young people

268

THE MARKETING OF ADOLESCENCE IN JAPAN

themselves are well aware that they are not part of a monolithic single-class society, however useful such a fiction might be to industry and other institutions.

Since the 1960s, developing trend items and clothing styles specifically for youth has served to accentuate separateness from adult society while creating as predictable and homogeneous a shopping cohort as possible.[7] The market in its own way encourages conformity, for volume – the goal is 100 per cent saturation of a fad – efficiently produces high profit. But at the same time, market dynamics has produced subsegments – different lines, for example, of clothing or trendy goods, even within a given age and gender slot. Thus, magazines promote fashion 'types' such as *ame kaji* (American Casual, a relaxed American college campus style), *shibu kaji* (Shibuya Casual, a sort of fusion-dressing common to the hangers-out in the favored Shibuya section of Tōkyō), New Trad (in America, similar to preppy, favoring penny loafers, blazers and oxford cloth button down shirt collars from Brooks Brothers clothiers), Country (outdoor gear, hiking boots, and anything from the L.L. Bean catalog, or for girls, calicos and ginghams in a deliberately 'Little Town on the Prairie' look), Ethnic (usually Indian or Afghan, reminiscent of the mixed styles of the American late 60s) and so on. Some of these styles, like Seattle Grunge, are borrowed more or less wholesale from overseas, but others are local. Many are indeed created by teens themselves in an interactive relationship with the media – either formally established through teen fashion focus groups or less directly through market research, observation and testing of new ideas.

In the same way that personality quiz-tests are popular among children seeking to define themselves, so do these fashion types establish templates and models for the child to follow. As an aspect of the media training, 'role perfectionism' exploits its own inherent insecurities. Young people, the marketers discover, *like* to belong to a type, like to feel that they are doing fashion 'the right way', even as they want the option of a range of 'fashion personalities'.

Magazines also provide shopping training for their readers' future lives. Girls have the opportunity to glimpse, through home decoration and cooking, their future roles as homemakers (though they are also encouraged to dream of other experiences as well), and boys are taught to consider quality in their future options to buy cars and other big-ticket items. Here, as in other areas of the curriculum, a sense of guided choice is promoted.

269

Infomaniacs and Magatrends

In magazines, the incorporation of curricula for youth, along with the crystalization of the four 'identities' outlined above, have taken place with the understanding that youth wants to *know*. Editors indeed call these data-hungry young people 'infomaniacs' (*infomaniakku*), insatiable for more information to enable them to keep up and move on ahead. Some teen magazines read like catalogs of goods including tie-ins to special featured seasonal promotions at department stores,[8] and young people use them more as reference works to locate products and the shops where they are sold.

In order to satisfy the need for novelty, as well as to perpetuate it, magazines have spawned a variety of trends, mostly short-lived, suiting the audience's and the market's need for rapid turnover. But some of these have become more enduring aspects of youth culture – such as the custom of girls and (usually unmarried) women giving chocolates to male friends and colleagues on Valentine's Day, followed a month later by White Day on which males return the favor in the form of white chocolate, or lacy undies, or other white items.

Another trend is towards obsessive cleanliness, pushing sales of soap and shampoos whose formulae are concocted especially for morning washes. Though, as Lise Skov has pointed out in an earlier chapter, some ecologists concerned about water use have recently railed against this *asashan*, or morning shampoo, it might be said that this custom emerged as an affluence-enhanced way for teens to separate themselves from adults who bathe at night, with body-care regimens of their own (*Japan Times* August 18, 1989).

Food fads have been significant since *Hanako* first launched *tiramisu* as the trendy dessert in the early 1980s, citing the best places to eat it in Japan. This forced other restaurants to keep up by offering it; and even fast food shops and neighborhood bakeries began selling it. Since then, there has been a new fashionable dessert each year, mostly European, including creme brulée, and, in 1994, Belgian waffles with ice cream and chocolate sauce. In 1993, however, a coconut dessert from the Philippines, *nata de coco*, was popular.

Ironically, the recession has also created its own consumer trends. Magazines have recently begun to promote cheap generic clothing as a fad, and even touted the trendiness of eating such inexpensive foods as chicken gizzard stew. Do-it-yourself kits for home-made gifts became popular, and magazines also give directions for knitting, baking or constructing appropriate gifts. Entertaining is also included in the recessionary curriculum which offers advice on giving 'home parties', rather than entertaining in restaurants and other expensive places. The force of the market has thus created unforeseen side-effects – including an awareness of economic diversity running counter to received notions of homogeneity. We may witness, though, the establishment of homogeneous subsets, rather than a wide-open pool of diversity.

Outcomes, Intended or Novel

Japanese youth are not unique in wanting to be like their peers. Nor are Japan's consumer industries unique in attending to them as a target audience. But the pace, volume and intensity of media production and consumption have brought about something more than well-trained and loyal consumers.

The very qualities which marketing has exploited in teens – the intensity of their relationships, the desire to be appropriate – have produced a cohort which is performance-anxious and acutely aware of economic disparities. Like schools, meant to provide training and confidence, popular media also attempt to create a well-socialized, receptive, high-performing youth population. But performance perfectionism, a curriculum of conformity, and high demands (in money, if not time) have also produced anxieties similar to those of the educational system. Keeping up, getting ahead, doing it the right way, and being on top are hard in the consumer world as well.

Adults decry these pressures on young people, and some critics have pointed out that teens are no longer confident in any kind of performance. They see the prevalence of 'manuals' – either inserts into magazines instructing young people in all aspects of life, or separately published life-guides – as evidence that young people have grown too dependent on authority and have lost the ability to manage on their own – a problem which they have labelled the 'manual syndrome'. Manuals are different from school curricula and parental advice in that they are voluntarily chosen, their messages are upbeat and non-admonitory. They allow teens noncritical support. Unlike the directives of teachers and parents, and unlike the standardized curriculum of the Ministry of Education, manuals are located in the teens' own language.

Adult criticism of such manuals contains a contradiction because adult society itself has produced the expectations for performance in institutions which determine a young person's life chances – and thereby his or her ensuing pressure and lack of confidence. Criticism of the manuals may indeed be related to the fact that, in their tone and priorities,

271

they appear to be teen-generated. Adult critics may exhort the young to be more independent of outside authority, while they may still hope that their own authority will not be subverted. Obviously, adults may be wary of the power of the media which interacts with, and reflects, young people's lives more directly than other (adult-created) institutions, whose dictates emerge from centralized authorities. The discussion of youth 'trend slaves' and 'media zombies' might be more usefully folded into the wider debates on education and workplace reform.

What the economic boom of the 80s has produced is diversity – which is clear from the ways in which magazines encourage young people to 'express themselves' through a choice of styles and trends, while also offering training in doing so. The debate over a new Japanese identity, the perennial one now recast as the 'new Japaneseness' (*shin nihonjinron*), has produced some punditry on the effects of affluence and human resources. A key question is how Japan can be an affluent society, a leisure society, without losing its commitment to work and improvement which so far has only been learned through scarcity and self-discipline. Indeed, those whose lives are marked by scarcity now experience an, often alienating, deprivation, rather than a source of motivation, in the face of a dominant image of affluence.

Teens are among the first to discover the new realities; they are actually very good social critics. Ironically, the very industries that have instructed them and responded to their desires have also forced them to face the fact that not all are equally able to participate in the culture they were created to consume. Several examples of this emerged in my interviews: many young women conscious of name brand distinctions worried about their best friends who couldn't afford these, so themselves switched to generic clothing to preserve their friendship; young men avoided Sunday shopping trips with their friends, too embarassed because they couldn't afford to keep up. One of these was a high school boy, who works every day after school in his father's gas station in a town in Chiba. He will take over the gas station when his father retires. He says he might have liked to go on for a technical degree in auto engineering, but his family can't spare him to study after school and has no money for tutors to help him get into a special program. He says the system is supposed to be fair, but it is not, and he consoles himself by trying to save for a motorcycle.

Teens are only incompletely socialized into the polite gap between *tatemae* and *honne* that keeps uncomfortable realities at bay, and they know that acceptance of the gap is required. But for a short time, they reveal their discomfort with the public face of tatemae, saying that adult

272

expectations – such as the notion that they are all alike, all middleclass – simply aren't true, and that accepting adult social values makes them feel as if they are 'cheating' (*zurui*). Listening to the teenagers, we hear voices very different from those which tell us that Japan is a homogeneous middleclass society – and even the manufactured culture of the teen media has contributed to this revelation.

NOTES

1 Much of the material for this essay was gathered in conjunction with the research for my book, *The Material Child: coming of age in Japan and America*, New York: Free Press, 1993.
2 *Duet* magazine editor, Mr. Kitabatake, said that *Duet* has attempted to keep the price of the magazine low, at ¥300, to allow middle schoolers to buy it easily and to keep a wide readership.
3 Kondō Sumio, personal communication.
4 Kai Erikson (1966:13) argues that deviants are 'functional' as indicators of the boundary between normal and abnormal in a society. Teens in Japan have engaged in bullying which has in some cases become quite violent, directly or indirectly causing the death of victims. Some have speculated that slightly marginal children are targetted and their differences amplified to highlight the 'normality' of the others.
5 Mr. Kitabatake, personal communication.
6 Mr. Kitabatake, personal communication.
7 Fujiwara Mariko, HILL, personal communication.
8 Kanda Chiaki, personal communication.

8

YOSHIMOTO BANANA'S *KITCHEN*, OR THE CULTURAL LOGIC OF JAPANESE CONSUMERISM

John Whittier Treat

The July 1993 summit in Tōkyō of the leading industrial democracies (the 'G-7') was another of the now routine media performances by a select international cast of politicians intended for global consumption. Yet despite a full schedule of meetings, receptions, banquets and public declarations, something seemed missing. The G-7 leaders were 'seven characters in search of an author': the well-made play they intended us to view via the proscenium stage that is the television set was a disappointing drama missing both antagonist and protagonist. Without a villainous Soviet empire, or a rapacious Arab cartel, there can nowadays be no dramatic resolution, no tragedy or comedy. Presidents and prime ministers struck poses before high-tech footlights nonetheless thoroughly high-bourgeois, worthy of Ibsen but without the luck of his scripts – ready for a modernist plot that, like Godot, did not come.

For some playwrights, of course, such absurdity is precisely where the modern theater begins. Directing and starring center-stage in this particular production was the host country, whose Foreign Ministry went to the usual unusual lengths to 'explain Japan' to those in attendance and those watching around the planet. As it turned out, the Ministry meant to decipher more than just Japan: something new, we learned, was afoot worldwide. Added to each press kit for foreign journalists covering the summit was a copy of the recent English translation of Yoshimoto Banana's prize-winning 1988 novel, *Kitchen*. The slender first work by a young woman slighted by many critics at home for its kinship with comic books and other teenage schlock, *Kitchen* would hardly seem the stuff of summitry reading. But the Foreign Ministry, eager to edify as well as entertain, thought otherwise. 'There should be some element in her book that can be shared, not only by the Japanese, but by the younger generation all over the world', explained Ministry

Figure 8.1 Bananamania (Courtesy of Grove Press)

spokesman Amano. But as to what element – reporters understandably pressed Mr. Amano on just this point – all he could respond was 'I don't know'.

Others share both the Foreign Ministry's sense of *Kitchen*'s importance and its confusion over just what that importance is. Tersely described by the *Wall Street Journal* as the story of 'a young Japanese woman with a kitchen fetish' (Bussey and Williams 1993), its original publication in Japan was a milestone event, both in its commercial success and in the dumfounded consternation it occasioned among critics. Less than two years after it initially appeared in the literary

275

journal *Kaien*, the novel was already in its fiftieth printing, and the combined sales of Banana's Japanese-language editions alone totaled some six million copies. But her *Kaien* award for best new writer of the year was an exceptional event in Japanese literary history not on account of her youth,[1] but because, in the published summary of their deliberations, none of the judges praised the work. At a loss of what to say about this scant story so redolent of Japan's distinctly low-cultural female adolescent (*shōjo*) culture, the judges rather seemed resigned to award the prize on the basis of their nebulous impression that they were witness to something 'new' in Japanese literature – even if they did not know exactly what, and even if they were disturbed by that failure of reading. 'This is a work', wrote senior critic Nakamura Shin'ichirō,

> written on a theme and with a sensibility that the older generation of which I am a part could not have imagined. It is the product of an abandon completely indifferent to literary traditions. Its naive rejection of the very question of whether it does or does not conform to conventional concepts is precisely what makes it strike me as a new sort of literature.
>
> (Mitsui and Washida 1989:143)

It has recently been observed that most critics in Japan have either ignored Yoshimoto Banana or treated her works with a scarcely concealed contempt. The reason for this may be, it is suggested, that critics cannot discern anything in Banana's works to discuss, i.e. that they are functionally 'illiterate' when it comes to reading her (Tsuge 1994: 82–83). In hindsight, what helped to propel *Kitchen* to the ranks of award-winning fiction was, no doubt, its author's bankable parentage. Banana's father, Yoshimoto Takaaki, is himself a prominent and controversial poet and intellectual whose ruminations on that same Japanese 'mass culture' that his daughter may now epitomize were standard reading for intellectuals in the 1960s and 1970s. He still commands a large readership, although his theories are notoriously difficult to master. As Ian Buruma (1993:29) quipped of Takaaki's daughter when he reviewed *Kitchen*, it is 'as though there were a young German novelist called Banana Habermas'.

Increasingly, both Banana and Takaaki have raised the ire of critics alarmed by Japan's consumer culture and worried about the prospect of ever challenging its drive to commodify and reify. Masao Miyoshi and H. D. Harootunian (1989b: xvi) dismiss Takaaki's suggestion that consumption might in fact work to undermine capitalism as an 'absurdist conviction'; and Miyoshi (1991a:236; 1991b:38) declares Banana's writings – which he admits 'sell by the millions' – as 'baby talk, uninterrupted by humor, emotion, idea, not to say irony or intelligence'. What incites such censure is surely the nervous fear that the potential of intellectual discourse on one hand, and modernism on the other, to conceptualize and critique the ways we live is now nearly impossible under the relentless onslaught of the commodity, and under the terms of the postmodern 'cultural logic' it has inspired.

But as Andreas Huyssen (1986a:191) has pointed out, 'Mass culture has always been the subtext of the modernist project', and the success of *Kitchen* is yet another opportunity to consider the premises of this perennial modern combat between the forces of popular taste and those of its intellectual conscience. We can begin with the irrefutable: *Kitchen* and its marketing do exhibit many characteristics of an expanding consumerism – and not just in Japan, though the 'boom' that surrounds Banana's works is a perfect example of how, in the words of Mitsuhiro Yoshimoto (1989:9) (no relation), 'the massive forces of commodification currently at work in Japan' are structured by booms in order to create (marketable) differences. What is new, for Japanese *literature* at least, is the globalization of that boom. Quickly translated first into Italian and then many other languages, this Japanese novel has traveled like no other – although, aside from the Chinese, the original English title *Kitchen* has been retained in every version.² At the time when the publishing industry, despite the linguistic barriers posed by its products, was becoming as multinational as the oil majors,³ Grove Press marketed Banana's work in North America on an unprecedented scale, and did so without coloring it as exotically Oriental. 'Bananamania is coming', excitedly trumpeted full-page ads designed by, among others, the famous creator of the Holocaust comic *Maus*, Art Spiegelman. Run in newspapers and weeklies across the United States, such copy recalls the benign 'British invasion' campaign that primed the similarly pop 'Beatlemania' of a generation ago. But such frenzy was soon and predictably tamed: *Kitchen* became a featured selection in a popular book-of-the-month club whose come-ons, in contrast to the *Wall Street Journal*'s more pathological blurb, describe it blandly as 'a novel of a young Japanese woman who finds comfort in the warmth of kitchens'(Figure 8.1).

A Global Banana

One might well marvel that any novel whose story can be reduced to an affection for a room sells at all. But sell it does, and both the middle-brow literary journal that launched the 'Banana Phenomenon' domestically

– *Kaien* – and the more scholarly academic journal *Kokubungaku* devoted their February 1994 issues to the spectacle of 'Yoshimoto Banana Around the World' (as *Kokubungaku* put it) and 'Yoshimoto Banana In the World' (as did *Kaien*).

Both journals convened a panel of critics – including an unusual number of foreign ones – to comment upon the event of a new Japanese writer whose works have been marketed globally with remarkable dispatch. This event has been a riddle from the start, as evidenced when the Japanese business journal *President* asked in 1989 simply: 'Why Does "Yoshimoto Banana" Sell So Well?'. But now the question has to be, as one scholar recently posed it, 'Why, among the numerous writers in Japan today, is Yoshimoto Banana the first to go global?' (Tsuge 1994:78). Global, that is, commercially and not critically: but the two registers are hardly unrelated. Speaking specifically of *Kitchen*'s success in Italy, a country not known for a devotion to Japanese literature, Suga Atsuko ponders:

> Why, in a country with cultural traditions, tastes, lifestyles and social customs so utterly different from Japan's, has a novel like *Kitchen* achieved in Italy unprecedented sales on the order of 90,000 copies? . . . There is no other example of a book that has sold so spectacularly well.
>
> (Suga 1994:29)

Part of the answer lies simply in the amount of money spent promoting *Kitchen* in the west, not only via Spiegelman's ads in North America but, for example, by a correspondingly ambitious campaign by the book's Milanese publisher – a campaign that included featuring it in a popular Roman bookstore which, unlike other Italian shops but very much in keeping with the new patterns of 'international' marketing making inroads in Italy, is open during lunch and closes for no holidays (Natili 1994; Suga 1994). The attention lavished on Banana shows up in unusual places: one might expect a book review in the pages of *Der Spiegel* (dubbing her the 'kindliche Kaiserin der japanischen Jugend'), but how about an extensive interview with her in Italy's once communist party organ, *L'Unita*? ('Il Mondo', Banana was quoted in the article's headline, 'Non Sarà Un Grande Giappone' – reassuring readers that she represents no new hegemony.) In other words, the demand for *Kitchen* owes much to its global marketing – and not the other way around. With no clue to book's content other than that 'Bananamania is coming', the collaboration of the publishers with the media fostered a curiosity about an Asian young woman named after a tropical fruit that only the exchange of cash for a commodity could satisfy.

Critics who contributed to the special 'World Banana' issues of *Kaien* and *Kokubungaku* were, however, unanimous in their view that the contents of *Kitchen* communicated something new and 'popular worldwide', and thus could attribute its success to something other than the sheer manipulation of the marketplace. An American, Elizabeth Floyd, called Banana's writings 'something that young people the world over, regardless of nationality, can enjoy' (Tsuge *et al.* 1994:91); and while both the Italian Donnatella Natili and the Chinese Yin Hui'e noted that some part of *Kitchen*'s appeal in their respective countries was the novel's embodiment of a new, postmodern Japan with less cultural uniqueness and more economic clout ('From samurais to computers', as Natili put it), both also noted that there was something distinctly *non*-Japanese about the book that was 'universal' to the extent it was deracinated. 'The name of Banana, along with her works, is known by many people around the world regardless of national borders', claimed Yin, and Natili described the scene of the novel's story, Tōkyō, as 'an international city' without a strictly Japanese identity (Tsuge et al. 1994: 92–93; Natili 1994:109).

Most insistent, however, on the changed character of a once-provincial Japanese literature after Yoshimoto Banana is the German scholar Hilaria Gossman. She acknowledges that *Kitchen*'s 'German edition marked an important shift among publishers in German-speaking countries. Rather than present the work as one with a uniquely Japanese theme, we were told that here was a novel to which young people all over the world could relate'. Gossman believes this to be true: the 20,000 copies that sold immediately 'is evidence that those who read it were not only people with an interest in Japan, but indeed included those with a broad interest in the lives of young people' (Tsuge et al. 1994:90).

In other words, Foreign Ministry spokesman Amano's claim that *Kitchen* contained 'some element . . . that can be shared . . . by the younger generation around the world', however inexplicable that element is to Amano and others, appears to be widely accepted. *Kitchen* may in fact be Japan's first 'intellectual' global commodity, a status attested to not by its critics' comments, but by Mr. Amano's boasts that his government's purchase of 800 copies of the English-language *Kitchen* was proof that Japan is indeed 'import-oriented'.[4] As the *Kaien* judges uneasily observed, something new is at work here, and whatever it is, literature is not exempt from its logic: a 'cultural logic', one that is poorly understood but which surely exists, if only because nothing less basic could so puzzle critics and yet interest millions of readers. The key to what has happened is found at home – the homes not only where Banana's bizarre families comprised of orphaned children and sexual changelings reside, but where her older critics' own journey towards personal and intellectual adulthood unfolded according to the script of an even older, and scarcely more plausible, Greek myth.

Yoshimoto Banana and Late Capitalism

'The people recognize themselves in their commodities', wrote Herbert Marcuse (1964:9) in *One-Dimensional Man*, 'they find their souls in their automobiles, hi-fi sets, split-level homes, kitchen equipment'. Marcuse's scorn might seem justified if only in the case of *Kitchen*, where Mikage Sakura,[5] the novel's narrator, is told by a new friend to 'pick a room, then I'll know what kind of person you are' and goes directly to the disdained 'kitchen equipment'. 'Lots of tea towels, dry and immaculate', a giant white American-style (but assuredly Japan-made) refrigerator stuffed with delicacies enough 'to get through a winter'; the open cupboards crammed with English country crockery, Swiss cutlery, futuristic Japanese home appliances; 'a Silverstone frying pan and a delightful German-made vegetable peeler': the dense tableau of colors and shapes is the late-twentieth century Japanese update of the classic Dutch still-life – this is the kitchen that Mikage claims is the 'best in the world'.

Yet if this fictional kitchen is the 'best in the world', it is not *of* the world – at least of any we are apt to inhabit. It is indeed a room that one might fancy, a luxurious 'home' that reeks with nostalgia for family and its old-fashioned comforts, a place where the bread rises, the cookies bake and the *miso* soup simmers. But of course, outside of those Nescafé and Vermont Curry commercials on Japanese television, it is a room that hardly exists – least of all in Japan, where the exigencies of modern life mean that many meals come out of the microwave, if not the corner Seven-Eleven. Such evocations of the old-fashioned hearth and the possibility of a family assembled beside it are the modern consumer's dream; and as a dream, it is both unreal and powerful. ('Dream kitchens', muses Mikage. 'I will have countless ones, in my heart or in reality'.) Banana's spare prose describes a place as amiably crowded with things as those California households staged by her favorite Hollywood director, Steven Spielberg. It celebrates a warehouse of culinary tools that the novel's *New Yorker* reviewer correctly observes is 'under-utilized', to say the least (Garrison 1993:110). Banana's kitchen is a place that can only be imaginary, as any desire must, yet at the same time it is the material product of a postmodern Japanese consumerism that has generated aesthetics as well as profits.

That it is a teenage woman in *Kitchen*, and not her housewife mother, who surveys this kitchen is both paradigmatic within the logic of this Japanese consumerism, and something of an exception to the way in which many have theorized consumerism in the west. In the United States at least, it has been typical to read the relationship between women and consumption in two different and not wholly compatible contexts. First is that of woman as the passive *object* of consumption, herself an article of (kinship, sexual, economic) exchange. The second is that of woman as the groomed *subject* of consumption, that smart housewife in the ads who buys the newest detergent, the easiest floor wax. This double function has been dubbed a 'paradox', an 'essential tautology' (*Quarterly Review of Film and Video*, 1989, p.vii). Mary Ann Doane (1989:30), for example, notes that the female consumer 'is the subject of a transaction in which her own commodification is ultimately the object'. This conflation of sexual value and material desire with its converse – sexual desire and material value – is one that is constituted in Japan with significant difference, if only because the adolescent female (shōjo) is not precisely a woman (*onna*). One might well argue that shōjo constitute their own gender, neither male nor female but rather something importantly detached from the productive economy of heterosexual reproduction. Anthropologist Jennifer Robertson points out that 'Literally speaking, shōjo means a "not-quite-female" female . . . . Shōjo also implies heterosexual *inexperience* and homosexual *experience*' (Robertson 1989:56) – presumably homosexual because the emotional life of the shōjo is essentially narcissistic in that it is self-referential, and self-referential as long as the shōjo is not employed productively in the sexual and capitalist economies. A distinct gender, a distinct age cohort and a distinct status as consumer: the Japanese shōjo is a sign, one uniquely positioned as a master trope for all social forms of consumption. Sociologist Merry White correctly notes that 'Japanese define teenagers as a category because they are a market . . . Japanese teens have appeared and been identified . . . as the economic boom of the late 1970s and 1980s targeted and reached a new "youth market"' (White 1993:48, 7), but Japanese social scientists have proposed something more. 'The Japanese are no longer producers', writes anthropologist Ōtsuka Eiji, but instead

> Our existence consists solely of the distribution and consumption of 'things' brought us from elsewhere, 'things' with which we

play. Nor are these 'things' actually tangible, but are instead only signs without any direct utility in life . . . . What name are we to give this life of ours today?

The name is shōjo.

(Ōtsuka 1991:18)

The theory of the female consumer in the west typically declines to implicate men in its terms or distinguish adolescent women as a distinct group or subject. The situation is quite different in Japan, where the idea of the shōjo has in some analyses assumed the status of an increasingly hegemonic identity, one that extends to other ages and genders. Critic Horikiri Naoto, for example, speculates:

I wonder if we men shouldn't now think of ourselves as 'shōjo', given our compulsory and excessive consumerism, a consumerism that in recent years afflicts us like sleepwalking. We are no longer the shabby and middle-aged teacher Humbert Humbert who chased Lolita's rear-end in his dreams. We all have become the forever-young Lolita herself. We are driven night and day to be relentless consumers . . . . The 'shōjo', that new human species born of modern commodification, has today commodified everything and everyone.

(Horikiri 1991:114–15)

Yoshimoto Banana and her characters are said to be the archetypes of this 'new human species'. She was born in 1964, just as Japanese consumer capitalism and the subculture of the shōjo were being synchronized. She has defined her generation – male, female, and shōjo alike – as one that 'came into contact with exactly the same kinds of consumer products', products that include presumably Toyota cars as well as Hello Kitty notebooks (Yoshimoto 1990:239). Banana recognizes that her own works, hardly examples of 'high literature' but rather more like 'this year's model', are themselves commodities. She has stated, for example, that she wants all of her previously published books removed from bookshop shelves whenever she publishes something new (Yoshimoto 1990:279). But the contents of these books so easily consumed and discarded are filled with expressions of an intense longing for times and places that never truly existed. ('I was seized with nostalgia', says Mikage with her usual fervor, 'a nostalgia so sharp it was painful.') And it is here that Japan, so famously distinct from other advanced economies, begins to look familiar. The *New York Times*, for instance, has reported on the trend of southern Californians to seek out simpler lives in rural Montana and Idaho: as one such internal immigrant explains, 'There's this desire to return to a simpler, nostalgic life, even though we don't really have any idea what that is' (*New York Times* 1993:12).

But they do have images of it, those pictures of the last corral projected or beamed onto screens; images as real as Mikage's, who understands that all her life to date to has been 'total science fiction', and who has to refer to an American movie (*The Miracle Worker*) in order to explain how something seemed 'real' to her. Despite the intriguing ubiquity of the shōjo unique to contemporary Japan, *Kitchen* does indeed seem to suggest the Japanese version of the late-capitalist, postmodern 'cultural logic' sketched by Fredric Jameson in his 1984 essay, 'Post-modernism, or the Cultural Logic of Late Capitalism'. That comic books should inspire a novel which, in turn, goes on both to win high-cultural literary awards *and* become a popular movie does seem to confirm the blurring of distinctions between high and mass cultures that Jameson takes as one sign of the postmodern. And Mikage's inability to perceive anything without linking it to a mass-produced image (her favorite sofa 'looked like something out of a commercial. An entire family could watch TV on it') certainly suggests the postmodernist 'blank parody' that Jameson calls 'pastiche'. Moreover, nowhere in *Kitchen* is found the sort of 'nuclear family' that Jameson associates with modernist ideologies of individualism. Instead, in a phrase to which I will return, both postmodernism and Banana's stories are 'schizophrenic' in that one's sense of time, and thus of life, is, according to Jameson, no longer processed linearly but rather with attention to each individual signifier.

Such postmodernism is also our consumer society's logic, he argues, because its aesthetic is employed in commodification. If Mikage cannot conceptualize any part of her life as anything but the replay of a com-modified image, it may be because, as Jameson says,

> Cultural production . . . can no longer gaze directly on some putative real world, at some reconstruction of a past history which was once itself a present; rather, as in Plato's cave, it must trace our mental images of that past upon its confining walls.
>
> (Jameson 1984:71)

This is because 'aesthetic production today has become integrated into commodity production generally', since aesthetic innovation is now required to move goods and services. Banana – who, you will recall, wants her old books taken off the shelves when a new one comes out – seems to testify to this. That she also chose to be a writer as casually, she says, as she might have become an airline stewardess also makes

Jameson's point that late capitalism has destroyed the privileged 'semi-autonomy' of the cultural realm, and so too has eliminated the critical distance that once separated art from the 'rest' of modernity. This, states Jameson, is the predictable consequence of the 'third great original expansion of capitalism around the globe', an event that sponsors a cultural/social system both 'realistic' and 'diversionary' in that it mimics commodity production even while it obscures its own status as commodity.

In his essay 'Disjuncture and difference in the global cultural economy', Arjun Appadurai (1990) makes additional observations about the status of postmodern, late-capitalist culture that may make *Kitchen*, despite its eccentricity, the perfect proof-text for such theorizing. Appadurai rethinks Jameson's assertions globally to make the important point that global cultural flows are radically 'context-dependent' (as opposed to being rigidly predetermined) in a way that could make Japan's shōjo culture more fathomable within Jameson's general outline. In a comment useful for how I will explain both *Kitchen* and its queasy reception, Appadurai wants us to remember that 'if "a" global system is emerging, it is filled with ironies and resistances, sometimes camouflaged as passivity and a bottomless appetite in the Asian world for things western'. But most significant for *Kitchen*, Appadurai shifts his attention to what he terms 'a classic human problem': the status and function of the home in this new set of 'global cultural processes'.

> [H]ow do small groups, especially families, the classic loci of socialization, deal with these new global realities as they seek to reproduce themselves, and in doing so, as it were by accident, reproduce cultural forms themselves? . . . The task of cultural reproduction, even in its most intimate arenas, such as husband-wife and parent-child relations, becomes both politicized and exposed to the traumas of deterritorialization as family members pool and negotiate their mutual understandings and aspirations in sometimes fractured spatial arrangements.
>
> (Appadurai 1990:17–18)

Appadurai wonders how reproduction (of knowledge, of social relations, of everything) can be ensured, since nowadays 'family relationships can become volatile, as new commodity patterns are negotiated . . . Most important of all, the work of cultural reproduction in new settings is profoundly complicated by the politics of representing a family as "normal"'. These are the questions we might expect an anthropologist to pose; but they are also the same questions that should occur to any reader of Yoshimoto Banana, whose stories in general and *Kitchen* in particular raise in their own fashion the crucial question of the family, repro- duction, and late capitalism – as well as those 'ironies and resistances' that Appadurai predicts must occur even in a global system. Where we should start to look for answers to these questions is where family relationships, we have been told, are always volatile – Freud called them 'hostile . . . conflicts' but they are uncannily calm wherever Banana's people live.

Mikage and Her Queer Friends

'In Yoshimoto Banana's stories, girl baby talk drones on about the cool and abundant delights of gourmet commercial life', complains Masao Miyoshi. 'Yoshimoto's imaginary space is filled with floating zombies defined by the blurs of the brand goods they choose to buy' (Miyoshi 1991b: 38). Such a zombie is not, however, *Kitchen*'s Mikage Sakura, if in fact any of Banana's characters are. Indeed Mikage makes unam- biguous fun of such rampant consumerism. 'Truly strange' is how she first describes the plethora of consumer goods in the Tanabe apartment. 'I should have known these people would have a photocopier stashed away', she sardonically observes. 'These people', she concludes, 'had a taste for buying things that verged on the unhealthy'.

How Mikage ends up in a 'strange' apartment with its suspicious inhabitants is the first part of *Kitchen*'s story. The novel opens with the news of the death of Mikage's last surviving relative, her grandmother. A young college student who must now make ends meet on her small inheritance, Mikage sinks into a lonely melancholia until the day that Yuichi Tanabe, a young acquaintance of her late grandmother's, invites Mikage to visit his and his mother's nearby home one evening. When she does, she is immediately charmed by the Tanabe apartment's warm coziness, especially that of its kitchen ('everything was of the finest quality'). She spends the night on the Tanabe sofa ('so big, so soft, so deep . . . I loved the Tanabes' sofa as much as I loved their kitchen') at the kind insistence of Yuichi's mother, Eriko.

But into this homey *gemütlichkeit* comes the revelation the next morning that Eriko is not Yuichi's mother at all, but in fact his trans- sexual father. Yuichi explains that 'she had everything done, from her face to her whatever'. Living as a woman since the early death of his wife and Yuichi's biological mother, Eriko now owns a bar where she tends both the other transsexuals working for her and the ostensibly heterosexual men who patronize them. None of this news bothers Mikage, though she does admit to some initial surprise. ('I've never seen a woman that beautiful.') She soon welcomes Eriko's affection as genuine, and their friendship (one partly sisterly, partly filial) is consecrated over a breakfast that Mikage prepares for the two of them in that kitchen she so admires. Although Mikage eventually moves out into a new place of her own once she quits university for good and finds a job as an assistant at a cooking school, the half-year that she spends with the Tanabes is time that, even as she is in the midst of it, she nostalgically savors as time with the sort of family she never had.

> Someday, I wondered, will I be living somewhere else and look back nostalgically on my time here? Or will I return to this same kitchen someday?
>
> But right now I am here with this powerful mother, this boy with the gentle eyes. That was all that mattered.
>
> (Yoshimoto 1993:42)

It is thus a great shock for Mikage to learn from Yuichi, months after the actual incident, that Eriko has been murdered by a crazed admirer. ('He had spotted her on the street, and liked what he saw . . .') At first she has a hard time accepting this as true: 'I pictured a scene from a war movie'. But soon commiseration brings Mikage and Yuichi – with whom Mikage had earlier feared falling in love – back together again in a 'complicated, fragile relationship' that Mikage recognizes as both 'brother and sister' and 'man and woman in the primordial sense'. Eriko's death, coming so soon after that of Mikage's grandmother, makes the two of them orphaned sibling-lovers standing on what Mikage calls 'the cauldron of hell', into whose fires any family can disappear in an instant. 'For some reason', Mikage says to Yuichi, 'there's always death around us'. Later she describes the two of them as standing at 'the epicenter of death'. Their mutual solitude – Mikage cries at 'having been left behind in the night, paralyzed with fear' – makes both of them miserable, disconsolate without the odd maternal love that Eriko had provided.

In the last pages of *Kitchen* (for several reasons one cannot call it a 'climax'), Mikage acts to fill this void. At the same time that Mikage is on a business trip to the resort area of the Izu peninsula with the owner of her cooking school, Yuichi is at another inn some fifty kilometers away licking his emotional wounds. Neither Mikage nor Yuichi seems to be enjoying her or himself. A phone call between the two reveals that both inns have served almost inedible dinners. A famished Mikage is in a nearby restaurant that serves her exceptionally delicious *katsudon* (fried pork on top of rice with broth – one of the great Japanese comfort foods) when she has an idea: she'll get another order of katsudon to go, and take it by taxi, despite the extravagant cost, to a surprised Yuichi. When Mikage arrives at Yuichi's inn, she must figure out how to gain entrance to Yuichi's locked room. Making her way to the building itself via its illuminated garden – 'The scene reminded me of the Jungle Cruise at Disneyland' – she scales the inn's exterior wall with no little difficulty to reach Yuichi's window. An appreciative Yuichi attacks the katsudon with gusto as Mikage, bloodied with wounds earned on her assent, watches with all the joy of a nursing mother:

> My spirits began to lift; I had done all I could.
>
> I knew it: the glittering crystal of all the good times we'd had, which had been sleeping in the depths of memory, was awakening and would keep us going. Like a blast of fresh wind, the richly perfumed breath of those days returned to my soul.
>
> More family memories.
>
> (Yoshimoto 1993:100)

Yuichi's mood, too, seems to improve suddenly and just as markedly. 'It must be because we're family', he theorizes; and indeed, as Mikage observes, 'Even in the absence of Eriko', their past happiness has resumed. While Yuichi continues to enjoy his simple repast, Mikage tells him that the future is theirs to enjoy together if only they want it. 'Yuichi's smiling face seemed to sparkle. I knew I had touched something'. But her waiting cab means that she has to leave before Yuichi can give her a definite yes or no. Mikage is still uncertain of Yuichi's future intentions for them when, late the following night while making herself some tea, she gets a phone call from him in his Tōkyō apartment. As soon as he asks, 'I'm picking you up at the station tomorrow . . . what time are you getting in?', Mikage knows the answer, and the last paragraph of *Kitchen* is this happy ending: 'The room was warm, filling with steam from the boiling water. I launched into what time I'd be in and what platform I'd be on'.

The banality of this simple story, with its over-wrought sentimentality and its embarrassing excess of adolescent anxieties and passions, is unquestionably hard to take seriously – despite Grove Press's attempt to convince us that *Kitchen* recalls 'the early Marguerite Duras', or the Italian translator's valiant comparison of its style to Nobel Prize winner Kawabata's. But apparently, seriously is exactly how a panel of distinguished arbiters of literary merit did take it, and *Kitchen* remains a work that has intrigued critics. It represents, on the one hand, the 'novelization' of the shōjo comic book, or *manga*, that plays such a large part in contemporary Japanese culture, and as such underscores how the emotional tenure of the world of shōjo has come to typify some part of the experience of everyday life in Japan, and not just that of teenage girls. One of Banana's critics, both male and middle-aged, has written of his and his wife's startling and exciting experience of identification with the vacuous sense of life communicated in Banana's works (Matsumoto 1991:16). On the other hand, *Kitchen* is also the 'manga-fication' of mainstream fiction, a transformation that threatens not only to degrade an accomplished art form, but to destroy its potential to conceptualize and critique that same 'everyday life'. Consequently, *Kitchen* can appear simultaneously as both an advance for fiction and a parody of it.

Conspicuous to both *Kitchen*'s fans and detractors is its stubborn, thematic obsession with kitchens: a room indispensible to everyday life, whether that life is something we want nowadays to celebrate or denigrate. 'The place I like best in the world', reads the novel's first line, 'is the kitchen' – an opening that could hardly endear it to readers who prefer fiction that aspires to grander utopias. In fact, *any* kitchen will apparently do: clean or dirty, large or small. Mikage's penchant for kitchens is clearly a fetish, an obsession with a part that has come to symbolize an unattainable whole. Only sleeping in the vicinity of the refrigerator consoles her after her grandmother's death; and the kitchen is where, when her own time comes, she hopes to die. Just why this should be is unclear to Mikage: 'to me a kitchen represents some distant longing engraved on my soul'. But even the least attentive reader will conclude that the kitchen is a metonym for the family, the sign of a nostalgic desire for what the orphan Mikage never had.

That 'underutilized' kitchen in the Tanabe household provides Mikage with a golden opportunity: to put its many appliances and features to their fullest use. During her stay there Mikage gives full vent to her culinary ambitions. She perfects her recipes on two happy consumers of them. '[F]or the whole summer I went about it with a crazed enthusiasm: cooking, cooking, cooking. I poured all my earnings from my part-time job into it, and if something came out wrong I'd do it over again till I got it right. Angry, fretful, or cheery, I cooked through it all'. Why? Because she has others to cook for, an audience for her performance. 'I lived like a housewife', exults Mikage. 'I was thrilled'. But like all those images that she can summon to name each of her experiences, this too is merely a role at which she plays. Her joy seems genuine, her desire to please authentic: but these are 'feelings' that can be easily disassembled and reassembled, never tied to any 'natural' setting of biological family, or permanent home. In fact, the referent of both that joy and desire – the experience of family – seems distinctly postmodern. In her essay entitled 'Family' (*Famirii*), Banana says that

> Usually the world is a terribly difficult place to be, and lots of times we end up living our lives apart from each other. That's why the family is a fort built for us to flee into. Inside that fort both men and women become symbols, and there protect the home. I like that fact. I really think it's necessary, even when it's hard.
>
> (Yoshimoto 1989:39–40)

These are certainly the sentiments of Banana's Mikage Sakura, and certainly her predicament, where in the Tanabe home notions of 'mother' and 'brother' – not to mention the genders of male and female – seem distinctly rehearsed. When the Victorians called the family 'a tent pitch'd in a world not right', 'the place of peace; the shelter, not only from all injury, but from all terror, doubt, and division' (Zaretsky 1976: 51), it was the *natural* family that compensated the individual for his labor spent in the *unnatural* arena of the factory: but in Banana's world, what makes 'the world a terribly difficult place to be' is not the smokestack, but the uncertainty of the familial relations that once promised nurturing sanctuary from it; and what makes her *famirii* a 'fort' is its 'production' – not any refuge it offers from the same. This is why a space – the kitchen – and not any biological origin or relation defines the family. All that remains constant is that space defined as 'kitchen', or rather that such space always exists. Indeed, one could argue that in the final pages of *Kitchen* Mikage effectively turns the entire Izu peninsula into a kitchen as she races across with her hot dinner-to-go for lover/ brother Yuichi. Via a trip no different, other than in sheer distance traversed, from taking a casserole from the oven to the dining room table, Mikage may find the traditional way to her man's heart: but the upshot is to form a most untraditional family. Just as there is no fixed 'inside' to Banana's families, nor is there any necessary 'outside' to them either. The strict isomorphism once imposed upon the units in which we dwell has given way to something decidedly more polymorphous.

This story, while fictional, does occur in a country where reportedly 'family members' can now be rented by the hour in order to perform those ritual obligations one is just too busy to do oneself anymore; where the small place that industrial capitalism once exempted from commodification is, under its present successor, no longer excused. This is a story that seems to confirm just that sort of 'postmodernism' in which Jameson says 'the logic of the simulacrum, with its transformation of older realities into television images, does more than really replicate the logic of late capitalism; it reinforces and intensifies it'. If these 'older realities' include the family, then perhaps we have arrived at just what it is that fascinates some readers of Banana and irritates others for its 'diversionary' tactics in masking the allegedly late-capitalist underpinnings of such vacuousness. Then again, perhaps we should look further at what happens in *Kitchen*. Perhaps we have to ask a little more about what happens when Banana, or anyone else, begins to question our literal 'legitimacy' as the sons or daughters of both our families and of a progenitive modernity for which some literary critics themselves nostalgically pine.

Sometimes a Banana Is Just a Banana

Early in *Kitchen*, Mikage tells us that she is 'tied by blood to no creature in this world'. Indeed, with the death of Eriko (who, according to Mikage, 'didn't look human') neither is Yuichi. Neither adolescent is the issue of any certain genealogy; neither descends from parents unproblematically 'fathers' or 'mothers'. The typical denouement of such situations in literature is the orphan's happy reunion with long-lost family. But in Yoshimoto Banana's novels, orphans are happy to be orphans.

This is not an entirely new ending in Japanese literature. Critic Fujimoto Yukari has pointed out not only that Japanese girls' comics in the early 1970s began the kind of 'trans-gender experiment' so prominent in *Kitchen*, but that these comics depict a changing family structure: no longer 'natural', but nonetheless 'happy and normal'. Fujimoto notes of such families that there is 'an increasing number . . . in which, unlike the traditional family, there are absolutely no blood or kinship relations' (Fujimoto 1991: 54–55). Such carefree indifference to parentage (indifference that parallels Banana's own to those 'literary traditions' noted by Nakamura) has to raise certain psychoanalytical speculation. *Kitchen* describes a fertile ground for all manner of neuroses. Yuichi – narcissistically described by Mikage/Banana as an effeminate 'long-limbed young man with pretty features' who works in a flower shop – is suspected by Mikage of being her grandmother's secret lover. But this is only the first of many taboos to be transgressed. The quasi-sibling, quasi-sexual relationship between Mikage and Yuichi always teeters on the incestuous. Their relationship repeats that long ago of Eriko and his deceased wife: from Yuichi we learn that Eriko, an

YOSHIMOTO BANANA'S *KITCHEN*

apparent orphan him/herself, was as a child 'taken in by [his future wife's] family. I don't know why. They grew up together'. Then, of course, once Eriko becomes a woman, that all important phallus – the threatened loss and promised transfer of which Freud tells us is the currency required for the successful resolution (repression) of the Oedipal complex – disappears entirely. The only thing 'made' in the Tanabe apartment are Mikage's meals – any other kind of reproduction is patently impossible. The situation, in other words, is hardly set up for the traditionally 'normal' development of either Yuichi's or Mikage's adult sexuality.

Given the steady reference to kitchens, food and eating in this novel, one might be tempted to suggest that all its characters are, psychically speaking, stalled in the 'oral stage' and are thus regressively 'pre-Oedipal'. 'Why is it that everything I eat when I'm with you is so delicious?', ponders Yuichi. 'Could it be', suggests Mikage, 'that you're satisfying hunger and lust at the same time?' The child who sucks at its mother's breast does not yet know the terror of the father and his power: no small part of *Kitchen*'s charming innocence comes from this blissful ignorance. But what we may have in *Kitchen* is in fact an anti-Oedipal scenario, one in which the kitchen and Mikage's recipes have superceded the traumatic conflicts that Freud predicts for us; in which *Kitchen*'s warm and fuzzy feelings have replaced the struggles that 'normal sexual development' mandates.

Why would such an environment be attractive to Mikage, Yuichi and Eriko? For one, it does away with the stern discipline, enforced by punishment, associated with the fear of castration by the father. Eriko, it should be remembered, willingly surrendered her own penis when she became a woman in order, she tells us, 'to adopt a sort of muddled cheerfulness' apparently unavailable to her as a man. Masculinity of any sort seems lacking in this novel, as does the sort of femininity predicated on an essential difference from masculinity. Very brief and thoroughly unpleasant appearances by Mikage's former boyfriend and then by Yuichi's former girlfriend are the two exceptions which prove the rule. One is struck by the absence of explicit sexual contrast – like the absence of sex itself – from *Kitchen*. Mikage and Yuichi, like the so-called boy-girl pairs in all of Yoshimoto Banana's works, retain unarguable signs of maleness and femaleness only in the gender of their names.

But one is also struck by the narcissism rife in the Tanabe household, where every character seems to mirror every other. Perhaps we can imagine another rationale for the popularity of *Kitchen* with the Japanese Foreign Ministry and public alike. One might argue that it is not coincidental that the way we consume commodities to express ourselves also resembles how we enjoy a dangerous intimacy with the images we perceive. Commodity fetishism might, in fact, be most accurately situated as a form of narcissism. In other words, could the Tanabe household – dephallicized, yes, but very much in love with itself – represent a kind of paradigm for how we are to submit to the allure of consumer capitalism and its demands for our psychic identification with those things we are thus convinced to buy?

But such an analysis, in implying that the psychology of consumer capitalism is somehow a 'deformed' psychology, still takes Oedipal trajectory as the norm – even if it is resisted or reworked. If narcissism, which Freud rules a stage that we ordinarily pass through on our voyage to adult heterosexuality, is now to double as the state of how we exist as consumers, then our development (or rather, our lack of it) has to be regarded suspiciously as 'arrested'. I would propose instead that our stubborn commitment to the Oedipus myth has much to do with the evident frustration of intellectuals over the queer story that Banana tells in *Kitchen*. Her novel's absurd situation upsets some as the unraveling of the same transfer of psychic identification that underlines not only classic psychoanalytic theory but modernity – whose master trope has always been the 'struggle' against chaos or control – and the self-sowing critique of itself.

It is no coincidence that Freud calls Oedipus a 'revolutionary event'. He means that it sets into motion the development of our civilized selves. It is no less revolutionary for modern writers and critics, whose 'anxiety of influence', we are told, leads to literary and intellectual innovation. No liberation, in other words, without repression. A modern novel without Oedipus is a novel without the scripted wherewithal to wrest power from that social or political authority that modernism is said to contest. But none of this can be found in *Kitchen*. It provides no model for how we are to become such fully wrought 'individuals', and therein lies one reason for panic: *Kitchen* would indeed frighten any critic worried about how we are to oppose the tendency of modern consumer capitalism to reduce our ken of action to that of simply choosing the colors of our cars. But before we object to Yoshimoto Banana too strenuously, we should consider two things closely. One, is our own position as oppositional critics linked to the same Oedipus that engenders the commodification we would oppose? And two, does a post-Oedipal cultural logic really deny us all opportunity to resist that commodification?

292

Oedipus and Japanese Consumerism

Twenty years ago Gilles Deleuze and Felix Guattari argued that Oedipus is our very modern story, and one that indispensably functions as that story that convinces us to desire our own repression. *Anti-Oedipus: Capitalism and Schizophrenia* may well provide some clue to the real issues at stake in the dissonance not only between *Kitchen*'s global success and its critical ill-repute, but between the capitalism we inherited and the one we now see unfolding before us. Deleuze and Guattari's cynical historicalization of Oedipus, and their disclosure of how it duplicates the structure of our capitalist economy as well as accounts for that of our psyches, can from afar predict the moment that has produced both Yoshimoto Banana and the anxiety she prompts in critics.

I begin with Deleuze and Guattari's insight that the 'political economy' and the Freudian 'libidinal economy' are not unrelated. In fact, insofar as they similarly manage our desires, they overlap. 'The flows and production of desire will simply be viewed as the unconscious of the social productions. Behind every investment of time and interest and capital, an investment of desire, and vice versa'. Hence Deleuze and Guattari must return repeatedly to Oedipus, to what they deride as 'the holy family: daddy-mommy-me', for it is in the Oedipal code that the libido 'is converted into the phallus as detached object, the latter existing only in the transcendent form of stock and lack', just as in the capitalist code and its own triangular expression, where 'money as detachable chain is converted into capital as detached object' (Deleuze and Guattari 1983:73). The phallus works in Oedipus much as the commodity does in capitalism, another system whose tendency is to substitute for fixed and limiting relations between people and things an abstract unit of equivalence that allows for the free exchange of everything for everything. Consequently, the Oedipal family structure becomes the means of disciplining desire: the Oedipal complex/system guarantees that human desire will be housed within the modern nuclear family, while only a commodified desire will invest the larger social field.

In their section of *Anti-Oedipus* subtitled 'Oedipus At Last', Deleuze and Guattari speculate on just how such a synchronization of codes has come into being. Once, in those systems (the primitive, the despotic) that existed before (or now exist alongside) capitalism, 'social economic production is never independent of human reproduction, of the social form of this reproduction'. The family, in other words, is the real and not just virtual site of all (re)production. But with capitalism comes a real

293

and symbolic privatization and semiotization of the family. Just as Marx saw when he understood 'wealth' as the representation of productive activity, representation generally and including that of the family 'no longer relates to a distinct object, but to productive activity itself'. Capital now assumes 'the relations of alliance and filiation . . . . [T]he family is now simply the form of human matter or material that finds itself subordinated to the autonomous social form of economic reproduction'. Consequently, the family is a trope, a figure best 'suited to what it no longer dominates . . . . Father, mother, and child thus become the simulacrum of capital ("Mister Capital, Madame Earth", and their child the Worker)'.

Once, argue Deleuze and Guattari, the entire social field is reduced symbolically to this triangle of the family, then and only then 'Oedipus arrives: it is born in the capitalist system of the application of first-order social images to the private familial images of the second order'. In other words, when capitalism turns the family from that place where things are made, to the place where things are consumed, Oedipus is required to produce those cannibalistic desires that would have us identify with our mothers and fathers: 'it is father-mommy that we consume'. Oedipus is not only linked to capitalism, it is inconceivable *without* capitalism. 'It is not via a flow of shit or a wave of incest that Oedipus arrives, but via the decoded flows of capital-money'. Mother must become the simulacrum of our origins, and father that of the 'despotic Law' – and we, with our 'slashed, split, castrated ego, are the products of capitalism . . . . The family has become the locus of retention and resonance of all the social determinations'. Just as, according to Marx, capital fools us into thinking that it is responsible for production (rather than the other way around), Oedipus tricks us into thinking that it is what makes the family reproduce itself, when in fact it is what makes things not happen.

Such a grim collusion of the psychoanalytic and capitalist regimens that make us adult and modern is not, however, without its advantages. For Deleuze and Guattari, the Oedipal code – like the capitalist code – is not primitive or despotic, which is to say rigid and without fluidity. Rather, it is the very nature of capitalism to encourage desires even as it works to restrict them. Deleuze and Guattari say that 'capitalism therefore liberates the flows of desire, but under the social conditions that define its limit and the possibility of its own dissolution, so that it is constantly opposing with all its exasperated strength the movement that drives it toward this limit'. The same then, is also true of the Oedipal code: it is a 'poorly closed triangle, a porous or seeping triangle from which the flows of desire escape in the direction of other territories'

(Deleuze and Guattari 1983:96). The breakdown before our very eyes of Oedipus is evident in Yoshimoto Banana's *Kitchen*, where we find plenty of what had to be diagnosed with psychoanalytical theory in order to be repressed: the 'schizophrenic', whose schizophrenia is the 'exterior limit' to the 'interior limit' of capitalism – Oedipus. Schizophrenia in this usage is not a clinical diagnosis: it is the name Deleuze and Guattari give happily to the escape any of us make into what their most fluent interlocutor, Brian Massumi, calls the 'unstable equilibrium of continuing self-invention' (1992:92). It is the schizophrenic who 'explodes the Oedipal genealogy' because he or she (the 'or' here assumes special significance) refuses to understand his-or-her desire as that for the parent or for any kindred authority that creates desire by threatening to deprive others of what it paranoically has; the delirium of the father simply does not work here. His/her desire, rather, does not submit to such reasoning, or structure; the schizophrenic 'is not simply bisexual', for Freud could easily agree with that – the schizophrenic is 'between the two, or intersexual. He is transsexual'.

And so we are back to *Kitchen*. Not just in the schizophrenic/ transsexual Eriko, *né* Yuji, who gladly paid to have himself castrated for the sake of a 'muddled cheerfulness' and so lose the leverage of the phallus with which to organize and discipline his-or-her 'family', but also in Mikage and Yuichi, who are just as schizophrenic and just as anti-Oedipal. Neither can imagine oneself the issue of the daddy-mommy-me that Freud and his age mandated. The lack of overt sexual difference between the two is not really a 'lack': they are different genders, of course, but as Deleuze and Guattari indicate, such difference is not the basis of (different) subjectivity – 'Mikage' and 'Yuichi' are only 'oppositional terms'. Is their sexuality, too, 'muddled'? The products of bad object-choices, or of no object choices at all? Wrong: they are the 'orphans' of which Deleuze and Guattari speak as one of the directions in which anti-Oedipal, schizo flows may go, and go gladly. 'For what is the schizo', they say, 'if not first of all the one who can no longer bear "all that": money, the stock market, the death forces', those things that capitalism and psychoanalysis convinced us of? These people, too, 'can no longer bear "all that"'. Eriko becomes a woman after the death of his wife; Mikage and Yuichi become a family after the death of Eriko. But in the end, the consequence of giving up 'all that' seems to be the gain of something. What family in modern Japanese literature, after all, is as happy as Mikage, Yuichi, and Eriko?

Still, *Kitchen* has its moments of anxiety, though that anxiety can now be thought the consequence of its anti-Oedipal verve. What frightens both Mikage and Yuichi after the deaths of the former's grandmother and Eriko is the immediacy of those deaths and their demonstrated potential to leave one family-less at any time, stranded and alone. 'Someday, without fail', muses Mikage, 'everyone will disappear, scattered into the blackness of time'. What both fear is the disappearance of just that social field once ruled over by Oedipus, for even if we were orphaned, we were still someone's *daughter*, someone's *son*: titles that, even when Mikage and Yuichi assume them, are roles and not identities.

Mikage's blackness is one that Deleuze and Guattari predict as precisely the consequence of being anti-Oedipal: 'Oedipus informs us: if you don't follow the lines of differentiation daddy-mommy-me, and the exclusive alternatives that delineate them, you will fall into the black night of the undifferentiated' (Deleuze and Guattari 1983:78). The deaths that surround Mikage and Yuichi – so many, in fact, that Yuichi gloomily jokes that they should rent themselves out as '*de*construction workers' – *de*territorialize the Oedipal triangle and its penchant for wrecking 'the assemblage of desire'.

What remains is its reterritorialization. The response of the characters, and that which completes the bizarre comedy that is *Kitchen*, is to refashion that field for themselves. 'What a muddle, what an emulsion the family is', warn Deleuze and Guattari, 'agitated by backwashes, pulled in one direction or another, in such a way that the Oedipal bacillus takes or doesn't take'. But remember that it is for the sake of a 'muddled *cheerfulness*' that Eriko undergoes the knife to make himself a woman and a mother: there is something to be gained in breaking the rules. When Mikage first hears the news of Eriko's death, she feels 'powerless to stop the energy rushing out of my body; it seemed to dissipate with a hissing sound into the darkness', but that energy is the flow of a liberated desire, and the darkness is the anti-Oedipal void in which she will indulge that desire. When she orders katsudon to go, and races to Isehara to deliver it, she binds herself and Yuichi in that 'fort' that author Banana calls the famirii, a word taken from English precisely to deterritorialize it.[6] Her and Yuichi's family is not easily schematized as boyfriend and girlfriend, or mother and son, or brother and sister. It is 'undifferentiated' in the way that Deleuze and Guattari characterize the world of the schizophrenic; it is 'anti-Oedipal' in the way that they would schizoanalyze capitalism.

Obviously, one can debate whether all this is genuinely liberating, or hopelessly repressive/regressive. If *Kitchen*'s is a family that can be compared to any other, it is the family composed of all those images, nostalgic, cinematic, and otherwise, of the family that Mikage is heir to.

One could, with Jameson, see such a production as indeed the mark of the postmodern, namely 'the transformation of the real into so many pseudo-events'. (Though if the real in this instance must be the Oedipal 'real' of the family, then this could still be more cause for celebration than censure.) But I do not mean to suggest that the schizo-anything of *Kitchen* is the 'potential for revolution' that Deleuze and Guattari see in the schizo process elsewhere. Indeed, *Kitchen* is rife with the kind of diversionary 'intensities' that Jameson warns 'tend to be dominated by a peculiar kind of euphoria' in the style that accompanies late capitalism. Mikage does recall, after all, 'But – that one summer of bliss. In that kitchen'.

Can we say this: that the moment we now inhabit – one aptly characterized by what Appadurai in good Deleuzean fashion terms a 'rhizomatic' global capitalism, without real 'origins' and where the ideas of both 'consumer' and 'producer' are fetishes – is also one that can be, à la Banana, ambivalently 'anti-Oedipal'? Workers in Japan and other developed nations are told today that the 'new global economy' means that they will have to have several different careers over the course of their lives, that they will have to constantly adapt and change, abandon identities as forever *one* sort of worker or another. Some of us now telecommute from our homes and away from our bosses; others – the 'temporary employee' ever more common in the workforce – migrate like nomads *between* bosses. Does this make us more autonomous? Or merely cheaper to hire? The increasingly polymorphous shape of our economic lives finds its equivalent in families likewise more affinitive and less filial. Doesn't the newspaper tell us of families whose offspring derive from test-tubes? And promise cloning and transgenetic engineering for tomorrow? Where is the phallus there? Gone, or now the property of a high-tech corporation? Don't we speak worriedly of 'fatherless families', but hopefully of 'surrogate mothers'? Those 'families' in Japan that rent out by the hour may seem the final indignity heaped upon modern people so busy they cannot even visit their parents – but is visiting actually what we want to do with our time? Just how bizarre is the Mikage-Yuichi-Eriko household *really*? Perhaps not very. It could be that the immensely protean and adaptive nature of capital and labor today is reflected in the practice of the post-nuclear family, no longer spawned and contained by the father, but instead infinitely pliable as every family member now produces *and* consumes, in ways unimagined not only by Freud, but by Deleuze and Guattari as few as twenty years ago. Unimagined – but perhaps well intuited by Japan's Foreign Ministry last July, when copies of *Kitchen* were handed out to the world's media as a way of understanding 'the younger generation all over the world'. In 1994, just as its author has said she wants, *Kitchen* was banished from bookstore windows and replaced with *N.P.*, the second of her novels to appear in English. According to one reviewer, and in true keeping with the commodification of the literary work, *N.P.* features another of Banana's nearly identical 'young women adrift, sliding away from family into sensuous romance' – in this case, a sensuous romantic case of incest (Galef 1994). Such stories may disturb one generation of readers, but they may be attracting another one. Those 'younger people' around the world, cited by both the Japanese Foreign Ministry and Banana's foreign critics, might think the narcissism of parents and children in love with each other not so very different from a consumer culture that identifies what we desire with what we are. What is left to be understood is how this 'cultural logic', like Marx's bourgeois capitalism or Deleuze and Guattari's schizophrenia or Fredric Jameson's postmodernism, has to be both our worst news and our best chance for doing better.

NOTES

1 Half the submissions to Japan's many literary prizes reportedly come from adolescents, and nearly all the new writer prizes in 1991 were awarded to writers who were simultaneously young, female, and – in a testament to the power of both Japan's heralded 'internationalization' and its hyper-valued yen – living abroad.
2 The German publisher, Diogenes Verlag, considered the option of entitling it *Küche* 'offenbar zu banal': like other transnational corporate identities, 'Ford' or 'Coca-Cola', there is both market value and panache in English name recognition.
3 '(P)ublishers in New York and Tōkyō', wrote Herbert Mitgang (1990) on the eve of *Kitchen*'s international debut, 'are making a fresh effort to internationalize the market for Japanese fiction'.
4 Like those Ohio-assembled Hondas shipped to Japan, *gyaku-yunyū* 'reimportation' now brings the average consumer as well as foreign journalists the benefits of a globalized economy: Japanese bookstores in the fall of 1993 were encouraging shoppers to experience the 'English-version Banana'.
5 In the English translation of *Kitchen*, the characters' family and personal names have been reversed to mimic Western convention, and, in the case of Yuichi, have lost the diacritics usually used in Romanization.
6 Deleuze calls deterritorialized terms 'terms which are torn from their area, in order to reterritorialize another notion' (Deleuze and Guattari 1987:18).

REFERENCES

Akiyama Toyoko 1991 'Jakunensō no ishiki henka no tokuchō 1970 nendai – 80 nendai no henka o chūshin ni' (Changes in youth consciousness: from the 70s to the 80s), p. 55–81 in *NHK Hōsō Bunka Kenkyū Nenpō* 36.

—— 1983 'Nihonjin no heiwakan' (The Japanese outlook on peace), p. 2–15 in *Hōsō Kenkyū to Chōsa*, April.

—— and Muramatsu Yasuko 1986 'Josei no ishiki jūnen: katei fujin to yūshoku josei no bunseki o chūshin ni' (Women's consciousness over the last ten years: analysis of housewives and working women), p. 279–300 in *NHK Hōsō Bunka Kenkyū Nenpō* 31.

—— et al 1984 'Nihonjin no ishiki henka: danjobetsu, danjo nensōbetsu ni mita jūnenkan no henka' (Changes in Japanese consciousness: change over the last ten years divided by gender and age), p. 1–50 in *NHK Hōsō Bunka Kenkyū Nenpō* 29.

Anderson, Laurel and Marsha Wadkins 1992 'The new breed in Japan: consumer culture', p. 146–154 in *Canadian Journal of Administrative Sciences* 9 (2).

Aoki, Tamotsu 1994 'Anthropology and Japan: attempts at writing culture', p. 1–6 in *The Japan Foundation Newsletter*, XXII (3).

Appadurai, Arjun 1990 'Disjuncture and difference in the global cultural economy', p. 1–24 in *Public Culture* 2 (2).

Apter, David E. and Sawa Nagayo 1984 *Against the State: politics and social protest in Japan*, Cambridge: Harvard University Press.

Bailey, Stephen 1986 *Sex, Drink and Fast Cars: the creation and consumption of images*, London: faber and faber.

Barthes, Roland 1977 'The rhetoric of the image', p. 32–51 in *Image-Music-Text*, London: Fontana.

—— 1975 *S/Z*, New York: Hill & Wang.

—— 1972 'Ornamental cookery', p. 78–80 in *Mythologies*, New York: Hill & Wang.

—— 1970 *L'Empire des Signes*, Paris: Flammarion.

Baudrillard, Jean 1993 *Symbolic Exchange and Death*, London: Sage Publications.

Beck, Ulrich 1992 *Risk Society: towards a new modernity*, London: Sage Publications.

Berger, John 1972 *Ways of Seeing*, Harmondsworth: Penguin/BBC Books.

REFERENCES

Berman, Marshall 1988 (1982) *All That Is Solid Melts Into Air*, Harmondsworth: Penguin.

Blacker, Carmen 1975 *The Catalpa Bow: a study of shamanistic practices in Japan*, London: Allen and Unwin.

Bourdieu, Pierre 1984 *Distinction: a social critique of the judgment of taste*, London: Routledge and Kegan Paul.

Brinton, Mary 1993 *Women and the Economic Miracle: gender and work in Japan*, Berkeley: University of California Press.

Buruma, Ian 1993 'Weeping tears of nostalgia', p. 29–30 in *The New York Review of Books* XL (14), August 12.

—— 1984 *A Japanese Mirror: heroes and villains in Japanese culture*, London: Jonathan Cape.

Bussey, John and Michael Williams 1993 'Reporters' notebook: sumo champion makes pitch for his adoptive Japan', p. 2 in *Wall Street Journal*, July 7.

Cho, Haejoang 1986, 'Male dominance and mother power: the two sides of Confucian patriarchy in Korea', p. 277–298 in W. H. Slote (ed.) *The Psycho-Cultural Dynamics of the Confucian Family: past and present*, Seoul: International Cultural Society of Korea.

Clammer, John 1992 'Aesthetics of the self: shopping and social being in contemporary urban Japan', p. 195–215 in R. Shields (ed.) *Lifestyle Shopping: the subject of consumption*, London: Routledge.

Clark, Hazel 1994 'Eco fashion – conviction or conceit?', unpublished paper given at the AAH conference.

Clark, Rodney 1979 *The Japanese Company*, Cambridge, MA: Yale University Press.

Coward, Rosalind 1987 *Female Desire*, London: Paladin.

Creighton, Millie 1994 'The shifting imagery of childhood amidst Japan's consumer affluence: the birth of the 5 pocket child' in H. Eiss (ed.) *Images of the Child*, Ohio: Bowling Green State University Press.

Dalby, Liza 1983 *Geisha*, Berkeley and Los Angeles: University of California Press.

Dale, Peter 1986 *The Myth of Japanese Uniqueness*, London and Sydney: Croom Helm.

Deleuze, Gilles and Felix Guattari 1987 *Dialogues* (translated by Hugh Tomlinson and Barbara Habberjam), New York: Columbia University Press.

—— 1983 *Anti-Oedipus: capitalism and schizophrenia* (translated by Robert Hurley, Mark Seem and Helen R. Lane), Minneapolis: University of Minnesota Press.

Delfs, Robert 1992 'Leading the energy race', p. 49–50 in *Far Eastern Economic Review*, June 18.

Dentsū 1991 *Japan 1992: marketing and advertising yearbook*, Tōkyō: Dentsū Inc.

Doane, Mary Ann 1989 'The economy of desire: the commodity form in/of the cinema', p. 23–35 in *Quarterly Review of Film and Video* 11 (1).

Doi, Takeo 1973 *The Anatomy of Dependence*, Tōkyō: Kodansha International.

Dyer, Gillian 1988 (1982) *Advertising as Communication*, London: Routledge.

Economist, 1993 'Acid rain in Japan: passing the buck', p. 68–9, August 21.

Edwards, Walter 1989 *Japan Seen through its Weddings*, Stanford: Stanford University Press.

REFERENCES

—— 1987 'The Commercialised Wedding As Ritual', p. 51–78 in *Journal of Japanese Studies* 13 (1).

Eguchi Hiroyuki 1984 *Oshin o Tsukutta Oshintachi* (The Oshin-people who made Oshin), Tōkyō: Gurafusha.

Ehara Yumiko 1990 'Feminizumu no 70 nedai to 80 nendai' (Feminism in the 70s and 80s), in her (ed.) *Feminizumu Ronsō* (Feminism Debates), Tōkyō: Keisō Shobō.

Elias, Norbert 1976 *Über den Prozeß der Zivilisation* (The Civilising Process) 1–2, Frankfurt a.M.: Suhrkamp.

Erikson, Kai 1966 *Wayward Puritans: a study in the sociology of deviance*, New York: John Wiley and Sons.

Evans, David 1993 *Sexual Citizenship: the material construction of sexualities*, New York: Routledge Press.

Ewen, Stuart 1988 *All Consuming Images: the politics of style in contemporary culture*, New York: Basic Books.

Far Eastern Economic Review 1992 'Asia life styles', p. 35–51, September 10.

Featherstone, Mike 1991a *Consumer Culture and Postmodernism*, London: Sage Publications.

—— 1991b 'The body in consumer society', in M. Featherstone et al. (eds.): *The Body: social process and cultural theory*, London: Sage Publications.

Fiske, John 1991 (1989) *Understanding Popular Culture*, London: Routledge.

Fornander, Kjell 1992 'Risqué business', p. 28–35 in *Tōkyō Journal* (7).

Foucault, Michel 1980 *The History of Sexuality, Volume 1: an introduction*, New York: Vintage Books.

Frank, Arthur W. 1990 'Bringing bodies back in: a decade review', p. 131–62 in *Theory, Culture and Society* 7 (1).

Fujimoto, Yukari 1991 'A life-size mirror: woman's self-representation in girls' comics', p. 53–57 in *Review of Japanese Culture and Society* 4.

Fujioka, Wakao 1986 'The rise of the micromasses', p. 31–38 in *Japan Echo* 13 (1).

Funabashi, Kuniko 1991 'Das Frauenbild in der japanischen Pornographie' (The image of woman in Japanese pornography), p. 166–179 in E. Gössmann (ed.) *Japan – ein Land der Frauen?*, München: Iudicidum.

Galef, David 1994 'Jinxed', p. 23 in *New York Times Book Review*, February 27.

Garrison, Deborah 1993 'Day-O', p. 109–10 in *New Yorker* 69 (5), March 22.

Giddens, Anthony 1991 *Modernity and Self Identity: self and society in the late modern age*, Stanford: Stanford University Press.

Gluck, Carol 1985 *Japan's Modern Myths: ideology in the late Meiji period*, Princeton, NJ: Princeton University Press.

Goffman, Erving 1963 *Behaviour in Public Places*, New York: Free Press.

—— 1969 *The Presentation of Self in Everyday Life*, Harmondsworth, Penguin.

Goldstein-Gidoni, Ofra 1993 *Packaged Weddings, Packaged Brides: the Japanese ceremonial occasions industry*, doctoral dissertation presented to the Department of Anthropology and Sociology, School of Oriental and African Studies, University of London.

Gotō, Kazuhiko et al. 1991 *A History of Japanese Television Drama: modern Japan and the Japanese*, Tōkyō: The Japan Association of Broadcasting Art.

Hall, Stuart 1991 'The local and the global: globalization and ethnicity', in A. King (ed.) *Culture, Globalization and the World-System*, Binghamton: State University of New York.

REFERENCES

Hannerz, Ulf 1992 *Cultural Complexity: studies in the social organization of meaning*, New York: Columbia University Press.
—— 1991 'Scenarios for peripheral cultures', in A. King (ed.) *Culture, Globalization and the World-System*, Binghamton: State University of New York.
Harootunian, H.D. 1989 'Visible discourses/invisible ideologies', p. 63–92 in M. Miyoshi and H.D. Harootunian (eds.) *Postmodernism and Japan*, Durham and London: Duke University Press.
Harris, D. 1993 'Cuteness', in J. Epstein (ed.) *The Best American Essays*, New York: Ticknor and Fields.
Hasegawa, N. 1982 *The Japanese Character: a cultural profile*, Tōkyō and New York: Kodansha International.
Hashida Sugako 1984 *Oshin Jinseikun: yutaka na jidai no 'shin no kotoba'* (The Teachings in Oshin: words from the heart for an affluent age), Tōkyō: Simul Press.
Hebdige, Dick 1988 *Hiding in the Light*, London: Routledge.
Hendry, Joy 1993 *Wrapping Culture: politeness, presentation, and power in Japan and other societies*, Oxford: Clarendon Press.
HILL 1993a *Japanese Single Women: living in a world without signposts. Changing Lifestyles in Japan* 7, Tōkyō: Hakuhōdō Institute of Life and Living.
—— 1993b *'Hanbun Dake' Kazoku: famirī shōhi o dō miru ka* (The 'Half' Family: how to view family consumption), Tōkyō: Nihon Keizai Shinbunsha.
—— 1987 *Jiryū wa Joryū: mada mada kawaru Nihon no onna* (The Trend of the Times is Women's Trends: ever changing women of Japan), Tōkyō: Nihon Keizai Shinbunsha.
—— 1984 *Young Adults in Japan; new attitudes creating new lifestyles*, Tōkyō: Hakuhodo Institute of Life and Living.
Hobsbawm, Erik and Terence Ranger 1983 (eds.) *The Invention of Tradition*, Cambridge: Cambridge University Press.
Holland, Patricia 1992 *What is a Child? Popular images of childhood*, London: Virago Press.
Holliman, Jonathan 1990 'Environmentalism with a global scope', p. 284–290 in *Japan Quarterly* 37, July/September.
Horikiri Naoto 1991 'Onna wa dokyō, shōjo wa aikyō' (Women have mettle, shōjo have charm), p. 108–28 in H. Masuko et al. (eds.) *Shōjoron* (Essays on Shōjo), Tōkyō: Aoyumisha.
Hunter, Janet 1993 'Textile factories, tuberculosis and the quality of life in industrialising Japan', p. 69–97 in J. Hunter (ed.) *Japanese Women Working*, London: Routledge.
Huyssen, Andreas 1986a 'Mass culture as woman: modernism's other', p. 188–207 in T. Modleski (ed.) *Studies in Entertainment: critical approaches to mass culture*, Bloomington: Indiana University Press.
—— 1986b *After the Great Divide: modernism, mass culture, postmodernism*, Bloomington: Indiana University Press.
Hyodo, Hiromi 1991 'A new relationship between enterprises and the environment: examples of advertising campaigns with environmental themes in Japan', p. 70–81 in *Japan 1992: marketing and advertising yearbook*, Tōkyō: Dentsu Inc.
Imidas 1991, (Innovative Multi-Information Dictionary, annual series), Tōkyō: Shūeisha.

Inoue Teruko 1992 'Josei zasshi ni miru feminizumu' (Feminism as seen in women's magazines), p. 111–119 in H. Katō and T. Tsuganesawa (eds.) *Josei to Media* (Women and Media), Tōkyō: Sekai Shisōsha.

—— 1985 'The role of modern journalism', p. 79–93 in *Women in a Changing Society: views from Japan*, Geneva: Unesco.

—— et al. 1989 *Josei Zasshi o Kaidoku Suru: Comparepolitan – nichi, bei, mekishiko hikaku kenkyū* (Reading Women's Magazines: Comparepolitan – a comparative study of Japan, USA, Mexico), Tōkyō: Kakiuchi Shuppan.

Ivy, Marilyn 1993 'Formations of mass culture', in A. Gordon (ed.) *Postwar Japan as History*, Berkeley: University of California Press.

—— 1988 'Tradition and difference in the Japanese mass media', p. 21–9 in *Public Culture* 1 (1).

Iwao, Sumiko 1993 *The Japanese Woman: traditional image and changing reality*, New York: Free Press.

Jameson, Fredric 1991 *Postmodernism, or the Cultural Logic of Late Capitalism*, London: Verso.

—— 1984 'Postmodernism, or the cultural logic of late capitalism', p. 53–92 in *New Left Review* 146.

Japan Economic Journal 1990a 'Eco-fashion's painless way to make "statement"', June 17.

Japan Economic Journal 1990b 'Consumers seek global protection', June 23.

Jayawardena, Kumai 1986 *Feminism and Nationalism in the Third World*, London: Zed.

Johnstone, Bob 1991 'False economies' and 'Chemical reaction', p. 37–8 in *Far Eastern Economic Review*, September 19.

—— 1990 'The ozone player', p. 102 in *Far Eastern Economic Review*, June 21.

Kalland, Arne and Brian Moeran 1992 *Japanese Whaling: end of an era?*, London: Curzon Press.

Karatani, Kōjin 1993 'The discursive space of modern Japan', p. 288–316 in M. Miyoshi and H.D. Harootunian (eds.) *Japan in the World*, Durham and London: Duke University Press.

Kazama, Daiji and Akiyama Toyoko 1981 'Gendai no shōnenzō: 70 nendai o chūshin to shita shōnen no ishiki henka' (The image of modern youth: young people's consciousness in the 1970s), p. 1–58 in *NHK Hōsō Bunka Kenkyū Nenpō* 26.

Keizai Kikakuchō (ed.) 1992 *Kokumin Seikatsu Hakusho* (Citizens' Life White Paper), Tōkyō: Ōkurashō.

Kelly, William 1990 'Japanese no-Noh: the crosstalk of public culture in a rural festivity', p. 65–81 in *Public Culture* 2 (2).

Kinameri Yoshihisa and Ezaki Akira 1989 '"Imadoki no onna" ga torendo o umu' (Up-to-date women give birth to trends), p. 266–273 in *'Onna ga kawaru, shijō ga kawaru'* (Women change and the market changes), *President* 27 (10).

Kirkpatrick, R. Craig 1992 'Cleaning up Japan', p. 48–9 in *Far Eastern Economic Review*, July 30.

Knibbs, David 1992 'The Kansei factor: image making in Japanese advertising', p. 18–24 in *The Japan International Journal (JIJ)* 2 (1).

Kondo, Dorinne K. 1990 *Crafting Selves: power, gender and identity in a Japanese workplace*, Chicago: Chicago University Press.

REFERENCES

Konishi Akiyuki 1983 'How do we compile a newspaper?', p. 11–20 in *Orientation Seminars on Japan* 14, Tōkyō: Japan Foundation.

Lebra, Takie Sugiyama 1984 *Japanese Women: constraint and fulfillment*, Honolulu: University of Hawaii Press.

Lee, M. J. 1993 *Consumer Culture Reborn: the cultural politics of consumption*, London: Routledge.

Logan, F. 1983 'Tōkyō cute', p. 10–17 in *Tōkyō Journal*, April, Tōkyō: Yohan Publications Ltd.

Löfgren, Orvar 1990 'Consuming interests', p. 7–37 in *Culture and History* 7.

Maffesoli, M. 1990 *Au Creux des Apparences*, Paris: Plon.

Makita Tetsuo 1976 'NHK renzoku terebi shōsetsu no kōsatsu' (The concept behind NHK serialised television novels), p. 79–94 in *NHK Hōsō Bunka Kenkyū Nenpō* 21, Tōkyō: NHK Shuppankai.

—— and Janamoto Keifuku 1983 '*Oshin* būmu o saguru: Oshin to nihonjin chōsa kara' (Examining the *Oshin* boom: results from the Japanese people and *Oshin* opinion poll), p. 21–28 in *Hōsō Kenkyū to Chōsa*, December.

Marcuse, Herbert 1964 *One-Dimensional Man: studies in the ideology of advanced industrial society*, Boston: Beacon Press.

Massumi, Brian 1992 *A User's Guide to Capitalism and Schizophrenia*, Cambridge, MA: MIT Press.

Matsuda Seiko 1982 *Yume ni Aetara* (If we could meet in a Dream), Tōkyō: Wanibukksu.

Matsumoto Takayuki 1991 *Yoshimoto Banana-ron: 'futsū' to iu muishiki* (Yoshimoto Banana: the unconscious of the ordinary), Tōkyō: JICC Shuppankyoku.

McCracken, Ellen 1993 *Decoding Women's Magazines: from "Mademoiselle" to "Ms."*, London: Macmillan.

McNay, Lois 1992 *Foucault and Feminism*, Boston: Northeastern University Press.

Mitgang, Herbert 1990 'Letter from Tokyo: Brando, the Stones and Banana Yoshimoto', p. 13–14 in *The New York Times Book Review*, July 8.

Mitsui Takayuki and Koyata Washida 1989 *Yoshimoto Banana Shinwa* (The Myths of Yoshimoto Banana), Tōkyō: Aoyumisha.

Miwa Tadashi 1983 'Kodomotachi wa Oshin o dō uketotta ka' (How did children relate to Oshin?), p. 14–19 in *Hōsō Kenkyū to Chōsa*, November.

Miyake, Yoshiko 1991 'Doubling expectations: motherhood and women's factory work under state management in Japan in the 1930s and 1940s', p. 267–96 in G.L. Bernstein (ed.) *Recreating Japanese Women 1600–1945*, Berkeley and Los Angeles: University of Califoria Press.

Miyanaga, Kuniko 1991 *The Creative Edge: emerging individualism in Japan*, New Brunswick, NJ: Transaction Press.

Miyoshi, Masao 1991a *Off-Center: power and culture relations between Japan and the United States*, Cambridge, MA: Harvard University Press.

—— 1991b 'Women's short stories in Japan', p. 33–39 in *Manoa* 3 (2).

—— and H.D. Harootunian (eds.) 1989a *Postmodernism and Japan*, Durham and London: Duke University Press.

—— 1989b 'Introduction', p. vii–xix in M. Miyoshi and H. D. Harootunian (eds.) *Postmodernism and Japan*, Durham and London: Duke University Press.

Moeran, Brian 1996 *A Japanese Advertising Agency*, London: Curzon Press.

REFERENCES

—— 1993 'A tournament of value: strategies of presentation in Japanese advertising', p. 73–94 in *Ethnos* 58 (1–2).

—— 1991 'Media and advertising in Japan', *NIAS Working Papers* 4, Copenhagen: Nordic Institute of Asian Studies.

—— 1989 *Language and Popular Culture in Japan*, Manchester: Manchester University Press.

—— 1984 *Lost Innocence: folk craft potters of Onta, Japan*, Berkeley and Los Angeles: University of California Press.

—— and Lise Skov forthcoming 'Mount Fuji and the cherry blossoms: a view from afar', in P. Asquith and A. Kalland (eds.) *The Culture of Japanese Nature*, London: Curzon Press.

—— 1995 'Japanese advertising nature: ecology, fashion, women and art', p. 215–43 in O. Bruun and A. Kalland (eds.) *Asian Perceptions of Nature*, London: Curzon Press.

—— 1993 'Cinderella Christmas: kitsch, consumerism and youth culture in Japan', p. 105–133 in D. Miller (ed.) *Unwrapping Christmas*, Oxford: Oxford University Press.

Moon, Okpyo 1992 'Confucianism and gender segregation in Japan and Korea' in R. Goodman and K. Refsing (eds.) *Ideology and Practice in Modern Japan*, London: Routledge.

Morisette, Peter M. 1991 'The Montreal protocol: lessons for formulating policies for global warming', p. 152–62 in *Policy Studies Journal* 19 (2).

Muramatsu Yasuko 1979 *Terebi Dorama no Joseigaku* (The Study of Women in Television Drama), Tōkyō: Ontaimu Shuppan.

Myers, Kathy 1986 *Understains: the sense of education in advertising*, London: Comedia.

Nakano, Osamu 1988 'A sociological analysis of the new breed', p. 12–16 in *Japan Echo* XV.

—— 1985 *Marude Eirian* (Almost Alien), Tōkyō: Yubikaku.

Natili, Donnatella 1994 'Italy de no Yoshimoto Banana' (Yoshimoto Banana in Italy)', p. 108–12 in *Kokubungaku: kaishaku to kyōzai no kenkyū* 39 (3).

New York Times 1993 'Eastward, Ho! Disenchanted, Californians turn to the interior West', p. 12, May 30.

NHK International (ed.) 1991 *International Symposium: the world's view of Japan through Oshin*, Tōkyō: NHK International.

Nihon Zasshi Kōkoku Kyōkai 1990 *Zasshi Kōkoku Keisai Ryōkin-hyō* (Magazine Advertising Placement Rates), Tōkyō: Nihon Zasshi Kōkoku Kyōkai.

Nishibe, S. 1986 'A denunciation of mass society and its apologists', p. 39–43 in *Japan Echo* 13 (1).

O'Barr, William 1989 'The airbrushing of culture: an insider looks at global advertising', p. 1–19 in *Public Culture* 2 (1).

Okonogi Keigo 1981 *Moratorium Ningen no Jidai* (The Age of the Moratorium People), Tōkyō: Chūō Kōronsha.

—— 1978 'The age of the moratorium people', p. 17–39 in *Japan Echo* V (1).

O'Neill, P. G. 1984 'Organization and authority in the traditional arts', *Modern Asian Studies* 18 (4).

Ono, Keigo 1983 'Disney and the Japanese', p. 6–12 in *Look Japan*, July 10.

Oshin: NHK Dorama Gaido 1983, Tōkyō: Nippon Hōsō Shuppan Kyōkai.

Ōtsuka Eiji 1991 *Shōjo Minzokugaku* (Shōjo Ethnology), Tōkyō: Kōbunsha.

REFERENCES

REFERENCES

—— 1989 'The teenagers' cute emperor', p. 65–68 in *Japan Echo*, XVI (1).

Peak, Lois 1991 *Learning to Go to School*, Berkeley: University of California Press.

Pharr, Susan 1981 *Political Women in Japan*, Berkeley and Los Angeles: University of California Press.

Picone, Mary 1989 'The ghost in the machine: religious healing and representations of the body in Japan' in M. Feber (ed.) *Fragments for a History of the Human Body, Part 2*, New York: Zone.

Pierce, John C. et al. 1990 'Support for citizen participation: a comparison of American and Japanese citizens, activists and elites', p. 39–59 in *Western Political Quarterly* 43 (1).

Poole, Peter J. 1988 'China threatened by Japan's old pollution strategies', p. 78 in *Far Eastern Economic Review*, June 28.

Posener, Jill 1982 *Spray it Loud*, London: Routledge and Kegan Paul.

Pyle, Kenneth 1987 'In pursuit of a grand design: Nakasone betwixt the past and the future', p. 243–70 in *Journal of Japanese Studies* 13 (2).

Quarterly Review of Film and Video 1989 'Preface: female representation and consumer culture', p. vii–viii, 11 (1).

Robertson, Jennifer 1989 'Gender-bending in paradise: doing 'female' and 'male' in Japan', p. 50–69 in *Genders* 5.

Rosario, Louise do 1992 'Green at the edges', p. 39 in *Far Eastern Economic Review*, March 12.

Rosenberger, Nancy 1993 'Japanese young women and elite global identities: construction and contradictions', paper presented at the American Anthropological Association, Washington, D.C., November.

—— 1992a 'Tree in winter, tree in summer: movement in Japanese self', p. 67–92, in N. Rosenberger (ed.) *Japanese Sense of Self*, Cambridge: Cambridge University Press.

—— 1992b 'Images of the West: home style in Japanese magazines', in J. Tobin (ed.), *Remade in Japan*, New Haven: Yale University Press.

—— 1991a 'Gender and the Japanese state: pension benefits dividing and uniting', p. 178–194 in *Anthropological Quarterly* 64 (4).

—— 1991b 'Don't think! There's no time! Messages of individuality, freedom and status in young women's magazines', paper presented at the Association for Asian Studies, New Orleans, March.

Russell, John 1995 'Race and reflexivity: the black other in contemporary Japanese mass culture', in J. Treat (ed.) *Contemporary Japan and Popular Culture*, London: Curzon Press.

Saitō Kenji 1975 'Katei fujin to terebi shichō: shokugyōbetsu hikaku o chūshin ni' (Housewives and television ratings in a comparative perspective with other professions), p. 10–15 in *Bunken Geppō*, December.

Savigliano, Marta E. 1992 'Tango in Japan and the world economy of passion', p. 235–253 in J. Tobin (ed.) *Re-Made in Japan: everyday life and consumer taste in a changing society*, New Haven and London: Yale University Press.

Seikatsu Shikkihō 1992 *Eco Raifu no Shinten to 21 Seiki* (The Development of Eco Life And the 21 Century), Seikatsu Shikkihō, spring edition.

Shields, Rob (ed.) 1992 *Lifestyle Shopping: the subject of consumption*, London: Routledge.

Shilling, Chris 1993 *The Body and Social Theory*, London: Sage Publications.

306

REFERENCES

Shimamori Michiko 1984 *Kōkoku no Naka no Onnatachi* (Women in Advertising), Tōkyō: Daiwa Shobō.

Shimamura, M. 1990 *Fanshii no Kenkyū: kawaii ga hito, mono, kane o shōhai suru* (Research into 'Fancy': cute controls people, objects and money), Tōkyō: Nesco.

—— 1991 *Japan Times Weekly* cover story, January 5.

Shiraishi Nobuko 1993 'Hirari wa dō mirareta ka' (How was Hirari viewed?), p. 38–39 in *Hōsō Kenkyū to Chōsa*, May.

Sievers, Sharon 1983 *Flowers in Salt: the beginnings of feminist consciousness in modern Japan*, Stanford: Stanford University Press.

Silverberg, Miriam 1991 'The modern girl as militant' p. 239–67 in G.L. Bernstein (ed.) *Recreating Japanese Women 1600–1945*, Berkeley and Los Angeles: University of California Press.

Smith, Robert J. 1987 'Gender inequality in contemporary Japan', p. 1–26 in *Journal of Japanese Studies* 13 (1).

—— 1983 *Japanese Society: tradition, self and the social order*, Cambridge: Cambridge University Press.

Sōrifu (ed.) 1993 *Josei no Genjō to Shisaku: kawaru kazoku to josei no seikatsu* (The Present Situation of and Policy towards Women: the changing family and women's lives). Tōkyō: Ōkurashō Insatsukyoku.

Spiegel 1991 'Geldmaschine Greenpeace: McDonald's der Umweltsszene', (Money machine Greenpeace: The McDonald's of the environmental scene), 38 (September).

Suga Atsuko 1994 'Bashō wa banana no ki?' (Is a Bashō the same as a banana tree?), p. 28–31 in *Kaien* 13 (2).

Takemura, Tamio 1989 'The formation of a mass consumption society in Japan in the 1920s', unpublished manuscript.

Tamiya Takeshi 1992 'Masu komi hyōgen ni miru josei sabetsu' (Women's discrimination as seen in the language of the mass media), p. 92–110 in H. Katō and T. Tsuganesawa (eds.) *Josei to Media* (Women and Media), Tōkyō: Sekai Shisōsha.

Tanaka, Keiko 1990 'Intelligent elegance: women in Japanese advertising', p. 78–97 in E. Ben-Ari et al. (eds.) *Unwrapping Japan*, Manchester: Manchester University Press.

Thompson, John 1990 *Ideology and Modern Culture: critical social theory in the era of mass communication*, Stanford: Stanford University Press.

Tobin, Joseph J. 1992a 'Japanese preschools and the pedagogy of selfhood', p. 21–39 in N. Rosenberger (ed.) *Japanese Sense of Self*, Cambridge: Cambridge University Press.

—— (ed.) 1992b *Re made in Japan: everyday life and consumer taste in a changing society*, New Haven: Yale University Press.

—— 1992c 'Introduction: domesticating the West', p. 1–41 in his (ed.) *Re—Made in Japan: everyday life and consumer taste in a changing society*, New Haven: Yale University Press.

Tōkyō Asahi Shinbun 1933 *Changing Japan Seen through the Camera*, Tōkyō: Tōkyō Asahi Shinbunsha.

Treat, John W. 1993 'Yoshimoto Banana writes home: *shōjo* culture and the nostalgic subject', p. 353–87 in *Journal of Japanese Studies* 19 (2).

REFERENCES

Tsuge Teruhiko 1994 'Yoshimoto Banana no sekaiteki na imi' (The global significance of Yoshimoto Banana), p. 78–83 in *Kaien* 13 (2).
—— et al. 1994 'Sekai no naka no Yoshimoto Banana' (Yoshimoto Banana around the world), p. 88–106 in *Kokubungaku: kaishaku to kyōzai no kenkyū* 39 (3).
Tsurumi, Patricia 1990 *Factory Girls: women in the thread mills of Meiji Japan*, Princeton, NJ: Princeton University Press.
Turner, Bryan S. 1992 *Regulating Bodies*, London: Routledge.
—— 1984 *The Body and Society*, Oxford: Basil Blackwell.
Ueno Chizuko 1991 'Imēji no shijō: taishū shakai no "shinden" to sono kiki' (The image market: the 'temple' of mass society and its crisis), p. 3–136 in *Sezon no Hassō: māketto e no shinkyū* (The Development of Saison: searching for a market), Tōkyō: Librovert.
—— 1987 *'Watashi' Sagashi Gēmu: yokubō shimin shakairon* (The Search for 'Me' Game: a social theory of desire for selfhood), Tōkyō: Chikuma Shobō.
Ui, Jun 1985 'A citizen's forum: 15 years against pollution', p. 271–6 in *Japan Quarterly* 32, July/September.
Vos, George de 1973 *Socialization for Achievement*, Berkeley: University of California Press.
Wakiya Michihiro 1983 'Kokumin wa kako no sensō no rekishi o dō mite iru ka' (What do the Japanese think about the history of the last war?), p. 54–63 in *Hōsō Kenkyū to Chōsa*, May.
White, Merry 1993 *The Material Child: coming of age in Japan and America*, New York: Maxwell Macmillan International.
Williamson, Judith 1978 *Decoding Advertisements*, London: Marion Boyars.
Winship, Janice 1987 *Inside Women's Magazines*, London and New York: Pandora.
—— 1983 '"Options – for the way you want to live now" or a magazine for Superwoman', p. 44–65 in *Theory, Culture & Society* 1 (3).
Wolferen, Karel van 1989 *The Enigma of Japanese Power: people and politics in a stateless nation*, London: Macmillan.
Wolff, Janet 1985 'The invisible *flaneuse*', p. 37–48 in *Theory, Culture & Society* 2 (3).
Woodiwiss, Anthony 1991 'Postmodanizumu: Japanese for (and against) post-modernism', p. 111–118 in *Theory, Culture & Society* 8 (4).
Yamaki Toshio 1992 *Nihon Kōkokushi* (A History of Japanese Advertising), Tōkyō: Nihon Keizai Shinbunsha.
Yamane, Kazuma 1990 *Gyaru no Kōzō* (Structure of the Girl), Tōkyō: Sekaibunkasha.
—— 1986 *Hentai Shōjo Moji no Kenkyū* (Anomalous Teenage Handwriting Research), Tōkyō: Kōdansha.
Yamazaki, Tomoko 1985 *The Story of Yamada Waka: from prostitute to feminist pioneer*, Tōkyō: Kodansha International.
Yoshimoto, Banana 1993 *Kitchen* (translated by Megan Backus), New York: Grove Press.
—— 1990 *Fruits Basket*, Tōkyō: Fukutake Shoten.
—— 1989 *Painappurin* (Pineapple Pudding), Tōkyō: Kadokawa Shoten.
Yoshimoto, Mitsuhiro 1989 'The postmodern and mass images in Japan', p. 8–25 in *Public Culture* 1 (2).

REFERENCES

Yoshino, Kōsaku 1992 *Cultural Nationalism in Contemporary Japan*, London and New York: Routledge.

Yuasa, Y. 1987 *The Body: toward an eastern mind-body theory*, Albany: State University of New York Press.

Zaretsky, Eli 1976 *Capitalism, the Family, and Personal Life*, New York: Harper & Row.

CONTRIBUTORS

John Clammer is Professor of Sociology and Anthropology and Graduate Professor of Asian Studies at Sophia University, Tōkyō. His interests
include issues of identity, consumption and the sociology of culture, and
his most recent book is *Difference and Modernity: Social Theory and
Contemporary Japanese Society* (London, KPI).

Paul A. S. Harvey is working as an Assistant Professor at Ōsaka
University, Faculty of Language and Culture. He has written a number
of articles on cultural encounters in the Renaissance, and is doing research into popular culture in modern Japan, moving between television
drama and Kabuki.

Sharon Kinsella comes from a small pit town in the north of England,
and studied Economic History at the London School of Economics. She
has lived and worked in Japan for some years and is now doing the last
year of her doctoral thesis on Japanese comic culture and industry at
Oxford University, Faculty of Sociology.

Brian Moeran is a social anthropologist and Swire Professor of
Japanese at the University of Hong Kong. He has lived and studied in
Japan for more years than he can count and has written a number of
books and articles on various aspects of Japanese folk crafts, pottery,
popular culture, and advertising.

Nancy Rosenberger is an Associate Professor at Oregon State University. She is the author of numerous articles on Japanese women and
their relation to discourses of power, and she is the editor of *Japanese
Sense of Self.*

Lise Skov is a cultural sociologist doing research on fashion. After
having spent some years working on Japanese women's fashion and

media, she is now studying fashion design in a global perspective. She is affiliated with the Department of Sociology and the Department of Japanese Studies, University of Hong Kong.

John W. Treat teaches Japanese language and literature at the University of Washington in Seattle. He is the author of *Writing Ground Zero: Japanese literature and the atomic bomb* (Chicago: 1995), and editor of *Popular Culture and Contemporary Japan* (London: 1995) in the ConsumAsiaN book series.

Merry I. White is Professor of Sociology at Boston University and Research Associate at the Edwin O. Reischauer Institute of Japanese Studies, Harvard University. Among her publications are: *The Material Child*, New York: Free Press, 1993; *The Japanese Overseas*, New York: Free Press, 1987; *The Japanese Educational Challenge*, New York: Free Press, 1986. She lives in Cambridge, Massachusetts.

INDEX

Notes: All references are to Japan unless otherwise stated.
Reference to illustrations are in bold type.

internationalism 251 *see also* global
culture
interior design 113, 151, 154, 269;
magazines 158
Inoue, Teruko 5, 39–40, 44, 53, 59,
60, 119, 124, 144, 170
Iwao, Sumiko 15, 24, 27, 34–4, 39

Jameson, Fredric 48, 284
Japanese culture as masculine 13,
25, 101
Japaneseness 25, 54, 100, 115–6,
120–5, 132, 135, 137–8, 212–3

Katei Gahō 8, 35, 59, 61, 111–42,
**112, 115, 116, 128, 129, 130, 131,
134,** 212; isolation of women in
136–7, 138; readership of
111, 113, 139–40n, sales policy
112–4
Kaien 276, 278
kawaii *see* cute
kimono 17, 18, 118, 137
Kitchen (by Yoshimoto Banana)
274–98; plot outline 285–7;
reception of 275–80
Karatani, Kōjin 10
Kokubungaku 278
Kondo, Sumio 260
Konishi, Akiyuki 188–9
Korea 10, 24; Koreans 47, 156;
protests about biased teaching of
history 89–90, 94

language 50, 132, 156, 224–5, 271;
English 16, 224, 227–8, 255 (in
Japanese media 60, 178, 188);
slang 225
Lebra, Takie Sugiyama 25, 105
leisure 27, 29; women's private time
34
Liberal Democratic Party 11, 90
lifestages/lifecycle 8, 56–58, 154,
225–6, 260; and consumption 57
lifestyle 28, 33, 37, 59, 67–8, 165,
245, 259–61; labels in market
research 37; magazines 39, 62,
113, 144, 146, 158–9; *see also
under* magazines

literacy 50
loneliness 136–7, 138, 155, 242, 285–6
love 146, 152, 224, 286; charms 266;
hotels 41, 138 228, 268;
relationships 156, 286

magazine 197; circulation and sales
62, 200; covers **112,** 114, **115–6,**
116–8; flow in 125–32, 133; and
market segmentation 51, 59;
publishers 63–4; readership 8,
58–9, 65, 66–7, 69, 74n, 144
(crossover 64, 67, 262–3); titles
60, 114–5
Magazine House 63, 66
magazines, men's 64, 201, 205, 207,
208, 210; *see also under their titles*
magazines, teenagers 64, 262–71;
see also under their titles
magazines, weekly 158, 200, 201,
205–7; *see also under their titles*
magazines, women's 5–6, 28, 39, 51,
59–68, 72n, 73n, 111–42, 144–57,
158–9; comparison with western
women's magazines 117; editorial
line in 65, 69, 111–4; 'new
women's' 29, 60; *see also under
their titles*
Mainichi Newspaper 51, 63, 188–9,
225
Makita, Tetsuo 80–3, 97, 102
manga *see under* comics
marginalisation of women; in
discourses of Japanese society
12–3; on the labour market 9, 13,
26, 31, 47, 244; in society 177;
Marie Claire 61, 62, 180
market segmentation 37, 50–67
market research 8, 65, 68–9, 144;
discourses of 31–5; macro figures
37; 'women's view' in 33–4; *see
also under* HILL
marriage 40, 154, 143, 169n;
appropriate age for 40, 144, 165;
as cut-off point 162–4, 244;
women's attitudes to 161–8
married women *see* housewives;
work
Masako *see* Crown Princess

315

selfishness 155–6, 168, 249
service sector 12; women in the 16,
 17, 18, 21–2, 28, 33
Seventeen 265
sex 41, 148, 225, 263, 265;
 consumption of 31; representation
 of 54
sexuality 41, 44, 117–8, 145, 148,
 152–4, 157, 205, 207, 212, 214,
 243, 266, 268, 281, 290–1, 295;
 see also under female body;
 pornography
Shimamori, Michiko 16, 22
shinjinrui 29–30, 50, 72n, 139,
 259–60
Shōwa period 10, 22, 38, 103
shōjo 16, 58, 66, 244, 250, 276,
 281–2, 283, 288
Shufu no Tomo 65, 188
shopping 22, 67, 160, 247, 262,
 268–9, 272
shun *see* seasonality
single women 36, 143–69, 189; *see
 also under* work
student movements 10, 187, 225,
 250–1
Suga, Atsuko 28
Sunset Kittens 235–7

Takarajima 230, 246
Tamiya, Takeshi 41, 44
Taishō period 16, 221, 255, 258
tea ceremony 24, 124, 132; *see also*
 bridal arts
teenagers 8, 255–73; as children 66,
 261; as consumers 55, 66–7,
 256o662, 268–9, 281–2;
 compared to teenagers in the US
 257–8; emergence of 255, 259;
 magazines 64, 262–71; *see also*
 cute; shōjo
television 10, 28, 50–1, 71n, 75, 76,
 79–86, 99; representation of
 women in 44; women in television
 industry 85; *see also* asadora,
 Ohanahan, *Oshin*, NHK
Tōkyō Olympics (1964) 10, 80, 255
traditionalism/traditional values
 8–11, 30–1, 76, 86–8, 99, 132,

139, 212, 213, 224, 247, 251; in
 magazines 114, 120–3; *see also*
 confucianism
travel 36, 120, 148, 159–61;
 magazines 158
trends 8, 170–4, 178, 193, 224, 269,
 270–1, 282; as temporal market
 segmentation 55, 58
tourism *see* travel

Ueno, Chizuko 28, 60
UN International Year of Women
 (1975) 29, 84
urbanism *see* cities; life in
urbanization 28, 48, 84, 258
Urecco 201, 205, 210

Valentine's Day 57, 123, **233**, 270
25 ans 60, 61, 62, **64**, 181

war 10, 16, 84; attitudes to 89–97,
 92–3, 95; mobilization of female
 labour during 22*see also* history;
 textbook controversy
Weekly Playboy 201, **206, 209**, 210
westernness 8–9, 54, 118, 152; *see
 also* global culture
White Day 270
Williamson, Judith 217
Winship, Janice 31, 39, 59, 60, 117,
 118–9, 135, 136
with 52, 117
Wolferen, Karel van 51
women; as individuals 28; and
 power 37–47; as trend-setters
 32–3, 34, 177, 195, 243–4;
 visibility of 1–4, 12, 16–22, 26;
 see also industry; marriage;
 sexuality; single women; *see also
 under* consumer culture; work
work and women 21, **21**; comparison
 with western women 14–5; as
 enabling women to consume 9;
 equal opportunities 38–9, 71n, 72n;
 ethic 29–30; part-time 26; women
 in the workplace 155; and married
 women 26–7, 36, 162–3; and
 single women 25–6, 145, 148, 155
World War II *see* war